Assembly Language Techniques for the IBM PC

Assembly Language Techniques for the IBM® PC

Alan R. Miller

SYBEX®

Berkeley • Paris • Düsseldorf • London

Cover art by Dave Jensen
Book design by Ingrid Owen

PC DOS, TopView, and Professional FORTRAN are trademarks of International Business Machines Corporation.
WordStar is a trademark of MicroPro International Corporation.
Turbo Pascal and SuperKey are trademarks of Borland International.
SuperSpl, Advantage, and SixPack are trademarks of AST Research Inc.
CP/M is a trademark of Digital Research Inc.
Microsoft Word is a trademark of Microsoft.
Professional BASIC is a trademark of Morgan Computing.
Prokey is a trademark of Rosesoft.
Lotus 1-2-3 is a trademark of Lotus Development Corp.
SuperCalc is a trademark of Sorcim/IUS.
Grammatik is a trademark of Aspen Software.
SYBEX is not affiliated with any manufacturer.

ISBN 0-89588-309-0
Printed by Haddon Craftsmen
Manufactured in the United States of America
10 9 8 7 6 5 4 3 2 1

ACKNOWLEDGMENTS

I am sincerely grateful to Jim Compton, editor of the manuscript, for his helpful suggestions and to Joel Kroman for trying out the programs. Rudolph Langer made valuable suggestions during the initial stages of the book. Other SYBEX staff members who made contributions to the book are Dave Clark and Olivia Shinomoto, word processing; Donna Scanlon, typesetting; Ingrid Owen, design; and Merrilee Davis, proofreading.

Alan R. Miller
Socorro, New Mexico
March 5, 1986

CONTENTS

■2   The Disk-Operating System   27

■7   Reading Disk Files   165

PREFACE

When you use a large computer, you can concentrate on the tasks you want to do, leaving the operation of the computer to others. For example, you can create a FORTRAN source program with a text editor and then you can compile, link, and run your program. As a computer user, you do not have to worry about the operation of the printer, the disks, or the operating system (the software that runs the computer). These are the concerns of the computer operators.

The operation of a microcomputer is different. Here you are both the user and the operator. You can use a microcomputer more effectively if you learn about the hardware and the operating system, even if your primary goal is solving mathematical or business problems. For example, you should learn how to prepare new disks (placing the operating system on some disks but not on others.) Furthermore, if you establish a print buffer, you can do other tasks while the printer is working. As another example, establishing a virtual disk allows some programs to run faster.

In this book we explore both the hardware and the operating system of the IBM PC and we write auxiliary programs that will make this computer faster and easier to use. Our computer programs will be written exclusively in assembly language because such programs are smaller and faster than those written in other languages. However, we will use a construction known as a *macro* to make our work easier.

Several different operating systems are available for the IBM PC. However, we will only deal with PC DOS versions 2 and 3 since these are the most common. Furthermore, since these two versions are nearly identical, programs written for either version will generally also run on the other. There are many readily available programs for PC DOS, including spreadsheets such as Lotus and SuperCalc, editors such as WordStar and Word, compilers for BASIC, FORTRAN, and Pascal, and other programs such as spelling and syntax checkers.

There are introductory books on the use of the IBM PC, other books on the use of assembly language, and still others on the inner workings of the hardware. The present book, however, concentrates on small but powerful assembly-language programs that interact with the hardware. We write a macro library to avoid placing the same macros in each program.

I have been using computers since 1963, teaching programming methods to engineering students since 1967, and have been a contributing editor for two computer magazines since 1979. This book is similar in format and approach to my *Mastering CP/M*[1], which was written for the CP/M operating system.

Although each program is described in detail, the reader should have some prior experience with assembly language to understand the operation of each program as fully as possible. On the other hand, it is possible to type in and then use all the programs in this book without understanding how they work. Even though the programs can be used directly from the book, they are not trivial. They were written to solve problems that arose in my computer work. It is hoped these programs will be starting points for solving different problems encountered by the reader.

To obtain the fullest benefit of this book, it is necessary to have an IBM PC or PC copy with two disks, at least 256K bytes of memory, a Microsoft or IBM macro assembler, a linker, and a debugger.

The book begins with a brief survey of the IBM PC hardware including the ROM BIOS and the BIOS interrupts. The disk-operating system (DOS) and its interrupts are described in the second chapter. In Chapter 3 we discuss techniques for setting up your computer for easy operation, including the CONFIG.SYS and AUTOEXEC.BAT files. We also write batch files for easier assembly.

Assembly language is reviewed in Chapter 4, in which several different types of simple programs are written. Both the EXE and COM types are considered here. (Only COM files are written in later chapters.) The idea of macros and a macro library is also introduced in this chapter. Chapter 5 is devoted to the use of the debugger, called DEBUG. This program can be used to study the operation of other programs. It can also be used to study the hardware of the computer.

The remaining chapters are devoted to writing useful assembly-language programs and to expanding the macro library. In Chapter 6 we develop several short but useful programs that do such things as interchanging ports, changing cursor shape, and disabling the PrtSc key. Several programs that read disk files are developed in Chapter 7. These include a program to display the ASCII characters in WordStar files and in executable programs, a program to mark a file read-only or hidden, and two programs to execute hidden files. Additional macros, including the in-line macros—REPT, IRP, and IRPC—are included.

Programs that create disk files are written in Chapter 8. One program moves a file from one directory to another. A second program creates a disk file from the video screen or restores the screen from a previously saved file. Filters are written to change a file in some way. A program for encrypting a file is included. In Chapter 9 we write several sophisticated programs that perform tasks between the monochrome and color screens, interchanging keyboard keys, and expanding the usable RAM to 704K bytes.

The appendixes contain all the material needed to write assembly-langauge programs. Appendix A identifies the ASCII characters, including the IBM graphics characters. Appendix B gives the extended ASCII codes associated with the function and Alt keys. Appendix C briefly summarizes the 8086/8088 instruction set and Appendix D lists the assembler directives. Appendixes E and F identify the BIOS and DOS interrupts, respectively. The important DOS interrupt 21 hex functions are given in Appendix G and the keyboard scan codes are identified in Appendix H.

All the assembly-language programs given in this book were written with WordStar running on an IBM PC with either PC DOS version 2.1 or 3.1. The computer contained two floppy disks, an 8087 coprocessor, a monochrome screen, a parallel printer, a serial printer, and 704K bytes of RAM. However, 360K bytes of this memory were set aside as a RAM disk designated as drive C. Two other computers were available for testing the programs. A PC XT with a 20M byte hard disk and both a monochrome and a color screen was used to check the video-screen programs. An IBM PC AT with a 30M byte disk was also available. Besides the usual 640K bytes of RAM, it contained 512K bytes of RAM above 1M byte; this memory was used as a RAM disk. The programs were assembled with the Microsoft version 3 macro assembler. Many of the programs were also run with the IBM version 1 assembler.

The manuscript was created and edited with WordStar running on an IBM PC. The manuscript was checked with Spellix, a spelling checker and Grammatik, a syntax checker. Assembly-language programs were magnetically incorporated into the manuscript. Video screen output was written to disk with the DOS redirection feature so that it could also be magnetically incorporated into the manuscript. One figure showing details of the video screen was created with the IMCAP program. This resident program copies the video screen to a disk file without altering the screen. The complete manuscript was submitted to SYBEX on floppy disks for final editing and electrical transmission to the photocomposer. Consequently, except for editorial changes, the manuscript, including the computer programs, has not been retyped.

---

[1]A. R. Miller, *Mastering CP/M*, Berkeley: Sybex, 1983

A Brief Survey
of the IBM PC

INTRODUCTION

In this chapter we will briefly survey the hardware and software of the IBM PC computers as they apply to assembly-language programming. We will study the registers and methods of addressing memory locations for the 8088 family of CPUs. We will also briefly consider the associated math coprocessors. The memory organization, input and output ports, video screens, keyboard, and other peripherals will be considered next. The ROM BIOS will be summarized, followed by the corresponding interrupt vectors.

The IBM PC Family

The four members of the IBM PC family are the regular PC, the PC XT, the PC portable, and the PC AT. (Another member of the IBM family, the PC jr, will not be addressed in this book.) The first three of these computers are closely related to each other; they all use the 8088 CPU and can address about one megabyte of memory. The PC AT, however, uses the 80286 CPU, which employs a 16-bit data path and a 24-bit address bus. As a result, it is faster and can address more memory (up to 16 megabytes). Nevertheless, the programs we will write in this book can generally run on any of these IBM PCs.

There are many other computers that closely resemble the IBM PC; they are sometimes incorrectly termed "clones." Unfortunately, they are not exact duplicates (as clones should be); they all lack two features of an IBM PC—the IBM ROM BIOS and ROM BASIC. (We will discuss the ROM BIOS later in the chapter.) Of course, the PC copies also have a ROM BIOS, but it is not the same as the one in the IBM PC. Fortunately, the ROM BIOS in the PC copies is close enough for most purposes. Thus, many IBM programs, including most of those in this book, will run on PC copies. The PCs sold under the name Compaq appear to come closest to the IBM in software compatibility.

THE CPU

The Intel CPUs of the family that includes the 8086, 8088, 80186, and 80286 are similar in many respects. They are organized as 16-bit (two-byte) devices that can execute a common set of instructions. While all of these CPUs operate internally with 16-bit data, the 8088 has only an 8-bit data path to the outside world. By contrast, the others use 16-bit external paths.

These CPUs incorporate 14 memory locations, called registers, that are 16 bits wide. Because these registers are located on the CPU chip, they can be rapidly manipulated. The registers cannot all perform the same operations, and so they have each been given specialized tasks. As shown in Figure 1.1, they can be divided into several groups. Let us look at each.

The General-Purpose Registers

Four of the CPU registers are designated AX, BX, CX, and DX. These are general-purpose registers that can be used for manipulating data. However, each has also been assigned special tasks we will consider shortly. As

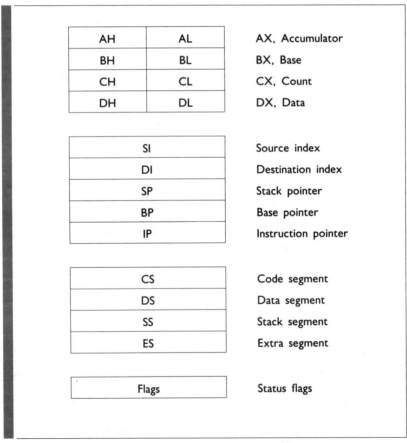

Figure 1.1: *The 14 CPU registers of the 8088 family.*

shown in Figure 1.1, these four registers can be used as either 16-bit or 8-bit entities. That is, either the left (high) half or the right (low) half can be individually addressed and, if desired, manipulated individually in various operations. Thus, there can be eight general-purpose registers, each holding one byte. In this mode the registers are designated as AH, AL, BH, BL, CH, CL, DH, and DL. The letter H and L, of course, refer to the high or low half of the corresponding 16-bit register. All of these registers will be used in the programs we write later in this book.

The special uses for these registers are suggested by the initial letter of the names. Thus, A stands for accumulator, B for base, C for count, and D for data. We will study these special operations when we use them in the programs.

■ The Pointer Registers

The next five CPU registers shown in Figure 1.1 serve as pointers to locate data in main memory. They are called the source index (SI), the destination index (DI), the stack pointer (SP), the base pointer (BP), and the instruction pointer (IP). We will specifically use the SI and DI registers in our programs, while the instructions we execute indirectly will use the IP and SP registers. We will occasionally use the BP register as a storage location.

■ The Segment Registers

The 8088 CPU uses 20 bits to form a memory address, so it can manage a little more than one megabyte of memory ($2^{20} = 1,048,576$). However, the CPU does not incorporate any 20-bit registers; all the CPU registers are 16 bits long. Therefore, a single register can reference only 64K bytes of memory ($2^{16} = 65,536$). It is necessary, then, to combine two registers for each memory reference. The 8088 CPU combines one of the nine general registers with one of the four segment registers (near the bottom of Figure 1.1) to form a 20-bit address. The segment registers are called the code segment (CS), the data segment (DS), the extra segment (ES), and the stack segment (SS).

For each type of memory reference, there is a default segment register and perhaps a default general register. For example, CS and IP are combined to locate the next instruction, and SS and SP are combined for stack operations. Sometimes we can override the default segment register by explicitly choosing a different segment register. Let us see how two registers are combined.

If we combined two 16-bit registers end-to-end, we would have 32 bits and we could then address over four gigabytes (2^{32} = 4,294,967,296). To address one megabyte, however, we only need four more bits beyond the 16 bits of the general register. The combination, then, is obtained by off-setting the segment register by four bits and adding the result to the general register to provide the 20-bit address. The result is called the *effective address* (EA). The effective address is placed on the *address bus* so that the corresponding memory location can be accessed.

We can think of an effective address as having two parts. The *segment register* defines a 64K-byte region of memory, and the *general register* specifies an *offset* from the beginning of the 64K segment (i.e. the byte address within the segment). We express an effective address by giving the segment register and then the general register. A colon separates the two. A memory address may be represented symbolically:

DS:SI

or expressed explicitly:

F000:E82E

In the first case, the 64K-byte segment is defined by the DS register, and the offset is contained in the SI register. In the second case, the segment is F000 hex and the offset is E82E hex. The effective address in the second case is FE82E hex. Notice that we shift the segment address by adding a zero to the right end. That is, F000:E82E becomes F0000 + E82E, or FE82E hex, the effective address.

THE 8087 AND 80287 MATH COPROCESSORS

The 8088 family CPUs can perform such arithmetic operations as addition, subtraction, multiplication, and division. They can also perform such logical operations as OR, AND, NOT, shift, and rotation. However, these operations are performed only on one-byte and two-byte integers. This size is acceptable for systems programs used to control the computer. In fact, the programs in this book can all use data of this size. But for, say, engineering applications, we need to operate on larger numbers and we frequently need to use floating-point numbers.

Some BASIC, FORTRAN, and Pascal compilers perform operations on 32-bit and 64-bit floating-point numbers by a bit of trickery. Calculations and manipulations of floating-point numbers can be performed *in software* using programmed routines written in the CPU's native 16-bit operations. But such software floating-point arithmetic operations are much slower than if the corresponding operations were performed by built-in hardware. One such hardware device is a dedicated, separate "math coprocessor" that can execute sophisticated number processing. Trigonometric and tran-scendental operations can be performed, as well as addition, subtraction, multiplication, and division.

Because of the importance of floating-point operations in scientific and engineering applications, Intel has provided a family of auxiliary processors for this purpose. The 8087 math coprocessor is coupled with the 8088 or 8086; the 80287 with the 80286. These devices are called "coprocessors" because they can perform their calculations concurrently with the regular CPU operation.

The 8087 and 80287 math coprocessors perform all calculations with 80-bit precision. There are seven distinct data types—three are integers, one is decimal, and three are floating-point. Common mathematical opera-tions such as sine, cosine, tangent, arctangent, logarithm, and square root are also included. Several compilers use the coprocessor with dramatic results[1]. The computations are obtained more rapidly and are more precise than the corresponding software implementation. For example, the 64-bit floating-point range extends to 10^{308}, whereas 10^{38} is the dynamic range for the software implementation.

MEMORY ORGANIZATION

As we have seen, the 8088 CPU can address a megabyte of memory by combining a general register with a segment register. IBM has assigned vari-ous activities to different parts of the one-megabyte memory space. One portion contains permanent general instructions for operation of the com-puter and its accessories, another holds the user's program and data, and a third is devoted to the video-screen memory.

Before we look at the memory organization, let us briefly review the two types of memory. Some of the memory cells in a computer can be read but not changed; this type is called *read-only memory* (ROM). A sec-ond type of memory can be readily altered. That is, it can be both read

---

[1] Professional FORTRAN (IBM), Turbo Pascal (Borland International), and Professional BASIC (Morgan Computing) are among those known to the author.

and written. This type should be called read/write memory. Unfortunately, the name *random-access memory* (RAM) has come to be used to designate this type of memory. The name is misleading, of course, because the ROM is also a random-access memory.

The ROM is permanent memory, available the instant the computer is turned on. It cannot be altered by a computer program (although it is possible to remove the ROM circuit and replace it with another). By contrast, the information contained in RAM is lost each time the computer is turned off. This memory must be reprogrammed each time the computer is turned on. Of course, the advantage of RAM is that it can be changed as needed.

A memory map for the IBM PC is shown in Table 1.1. Let us look at each of the 64K-byte segments. Some of these segments contain ROM, some contain RAM, and some may have neither. The address of each 64K-byte segment begins with a different hex digit (0–9 and A–F). Thus, there are 16 different segments.

The top 64K bytes contain ROM. The upper part of this region has the ROM BIOS (segment FE00 hex). This portion contains instructions for the power-on self test (POST) program and the operation of the peripherals. We will use routines in the ROM BIOS for some of our programs. The lower part of this ROM contains the instructions for the BASIC interpreter.

The next lower segments are not normally used but could contain RAM or ROM. The C800 hex segment may have ROM for operation of the hard disk

Address	Description
0000	BIOS interrupt vectors
0008	DOS interrupt vectors
0040	BIOS data area
0050	DOS and BASIC data area
A800	Enhanced graphics
B000	Monochrome adapter
B800	Graphics adapter
C800	Hard disk ROM
F600	ROM BASIC
FE00	ROM BIOS

Table 1.1: *A memory map for the IBM PC.*

if one is installed. Otherwise, this region will be empty. The B000 and B800 hex segments, which will be studied later, contain RAM for the video screens. The A800 hex segment is also allocated for enhanced-graphics video memory. However, it will be empty if the standard displays are used.

The remaining memory, from the beginning up through the 9000 hex segment, is allocated for working-space RAM. This can provide as much as 640K bytes, but there may be less memory actually installed. In the final chapter we show how to add memory above 640K bytes. The beginning of the memory contains the interrupt vectors, which will be considered later in this chapter. This area is followed by the disk-operating system (DOS), which we consider in the next chapter. Let us now look at the peripherals.

■ The BIOS Data Area

The memory region 400 to 48F hex, immediately following the interrupt area, is set aside for ROM BIOS data. This includes the addresses for serial and parallel ports, the equipment list of devices and internal equipment installed in the PC (at time of last power-up or reset), and the size of the working memory. We consider the addresses for the serial and parallel ports next; the ROM BIOS uses these data in its operation. In a program we write later in this book, we will change the equipment list to switch between the monochrome and graphics screens.

■ INPUT AND OUTPUT PORTS

We have seen that the CPU communicates with one megabyte of main memory through a 20-bit address bus. There is also a 1024-byte area, located at the beginning of memory, for 256 interrupt vectors. These vectors provide entry points into service subroutines located elsewhere in memory. The service routines communicate directly with the peripherals through registers known as input and output *ports*. Usually more than one port is assigned to each peripheral; one may be for status and another for data. Since port addresses are 16-bit numbers, there can be in principle as many as 64K different ports. The actual numbers, however, may change from computer to computer. For example, the address of the status register for the parallel printer is 3BD hex if a monochrome screen is present, but 379 hex when a separate port is used with the graphics screen.

Fortunately, we do not need to know the port addresses; we simply use the corresponding interrupt vector.

The Serial Ports

The IBM PC has provisions for two serial ports. The first port is called AUX or COM1; The second port is called COM2. These ports can be used for a phone modem, a serial printer, or direct connection to another computer. The addresses for the serial ports are given in the BIOS data area at locations 400 and 402 hex. Table 1.2 lists the port addresses normally found there.

Suppose you use two serial ports; you have a printer attached to COM1 and a phone modem connected to COM2. You want to transfer information through the modem using a communications program, but the program specifically requires the use of COM1. In principle, you can interchange the two serial ports simply by interchanging the two words at 400 and 402 hex. Unfortunately, this switch will not always work. Some application programs communicate directly with the desired port rather than use the address value at 400 hex.

The Parallel Ports

The IBM PC allows as many as three parallel ports. These ports are called PRN or LPT1, LPT2, and LPT3. The addresses for these ports are stored in memory at locations 408, 40A, and 40C hex. The normal value at any of these ports depends on the type of video screen. If you have a monochrome screen, its parallel port is designated PRN and has an address of 3BC hex. If you add a second parallel port, it is designated LPT2 and has the assigned address 378 hex. But if you have a graphics screen rather than a monochrome screen, there will not be an on-board parallel port. If you then add a separate parallel port, it will be called PRN, but the address will be 378 hex. These addresses are summarized in Tables 1.3 and 1.4.

The Monochrome Screen

As we have seen, the monochrome screen displays information written in the first 4K bytes of memory in segment B000 hex. The screen displays

Name	Address	ROM Data Address
COM1	3FB	400
COM2	2FB	402

Table 1.2: *The serial ports.*

Name	Address	ROM Data Address
PRN	3BC	408
LPT2	378	40A

Table 1.3: *The parallel ports with a monochrome screen.*

Name	Address	ROM Data Address
PRN	378	408
LPT2	278	40A

Table 1.4: *The parallel ports with a graphics screen.*

the regular ASCII characters and the IBM graphic characters (listed in Appendix A), but graphics such as circles and other curves cannot be displayed. The characters are formed within an array of 14 by 9 dots, and so they are very easy to read.

The monochrome screen can display 25 lines of text with a maximum of 80 characters in each line for a total of 2000 characters. However, the screen requires 4000 bytes, since two bytes are required for each character. The Monochrome Adapter card contains 4K bytes of memory. Since that equals 4096 bytes, there are 96 extra bytes of memory not used to display information. We will use one of these extra bytes in a program we write later. Let us now look at the details of the display.

For each 16-bit location in the screen memory, the first byte (the even address) is the character to be displayed; the second byte (the odd address) is the attribute that describes the appearance of the character.

There are four ways a monochrome character can be displayed—normal, bright, reverse-video (a dark character on a lighted background), and bright on a reverse-video field. Furthermore, each character can be made to blink, and normal and bright characters can be underlined whether blinking or not. Thus there are eight more forms that can be selected.

The bits that control the video attributes are illustrated in Figure 1.2. The lowest three bits of the attribute byte (on the right) turn on the foreground. Therefore, a value of 7 displays a normal character. The next bit controls the brightness (intensity), and so a value of F hex displays a bright character. The next three bits control the background; a value of 70 hex displays a reverse-video character. Finally, a value of 78 hex creates a bright character with a reverse-video background. An attribute value of zero, of course, turns off the character. That is, nothing is displayed, regardless of the character value.

The high-order bit controls blinking. Thus, if 80 hex is added to any of the four regular display bytes (normal, bright, reversed, bright-on-reversed), the corresponding character will blink. However, only two of the four types can be underlined; these are 1 for normal and 9 for bright. The corresponding values, then, are 81 and 89 hex for blinking. The thirteen attribute values are listed in Table 1.5.

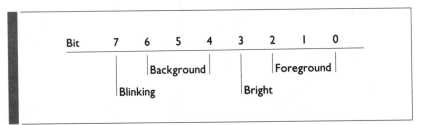

Figure 1.2: *Video attribute bits for the monochrome display.*

Foreground	Background	Normal	Blinking	Underline	Blinking Underline
Normal	Dark	7	87	1	81
Bright	Dark	F	8F	9	89
Dark	Normal	70	F0		
Bright	Normal	78	F8		
Dark	Dark	0			

Table 1.5: *Video attribute bytes for the monochrome display.*

As with the serial ports, you can in principle interchange the first and second parallel ports simply by interchanging the addresses at locations 408 and 40A hex. But, again, if an application program uses the port address without checking the value at location 408 hex, this method will not be effective.

Your program can check to see if a printer is connected to one of these ports and if it is ready to accept a character. The status address is greater than the given address. For example, if the address for PRN is 3BC hex, you can read 3BD hex and look for the value DF hex, indicating that the device is ready.

THE VIDEO SCREENS

As we have seen, the B000 hex segment is allocated for the video display. In addition, the A000 hex segment is used when the Enhanced Graphics Adapter is installed. In the usual installation, there is either a monochrome screen, a graphics screen, or both. The standard monochrome screen uses 4K bytes of memory starting at B000:0 hex; the graphics screen has 16K bytes of memory starting at B800:0 (B000:8000) hex. Any information written in these areas of memory will be displayed on the corresponding screen. Since the memory regions for these two screens do not overlap, it is possible to have both screens installed in the same computer. (Later in this book we will write a program to change from one screen to the other.) Let us consider the monochrome screen first.

We now turn to the graphics screen.

The Graphics Screen

The graphics screen is driven by the Color/Graphics adapter, which, as we have seen, contains 16K bytes of memory beginning at segment address B800 hex. While the monochrome screen has only a single text mode, the Color/Graphics screen has seven different modes. Furthermore, any of four different types of video screens can be attached to the Color/Graphics Adapter card.

Let us look at the seven graphics video modes.

The Graphics Video Modes

The regular Color/Graphics adapter can be set to any one of seven modes, of which four are text modes and three are graphics modes.

(The modes are listed in Table 1.6.) The text modes display either 40 or 80 characters on each line, in either color or black-and-white mode. (Color should be turned off when using any black-and-white monitor with the graphics adapter so the characters are easier to read.) If you have the Enhanced Graphics Adapter, there are four additional modes. (We will learn how to use the text mode later in this book, but we will not use the graphics modes.)

Let us see how to install both types of video monitor.

Combining Both Monochrome and Graphics Monitors

Since the two video adapters use different memory space, it is possible to have both installed in the same computer. A switch on the system board tells the CPU which adapter board to use. When both screens are present, the switch should be set for the monochrome screen. You can change from one screen to the other by running the MODE program, although you cannot turn on the color mode in this way. (MODE is found on the DOS diskette.) You can also switch from one type of graphics mode to another by running the MODE program. We will write a program later in this book that will let us change screens, turn on color, and switch modes.

Let us now look at the keyboard.

THE KEYBOARD

The IBM keyboard incorporates an 8048 microprocessor (similar to the 8080 CPU) to process the information. There is a 16-byte buffer in the keyboard, and so you can confidently type ahead while the computer is busy doing something else. The keyboard interrupt will temporarily stop the computer so that the keystroke can be detected and stored in a buffer. When the computer is ready for another character, the keyboard processor will send the next character to the main computer. The keyboard processor can also sense when a key is held down for a while and will then repeatedly send the character to the CPU.

The IBM keyboard is different from those usually found on a video terminal, in that it does not send ASCII characters. It sends a scan code instead. All the keys are numbered from 1 to 83 (the keyboard scan codes are given in Appendix H). When a key is pressed, the keyboard processor sends the corresponding key scan code number. When the key is released,

Mode	Type	Size	Color	Adapter
0	Text	40 × 25	Off	Graphics
I	Text	40 × 25	On	Graphics
2	Text	80 × 25	Off	Graphics
3	Text	80 × 25	On	Graphics
4	Graphics	320 × 200	On	Graphics
5	Graphics	320 × 200	Off	Graphics
6	Graphics	640 × 200	Off	Graphics
7	Text	80 × 25		Monochrome

Table 1.6: *The video modes.*

the keyboard processor sends another number—the scan code plus 128. For example, the scan code for the Esc key is I. Therefore, the keyboard processor sends the value I when this key is pressed and 129 (81 hex) when it is released. (Later in this book, we will write a program to interchange the meaning of two keys. To do so, we must look for the release scan codes as well as the press scan codes. That is, we must look for four different codes when changing two keys.)

VIRTUAL DISKS

One of the advantages of a hard disk, faster transfer between disk and memory, can be brought into a floppy-disk system by establishing a *virtual disk*. The technique makes a portion of main memory appear to be a floppy disk. Transfer between the virtual disk and main memory is very rapid, even faster than a hard disk. Of course, the information stored in the virtual disk is lost when the computer is shut off. You should therefore save any material created on the virtual disk to a regular disk before turning off the computer. Of course, copies of application programs such as your editor and spelling checker can safely be placed in the virtual disk, since you already have additional copies.

You can add extra memory in segments A000, C000, D000, and E000 hex for use as a virtual disk if you are not using these memory regions for other things. If you have a PC AT, you can place memory above the one-megabyte region for a virtual disk. We will see how to establish a virtual disk later in this book.

THE PRINTERS—PARALLEL AND SERIAL

It is assumed that the regular printer for the IBM PC is connected to a parallel port. You reference it as LPT1. However, the actual port address may have either of two values. If you have an IBM-style monochrome adapter, the printer port on that card will be LPT1. The status address is 3BD hex. An IBM-style Color/Graphics Adapter, however, does not have a printer port. If you have only this adapter, you will need to install a separate port, such as that found on the AST Sixpack. In that case, the printer port will still be referenced as LPT1, but the status address will be 379 hex. If you have both of these ports, the one on the monochrome adapter is LPT1 and the other is LPT2.

Now let us consider the interrupt vectors.

THE ROM BIOS INTERRUPT VECTORS

The first 1024 bytes of main memory (0 to 400 hex) contain 256 (4-byte) addresses that reference subroutines or data located elsewhere in memory. These address are numbered from 0 through FF hex and are known as *interrupt vectors*. Some of these vectors are directly accessed by hardware. For example, when you type information at the keyboard, an electrical signal interrupts the CPU and directs it to the address given for interrupt 9, located at 24 hex. The address is a keyboard-service routine contained in the ROM BIOS. After the keyboard routine completes its work, it returns control to the interrupted program. The printer can similarly interrupt the CPU when it needs another character. Table 1.7 identifies the interrupt vectors that branch into the ROM BIOS of the IBM PC.

We have seen how a hardware device can interrupt the CPU when it wants to be served. However, it is also possible to use the interrupt vectors through software. Since the vectors are located in memory, any computer program can use them to locate a desired routine. In fact, the 8088 instruction

INT X

(where X is the interrupt number) automatically generates a subroutine-like call to the address located in the corresponding vector. For example, the ROM BIOS video services begin at F000:F045, so this address is stored at interrupt 10 hex (address 40–43 hex). To use the ROM video services, you could program a subroutine call to this address. However, it would be easier to use this simple instruction:

INT 10h

Furthermore, the ROM BIOS changes from one model of PC to the next. However, the address at interrupt 10 hex will always contain the correct entry point to the BIOS routine.

Changing the Interrupt Vectors

Sometimes we want to alter the operation of the routines built into the ROM BIOS. We cannot, of course, alter the BIOS, since it is ROM. We can, however, intercept the corresponding interrupt vector. For example, suppose we want to interchange two of the keyboard keys. We can do this by changing the interrupt vector for keyboard service (interrupt 10 hex) so that it points into our program. Then we can check each keyboard character to see if it is one we want to change. We then branch to

Vector	Address	Function
5	14	Print screen
8	20	Timer
9	24	Keyboard scan code
10	40	Video screen
11	44	Equipment list
12	48	Memory size
13	4C	Disk/Diskette service
14	50	Serial transfer
15	54	Cassette tape and TopView
16	58	Keyboard character
17	5C	Printer
18	60	ROM-BASIC
19	64	Bootstrap loader
1A	68	Time of day

Table 1.7: *BIOS interrupt vectors for the IBM PC.*

the regular ROM BIOS keyboard routine to complete the operation. (We will write such a program later in this book.)

It is also possible to disable an interrupt vector. For example, if you press the PrtSc key while holding the Shift key, the information shown on the video screen is sent to the printer. But if no printer is attached, your computer will lock up. One solution to this problem is to change the printer interrupt vector so that it points to a Return statement in the ROM BIOS. Then, if you accidentally try to print the screen when no printer is attached, control will return immediately to you. (We will also write a program for this later.)

Let us look at some of the more important ROM BIOS interrupt vectors.

Interrupt 5: Print Screen

If you hold down the Shift key and press the PrtSc key, the information on the video screen is sent to the printer. Interrupt 5 is used for this purpose. Therefore, you can trigger the PrtSc operation from within a program simply by issuing the command

        INT 5

Alternatively, you can prevent the user from activating the PrtSc command by pointing this interrupt to a Return instruction. We will consider this technique later.

Interrupt 9: Keyboard Scan Code

As we have seen, the IBM keyboard sends scan codes to the CPU, rather than the usual ASCII characters, when a key is pressed. Interrupt 9 is used for this purpose. We can intercept the scan codes by changing this interrupt to point into our program. The scan codes are listed in Appendix H.

Interrupt 10 Hex: The ROM BIOS Video Services

The previous interrupt is very simple, performing only a single service. By contrast, interrupt 10 hex contains a variety of operations that can be selected through a function number. The more important ROM BIOS video services are summarized in Table 1.8. The desired function is selected

AH	Input	Return	Function
0	AL = mode		Set video mode
1	CH = starting scan line CL = ending scan line		Change cursor size
2	BH = page DH = row DL = column		Change cursor position
3	BH = page	BH = page DH = row DL = column CH = cursor start scan line CL = cursor stop scan line	Find cursor position
5	AL = page number		Select video page
6	AL = lines up CL = left column CH = top row DL = right column DH = bottom row BH = video attribute		Scroll up
7	AL = lines up CL = left column CH = top row DL = right column DH = bottom row BH = video attribute		Scroll down
8	BH = page	AL = character AH = attribute	Read character and attribute
9	AL = character BL = attribute BH = page CX = copies to write		Write character and attribute
Ah	AL = character BL = attribute BH = page CX = copies to write		Write character
Fh		AL = mode AH = screen width BH = page	Find video mode

Table 1.8: *The ROM BIOS video services.*

by placing the appropriate number in the AH register. Additional data are placed in other registers, and then we execute interrupt 10 hex.

We previously considered the eight video modes listed in Table 1.5; let us see how these modes are changed.

Function 0: Set Video Mode

As we have seen, the IBM PC can be fitted with either a monochrome screen, for displaying text, a graphics screen, or both. If you have only a monochrome screen, the video mode will always be 7. But if you have the graphics screen, you can use this function to switch to any of the seven modes (0–6) for the graphics screen. If you have both the monochrome and the graphics screen, you cannot use this function to change from one to the other without playing a trick. (We will write a program to do that later in this book.)

To change from one video mode to another, place the new video mode in register AL and the function number zero in register AH. Then issue interrupt 10 hex. This function clears the screen, even if the new video mode is the same as the previous one.

Function 1: Change Cursor Size

A blinking cursor on the video screen indicates where the next character will appear. Characters on the monochrome screen use a dot matrix of 8 by 13 pixels, while the graphics screen uses a dot matrix of 5 by 7 pixels. Initially the cursor is formed from the bottom two rows of the matrix. These are rows 11 and 12 for the monochrome screen and rows 6 and 7 for the graphics screen. (The first row is zero.) However, you can change the cursor so that it starts and ends on any row.

To change the cursor to a large solid block, start with row zero and end with row 12 or 7. You can also create a split cursor with one block at the top and another at the bottom of the character position. Make the starting row larger than the ending row, so that the cursor wraps around to the top. For example, starting at row 10 and ending at row 2 forms a split cursor on the monochrome screen.

To change the cursor size, put the starting row in register CH and the ending row in register CL. Set register AH to 1 and issue interrupt 10 hex.

Function 2: Change Cursor Position

As we have seen, each video screen has an associated cursor to indicate where the next character will appear. The monochrome screen has only one page of text, so there is only one cursor. However, the graphics screen has four pages for the 80-column mode and eight pages for the 40-column mode. Each page has its own cursor.

We can change the position of the cursor by putting the page number (normally zero) in the BH register, the new row number in the DH register, and the new column number in the DL register. The upper-left corner of the screen is row zero, column zero. The row number runs from 0 to 24; the column number runs from 0 to 79 for the 80-column mode and from 0 to 39 for the 40-column mode. Put the function number, 2, in the AH register and issue interrupt 10 hex.

Function 3: Find Cursor Position

The complement to the previous function—to change the cursor—is function 3, which can determine the present cursor position. Put the page number (normally zero) in the BH register, put function number 3 in the AH register, and issue interrupt 10 hex. On return from the interrupt, the DH register has the row and the DL register has the column. In addition, the cursor shape is identified. The CH register has the beginning row, and the CL register has the ending row.

Function 5: Select Video Page

We have seen that the graphics screen can have four pages in the 80-column mode and eight in the 40-column mode. We normally use page zero. However, it is possible to change the current page. Place the desired page number in register AL and the function number, 5, in register AH, and then issue interrupt 10 hex.

In 80-character mode it is possible to create different images on each of the four screens. Then you can use function 5 to switch from one to the next. In this way you can create an animated sequence.

Function 6: Scroll Up

It is possible to scroll all or a portion of the text on the video screen. Place the number of lines to scroll (0 to 24) in the AL register. (A value of zero clears the entire screen.) Put the left column number in register CL, the upper row number in register CH, the right column number in register DL, and the lower row number in register DH. As the text is scrolled up, blank lines appear below. The video attribute (Table 1.5) for the blank lines is placed in the BH register. This would be 0 for normal blanks, 70 hex for reverse video. Finally, set the AH register to 6 and issue interrupt 10 hex.

Function 7: Scroll Down

Function 7 is like function 6, except that the lines scroll downward. Notice that it is possible to scroll either the entire screen or only a portion of it.

Function 8: Read Character and Attribute

We have seen that the video memory contains, in alternation, bytes of characters and their attributes. We can determine the character and its attribute at the current cursor position with this function. First move the cursor with function 2, if necessary. Then set the BH register to the display page (normally zero), set the AH register to 8, and issue interrupt 10 hex. On return from the interrupt, the ASCII value of the character is found in the AL register, and the attribute is in the AH register.

Function 9: Write Character and Attribute

We can write one or more copies of a character with a particular attribute by using function 9. First we move the cursor to the desired position with function 2. Then the character we want to write is placed in the AL register, and the desired attribute is placed in the BL register. (Note the difference from function 8.) The page number is placed in the BH register, and the number of characters to write is placed in the CX (count) register. Set the AH register to 9 and issue interrupt 10 hex.

This function does not automatically move the cursor after a character is written. You must therefore move the cursor with function 2 after each write operation.

Function A Hex: Write Character

Function A hex is like function 9, except that we do not change the attribute; we only write one or more copies of the character. Set the AH register to A hex and issue interrupt 10 hex.

Function F Hex: Find Video Mode

Function F hex, which determines the video mode, is the complement of function 0, which changes it. Set the AH register to F hex and issue interrupt 10 hex. On return, the video mode is found in register AL. In addition, the video page is given in register BH and the screen width (80 or 40) is found in register AH. The video modes were summarized in Table 1.6.

■ Interrupt 11 Hex: Equipment List

The amount of memory on the system board and the number of peripherals are encoded in two bytes stored in the BIOS data area at address 410 hex (40:10). We can determine the information either by reading the two bytes directly or with interrupt 11 hex. On return from the interrupt, the information is located in the AX register. The bits are identified in Table 1.9.

■ Interrupt 13 Hex: Diskette Service

This entry to BIOS performs the fundamental operations of reading from and writing to the diskette. We will not use the BIOS for this

Bit	Meaning
F,E	Number of parallel ports
D	(Not used on PC)
C	Set if game adapter attached
B,A,9	Number of serial ports
8	(Not used on PC)
7,6	Number of diskette drives
5,4	Video mode 01 = 25 × 40 graphics
	10 = 25 × 80 graphics
	11 = monochrome
3,2	System-board RAM
1	(Not used on PC)
0	Set if diskette drives present

Table 1.9: *The bits of the equipment list.*

purpose; instead, we will use the more powerful DOS services. Nevertheless, we will find one interrupt 13 hex function useful. Because of a bug in DOS version 3, it is necessary to reset the disks with function 0 when the computer is first turned on. We put a zero in the AH register and execute interrupt 13 hex.

Interrupt 15 Hex: Cassette Tape and TopView

It was possible to purchase the first model of the IBM PC without disks. In that configuration, an audio cassette tape could be used to save and reload data, with interrupt 15 hex providing the entry into the BIOS for the cassette service routines. However, the cassette tape has given way to floppy disks and hard disks. Furthermore, the XT and AT models do not even have a cassette port. Therefore, it was logical for TopView, a multi-tasking environment, also to use this interrupt.[2]

The cassette services use functions 0–3, while TopView uses functions 10 hex and 12 hex. The cassette port triggers a hardware interrupt that branches into the ROM BIOS except when TopView is running. At such times, TopView replaces the interrupt with a pointer into itself.

SUMMARY

In this first chapter we have briefly surveyed the hardware of the IBM PC family of computers. We considered the CPU, its registers, and the method of addressing memory. We also considered the math coprocessor and how it can complement the CPU for floating-point operations. A summary of the memory organization showed the location of the ROM BIOS, video screen, program space, and vectored interrupts. The chapter concludes with a brief discussion of the ROM BIOS interrupts and some of their functions. In the next chapter we discuss the disk-operating system.

---

[2] A. R. Miller, *The Programmer's Guide to TopView*, Berkeley, Calif.: SYBEX, 1985.

The
Disk-Operating
System

INTRODUCTION

In the previous chapter we learned about the hardware of the IBM PC, particularly the CPU and its registers. We also considered the ROM BIOS—a set of software routines installed in permanent memory—which controls the peripherals. In this chapter we consider the disk-operating system (DOS), the interface between your programs and the ROM BIOS.

INTERACTING WITH THE ROM BIOS

We saw in the previous chapter that the ROM BIOS, located at the top of memory, contains routines for controlling the video screen, the keyboard, and the disks. Furthermore, we learned that the interrupt vectors located at the beginning of memory can be used to access the ROM BIOS routines. For example, interrupt 10 hex is the entry point to the routines that manage the video screen. Later in this book we will write programs that use some of these ROM BIOS routines. Nevertheless, it would be difficult to perform all necessary operations through the ROM BIOS, especially disk operations. For example, we would have to keep track of where we had stored information on each disk so that we could read it back again. Therefore, the IBM PC is provided with a disk-operating system to help us perform some of the common operations. It is known as PC-DOS on an IBM machine and MS-DOS on IBM copies.

THE DISK OPERATING SYSTEM

The IBM PC coordinates the activities of the peripherals through the disk-operating system (DOS). This is a software program that occupies the lower portion of memory, just above the interrupts and the data area. The DOS is an interface between the ROM BIOS and the programs that you run on the PC. It provides an extensive set of routines that complement the ROM BIOS services. As with the ROM BIOS, these DOS functions are accessed through a set of interrupt vectors; they are listed in Table 2.1. The DOS vectors start at interrupt 20 hex, just above the ROM BIOS interrupts. We will consider the DOS interrupts later in this chapter.

Some of the DOS functions are similar to those of the ROM BIOS. For example, there are routines to interact with the printer, keyboard, and video screen. The DOS functions, however, are easier to use. Consequently, we will generally prefer the DOS version of a function to its ROM BIOS equivalent. Sometimes, we need to use the BIOS because there is no corresponding DOS function. For example, we will use BIOS to read the keyboard scan codes and to change the video screen characteristics.

Direct Video Output

We will usually write information to the video screen using the regular DOS functions because they are so easy to use. Unfortunately, the DOS video functions are very slow. Consequently, programmers frequently write information directly to the video screen. Text editors such as Word-Star do so to refresh the screen instantly. The disadvantage of writing directly to the video screen is that the program may not run on the PC compatible computers. Another complication is that we must determine which of the two video screens is currently in use before we write the information. A third complication can occur when TopView is running. Top-View provides multitasking and window management by intercepting information sent to the video screen. However, programs that write directly to the video screen, and bypass DOS, cannot be managed by TopView. Then a special technique should be used for writing directly to the screen.

Management of Disk Files

Another important feature of DOS is the management of disk files. We could, in principle, transfer information to and from the disks using ROM BIOS, but it would be a hopelessly complex task. Consequently, we will always let DOS perform the disk operations for us. These include creating disk files, maintaining the disk directory, associating our chosen file name with the corresponding data on the disk, locating the various pieces of a file we want to work on, and deleting an unwanted file. We can also have DOS copy a program from disk to memory and then execute it for us. Let us look at the various parts of PC DOS.

Although we often consider DOS as a single entity, we can divide it into the five different parts that are provided on the DOS diskette: the three files IBMBIO.COM, IBMDOS.COM, COMMAND.COM, the DOS internal commands (actually a part of COMMAND.COM), and the external commands. We will look at each in turn.

When the PC is first turned on, instructions in the ROM BIOS are automatically executed. The power-on self test (POST) checks all parts of the computer. Then the ROM BIOS interrupt addresses at the beginning of memory are installed. The ROM BIOS then attempts to read the first sector from the diskette in drive A. This sector is called the *boot record;* it is automatically placed on each formatted diskette. If a diskette is available, the boot record is read into memory at 7C00 hex and control branches to that point. The instructions there copy the files IBMBIO.COM and IBMDOS.COM from the disk into memory. Control is then passed to IBMBIO. If a floppy diskette is not present in drive A, the BIOS attempts to read these two files from the hard disk. If the attempt is not successful, ROM BASIC is executed.

Two Hidden Files

If the bootstrap operation is successful, the two disk files IBMBIO.COM and IBMDOS.COM are copied from disk into memory. The disk versions of these two files are "hidden"; they do not appear on the disk directory. Therefore, you cannot readily tell whether they are present on a particular diskette. Once these two files have been copied into memory, they stay there until the computer is turned off. Therefore, it is only necessary to have them on the boot disk at startup time. Otherwise, these two files unnecessarily take up space (over 21K bytes) if they are placed on other diskettes.

You can get an idea of the purpose of these two files from their file names. The file IBMBIO (short for IBM BIOS) is relatively small, about 4K

Vector	Address	Function
20	80	Terminate COM program
21	84	General DOS services
22	88	Program terminate code
23	8C	Keyboard-break code
24	90	Error code
25	94	Absolute disk read
26	98	Absolute disk write
27	9C	Terminate but stay resident

Table 2.1: *The DOS interrupt vectors.*

bytes. It provides additional BIOS functions. The other file, IBMDOS, is much larger. It contains the disk-operating routines and other DOS functions. We will use many of these functions in our programs. The next part of DOS manages the keyboard.

The Command Processor

The third part of DOS is a processor for commands entered from the keyboard. Its job is to read the keyboard commands and then carry out the indicated operation. This part of DOS is also located on the DOS disk, under the file name COMMAND.COM. But unlike IBMBIO and IBMDOS, COMMAND is not a hidden file. Therefore, you can see if a disk has a copy just by reading the directory.

The COMMAND module is copied from disk into memory by IBMDOS. A small part of COMMAND, the *resident* portion, is placed at the beginning of memory, just after IBMDOS. The remainder, the *transient* part, is placed at the top of memory. The part that is loaded at the top of memory cannot be used after a program has begun operation. Therefore, an executing program can write over this portion to gain more memory space. Then, after the executing program has terminated, the transient portion of COMMAND must be reloaded. The fact that a program is small does not mean it will not overlay the transient part of COMMAND. Some programs place their stack of data at the top of memory. These programs always overlay the transient portion of COMMAND.

After COMMAND has been loaded into memory, it is given control of the computer. If the computer has just been turned on or rebooted by pressing the Ctrl, Alt, and Del keys, COMMAND looks for two disk files—CONFIG.SYS and AUTOEXEC.BAT. If these files can be found, COMMAND performs the indicated operations. If they are not present, COMMAND goes on to its next task. (These two files are not provided with DOS; you must write them yourself. We will create these files in the next chapter and tailor them to the type of system you are running.)

For the next step, COMMAND displays the prompt. Unless you have changed it to something else, this consists of a greater-than sign (>) and the name of the current disk drive. COMMAND then waits for a keyboard input.

The Built-in Commands   Some commands, such as DIR, COPY, and REN, are built into COMMAND.COM. If a built-in command is given from the keyboard, COMMAND immediately performs the operation since the necessary instructions are already located in memory. The DOS built-in commands are listed in Table 2.2. They are usually considered to be a fourth part of DOS, but as you can see, they are actually a part of COMMAND.COM. Of course, a drive name cannot be placed at the beginning of a built-in command, since no disk is associated with these commands. That is, the command A:DIR would not refer to a built-in command.

If the command given from the keyboard is not built-in, the command processor searches the referenced disk and directory for the corresponding program. If no disk is specified, the current drive is chosen. The command processor can process three kinds of files—those with extensions COM, EXE, and BAT. COM files can be executed directly, and so COMMAND simply loads the file into memory and branches to it. EXE files are not ready to run, and so a working area must be prepared. Then the COMMAND module has a little extra work to do. COMMAND then starts up the converted version of the EXE file. For a BAT file, COMMAND executes each line of the file as if it were a command entered from the keyboard. If the requested COM, EXE, or BAT file cannot be found, COMMAND issues an error message.

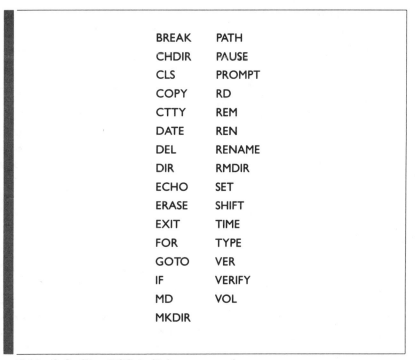

BREAK	PATH
CHDIR	PAUSE
CLS	PROMPT
COPY	RD
CTTY	REM
DATE	REN
DEL	RENAME
DIR	RMDIR
ECHO	SET
ERASE	SHIFT
EXIT	TIME
FOR	TYPE
GOTO	VER
IF	VERIFY
MD	VOL
MKDIR	

Table 2.2: *The DOS built-in commands.*

Each time an executing program has finished, control returns to the resident portion of COMMAND. A check is made to ensure that the transient portion at the top of memory is still intact. (Not all programs destroy the transient portion.) If this region has been altered, a new copy is written into memory from disk. Therefore, it will sometimes be necessary to have a disk containing a copy of COMMAND ready. If a copy cannot be found on the boot disk, DOS writes a message on the video screen requesting a disk with a copy of COMMAND. (Remember, we do not need to have copies of IBMBIO and IBMDOS on any disk after the computer is running.)

A fresh copy of COMMAND is normally read from drive A for a floppy-disk system and from drive C for a hard-disk system. However, we will later write a program that will direct DOS to look for a copy of COMMAND.COM on a drive of our choice; this will be drive C if we have two floppy disks and a virtual disk. Then COMMAND.COM will only be needed on the boot diskette. We will not need it on any other diskette, since DOS can now read it from the virtual disk.

The Last Part of DOS

The fifth part of DOS is a collection of utility programs known as external programs or external commands. Each is a separate entity that can be kept on any disk you want. Therefore, if an external program is available on a disk, the name is shown in the directory listing. Since these programs reside on disk, you must include the disk name in the command (unless they are located on the default drive).

You will find some of these programs so useful that you will want to keep a copy on your system disk or virtual disk. You may never need some of the others, so there is no reason to keep them on your system disk. A listing of the DOS external programs is given in Table 2.3.

FILE MANAGEMENT

We have seen that it is possible to access the peripherals in either of two ways—through the ROM BIOS or through DOS. For keyboard, video screen, and printer access we will sometimes use the ROM BIOS and at other times use DOS. For disk access we will always use DOS. The difference is that the keyboard, video screen, and printer are character devices, whereas the disk is a block device. That is, while we can write to the video screen and printer one byte at a time, we write to the disk one

ASSIGN	GRAPHICS
ATTRIB	LABEL
BACKUP	MODE
CHKDSK	MORE
COMP	PRINT
DISKCOMP	RECOVER
DISKCOPY	RESTORE
EXE2BIN	SELECT
FDISK	SHARE
FIND	SORT
FORMAT	SYS
GRAFTABL	TREE

Table 2.3: *The DOS external commands.*

sector (512 bytes) at a time. Furthermore, a file will usually consist of many sectors stored in different places on the disk. Consequently, we need a symbolic reference to the information stored on a disk.

When we create a disk file through DOS, we assign a file name that is associated with the corresponding information. Of course, we try to choose a name that suggests the contents or function of the file. For example, an assembly-language program for swapping two keyboard keys might be called KEYSWAP.ASM. We can access this file simply by giving its name. DOS creates a directory entry that records the file name and other information, such as the file length, date of creation, and location of the first part. The remaining parts are found by referencing the file-allocation table (FAT).

Entries in the FAT for floppy disks and some hard disks are 12 bits (1½ bytes) long. A hexadecimal display requires three characters to represent 12 bits. But since a hexadecimal display groups two characters for each byte, the 12 bits are spread over more than one byte. The situation is further complicated because we have mixed the reverse order of arabic numbers with the forward order of English text. Therefore the three characters of a FAT number appear to be scrambled with adjacent numbers. We shall devise a scheme for unscrambling the numbers in the last chapter. Larger hard disks (over 20 megabytes) use 16 bits for the FAT, and so there is less of a problem. In any case, we will not normally be interested in this table.

When we create programs that read and write disk files, we need a convenient way to refer to our file. The file name can consist of as many as eight characters for the primary name and three more for the extension. Furthermore, if the file is located on a hard disk, there can be one or more subdirectory names associated with the file name. Subdirectory names are separated by a backslash character. The complete specification is known as a *path name*. For example, this path name:

C:\ASM2\KEYSWAP.ASM

refers to the assembly-language program KEYSWAP.ASM, located in subdirectory ASM2 on drive C.

The first version of DOS required a direct reference to the file name (known as a file control block, or FCB). Starting with version 2, a new scheme, known as a *file handle*, was introduced. Because path names can become long if there are several levels of subdirectories, it is more convenient to reference a path name through a handle, a 16-bit identification number. We will use this method in the programs we write in this book, rather than the earlier method, since it is so much easier. Of course, the disadvantage is that programs written in this way cannot be run with DOS version 1.

To use this method, we give DOS the location of a path name, and DOS in return will assign a file handle. From then on, we can refer to our file with this handle (number) rather than the longer path name. Access through the file handle replaces the more complex file-control block of DOS version 1 and CP/M.

Let us now look at the DOS interrupts.

THE DOS INTERRUPTS

We saw in the previous chapter that routines in the ROM BIOS can be accessed by using interrupts 5 through 1A hex. In a similar way, DOS establishes interrupts 20 through 27 hex. We can use these interrupts to gain entry to useful DOS operations. The most important DOS interrupt is 21 hex because it can perform so many useful operations. We will look at it in detail in the next section. However, we will first consider three other DOS interrupts.

■Interrupt 20 Hex: Program Termination

We will generally terminate our programs with the DOS 20 hex interrupt because it is so easy to use. We only have to give this two-byte command:

    INT 20h

and control is returned to DOS. This method of program termination can only be used for COM programs. We cannot terminate an EXE program in this way. We will not find this to be a problem, since we will generally write our programs as COM files. Nevertheless, we will study ways of terminating EXE programs later in this book. See interrupt 27 and interrupt 21 function 4C hex.

■Interrupt 23 Hex: Intercepting Control-Break

It is often possible to stop an executing program by holding the Ctrl key and pressing the Break key. Sometimes Ctrl-C does the same thing. The keystroke combination causes a branch first to interrupt 23 hex and then to a DOS routine to stop the program. However, you can either prohibit the user from interrupting a program in this way or enhance the action by giving help or asking a question, by changing the interrupt 23 hex vector so that it branches back into your program. Then, when the user activates Ctrl-Break, control returns to you. You can also cause your program to stop by executing an INT 23 instruction.

Sometimes when you change an interrupt vector, you want the new value to remain in effect until the computer is turned off. At other times, you want to restore the original value before the program has finished. With interrupt 23 hex, DOS always restores the original value when the current program is done.

■Interrupt 27 Hex: Terminate Resident Program

The two previous interrupts are very easy to use because they always perform the same service; you just give the two-byte instruction. But when it is possible to change the action of an interrupt, we must provide additional information in a register. Interrupt 27 hex is an example. This instruction is used to install resident code, instructions that stay in place until the computer is turned off or reset. Usually the resident code will intercept another interrupt and alter its operation. It may also operate a peripheral. Device drivers and the code that operates a RAM disk and print spooler use this interrupt.

To use this interrupt we run a double program. One part comprises the installation instructions, and the other is the resident section. We point the DX register to the end of the resident section of the code and then issue an interrupt 27 hex instruction. The installation program is terminated, and control returns to DOS. However, DOS does not release all the memory allocated to the program. It reduces the size of the working memory by raising the starting address for executing programs, to protect the resident section just installed. The memory allocated to this resident program cannot be recovered until the computer is reset or turned off.

We will use this interrupt later in the book to interchange keyboard keys, change printer characters, and reduce the size of memory below 512K bytes (as required by some programs). Now let us look at some of the more useful functions available through interrupt 21 hex.

THE DOS FUNCTIONS

We have considered several of the DOS interrupts that only performed single services. We now consider a fairly complex service that can perform dozens of different tasks. This is DOS interrupt 21 hex. The desired operation is determined by the value in the AH register. Other registers may also have to be set. With this interrupt we can read the keyboard, write to the screen and printer, and perform disk operations.

There appear to be pairs of DOS functions that perform duplicate services. However, one set was designed for DOS version 1 and uses the concept of a file-control block (FCB). The second set was developed for DOS versions 2 and higher. It uses the concept of a file handle. We will only use the second method, because it is so much more convenient. Therefore, the functions that use the FCB method are not discussed here. Selected DOS functions are identified in Table 2.4 and are described more fully in the following section.

SUMMARY OF SELECTED DOS 21 HEX FUNCTIONS

The DOS 21 hex functions used in this book are described in this section, along with some potentially useful functions not used in this book. To use these functions, place the function number in register AH. Other registers may have to be established as described. Then the command

INT 21h

is given. Data may be available in one or more registers after return from the interrupt.

AH	Function
1	Keyboard input
2	Display character
3	Serial-port input
4	Serial-port output
5	Printer output
6	Direct input or output
7	Input, no display
8	Keyboard input, no tabs
9	Display string
A	Read keyboard buffer
B	Input status
25	Change interrupt vector
30	Get DOS version number
31	Terminate but stay resident
35	Get interrupt vector
3C	Create file
3D	Open file
3E	Close file
3F	Read file or device
40	Write file or device
41	Delete file
43	File attributes
4A	Change allocated memory
4B	Load and execute program
4C	Terminate program
4D	Determine error code
56	Rename file

Table 2.4: *The DOS functions for interrupt 21 hex.*

Function 1: Read and Display Keyboard Character

When this function is executed, processing stops until a key is pressed. That is, this function waits for input. If the corresponding character is ASCII, it is then displayed on the video screen. The tab character is automatically expanded to the end of the next eight-column field by adding spaces. Holding the Ctrl key and pressing Break terminates operation.

To use this function, set the AH register to 1 and execute interrupt 21 hex. The input character is returned in the AL register if it is ASCII. If the key corresponds to an extended code (see Appendix B), the AL register contains a value of zero. Then this function should be repeated to get the extended code. If the second value is less than 84, it represents the scan code of the pressed key. For example, a value of 30 indicates that the Alt key and the letter A were pressed, since the scan code for the letter A is 30. Similarly, a second value of 81 indicates that the PgDn key was pressed, since that is the scan code of this key. As a third example, a value of 59 indicates that the F1 key was pressed, because that is the corresponding scan code.

Values above 83 are more difficult to decode but they are given in Appendix B. For example, pressing Shift and F1 generates the number 84, while Alt and 1 returns a value of 120.

See functions 6, 7 and 8 for similar operations. You can determine whether a keyboard character is waiting to be read by using function B hex. Input can be read from another device or disk file by redirection of the standard input.

Function 2: Write Character to Video Screen

This function displays on the current video screen the character contained in the DL register. It is useful for writing one or two characters to the video screen. (Use function 9 for longer strings of characters.) This function is especially useful for displaying the dollar sign, since function 9 cannot do that. This function can also be paired with function 8, which reads keyboard characters but does not display them. The Backspace character moves the cursor to the left, but does not change (erase) the character there. The output can be sent to another device or disk file by redirecting the standard output with the greater-than (>) character.

Function 3: Read from Serial Port

Function 3 reads one character from the standard auxiliary input, defined as AUX or COM1. However, we can change the standard auxiliary port to COM2 by using the MODE program. This function waits until a byte is available. Place the value 3 in the AH register and issue interrupt 21 hex. The character is returned in the AL register.

Function 4: Write to Serial Port

Function 4 sends the byte in register DL to the auxiliary port AUX or COM1. Put the value 4 in the AH register and issue interrupt 21 hex. The other auxiliary port, COM2, may be selected with the MODE program.

Function 5: Write to Printer Port

Use this function to send the character in register DL to the standard printer port, PRN or LPT1. However, LPT2 or LPT3 may be selected with the MODE program. Put the value 5 in the AH register and issue interrupt 21 hex.

Function 6: Direct
Keyboard Input and Video Output

Function 6 can perform both input and output; it can also determine the input status. Unlike the other input functions, it does not wait for an input character. Also note that the input character is not automatically displayed and that the Ctrl-Break command does not terminate the operation.

As usual, the DL register contains the output character and the AL register receives the input character. You ask for input by placing the value FF hex in the DL register. Place the value 6 in register AH and issue interrupt 21 hex. On return from the function, the zero flag is set if no character is ready. If the zero flag is clear, it means a character was read into the AL register. If the DL register contains any other value but FF hex, that character is sent to the standard output device. Also compare with functions 7 and 8.

Function 7: Read Keyboard
Character without Echo or Break Detection

To use function 7, place the value 7 in the AH register and issue interrupt 21 hex. This function, like function 1, waits for a keyboard character to be entered. If an ASCII character such as a letter, number, or control character was entered, the ASCII value is returned in the AL register. The IBM graphics characters can be entered by holding the Alt key and typing the decimal value with the key-pad numbers. The number appears in the AL register. However, if an extended character such as a function key, cursor key, or Alt combination was entered, a value of zero appears in the AL register. The function must then be called a second time to determine the character. (The extended characters are given in Appendix B.) However, unlike function 1, this function does not display the input character. Furthermore, Ctrl-Break does not terminate the process. Also compare with functions 6 and 8.

Function 8: Read Keyboard Character without Echo but with Break Detection

Function 8 is like function 1 in that it waits for a character and terminates when Ctrl-Break is pressed. However, the input character is not displayed, and the tab character is not expanded. Place the value 8 in the AH register and issue interrupt 21 hex. Also compare with functions 6 and 7.

Function 9: Display a String of Characters

This function is useful for displaying a string of characters on the video screen. We have seen that functions 2 and 6 can display single characters, but function 9 is much easier to use for more than one character. Of course, unprintable characters (such as carriage return, line feed, and Esc) can also be included in the string.

To use this function, you place the string somewhere in memory and terminate it with the dollar sign. (Of course, you cannot include a dollar sign in the string; use function 2 for this purpose.) The address of the string is placed in the DS:DX registers. Set the AH register to 9 and execute interrupt 21 hex.

Later in this book we will write a macro that will make this function very easy to use. We will then be able to display a string with the simple expression

    @write 'This is a test of @write'

Function A Hex: Buffered Keyboard Input

We have seen that functions 1, 6, 7, and 8 read a single character at a time. But sometimes it is more convenient to read an entire line at once, so that the user can make corrections to the line before it is accepted by the computer. Function A hex is designed for this purpose. All characters typed by the user are entered into the keyboard buffer. The full power of the DOS editing keys, such as cursor left, cursor right, insert, and delete, is available. When the Return key is pressed, the line is placed into the input buffer.

Before you can use this function, you must establish a buffer in memory. There are two auxiliary bytes located at the beginning of the buffer. The first defines the maximum length of text that can be stored in the buffer; the second gives the number of characters that were entered by the user. You set the value of the first byte; DOS fills in the second byte after the buffer has been read. DOS also adds a carriage-return character to the end of the input string. However, the carriage return is not included in the count that DOS enters in the second auxiliary byte. Therefore, you should set the maximum size of the buffer to be one byte larger than you need.

To use the buffered keyboard, set the DS:DX registers to the first auxiliary byte, the byte defining the maximum buffer size. It is located two bytes before the text. Set the AH register to A hex and execute interrupt 21 hex.

■ Function B Hex: Keyboard Status

We have seen that functions 1, 7, and 8 wait for keyboard input. If no key has been pressed, the computer waits indefinitely until a key is pressed. However, we can avoid waiting for input when none is available by checking the status with function B hex. Set the AH register to B hex and execute interrupt 21 hex. On return from this function, register AL will contain a zero if no key has been pressed. Any other AL value indicates that a character is waiting to be read. This function does not read the character; use function 1, 7, or 8 for that purpose.

■ File-Control Block Functions

The next group of functions perform disk operations using the file-control block (FCB). However, this is such an awkward technique that we will not use it—or the associated functions—in this book. Instead, we will use an equivalent set of functions that reference a file handle. These are discussed later in this chapter. You'll notice that one function, 4D hex, can be used with either 31 hex, an FCB function, or 4C hex, a file-handle function.

Function 25 Hex: Change Interrupt Vector

We have seen that the beginning of memory contains interrupt vectors, four-byte addresses that refer to ROM BIOS and DOS routines. It is possible to change the action of these routines by changing the corresponding interrupt vectors. For example, we can disable the PrtSc command by changing interrupt vector 5 at address 14 hex.

We could, in principle, change an interrupt vector simply by writing the new value at the desired memory location. However, this method can cause unpredictable results if the interrupt is activated while it is being changed. Therefore, it is safer to let DOS change the vector with function 25 hex. The new 32-bit vector is placed in the DS:DX registers, and register AL is given the vector number. (Selected interrupt vectors are identified in Appendixes E and F.) Set the AH register to 25 hex and execute interrupt 21 hex. See function 35 hex for the complementary operation.

Function 30 Hex: Get DOS Version Number

Many useful functions were introduced with DOS Version 2. However, these operations cannot be used with the earlier DOS versions. Therefore, if you use these new features, you should first use function 30 hex to see that the version is 2 or later. If the version number is 1, you should terminate the program with an error message indicating that version 2 or later is required.

To use this function, set the AH register to 30 hex and execute interrupt 21 hex. The "major" version number will be returned in the AL register unless it is less than 2. In that case, the result will be zero. The AH register returns the "minor" version number, after the decimal point. Thus version 3.1 returns 3 in AL and 1 in AH, while version 1.1 simply returns zero in AL.

Function 31 Hex: Terminate but Stay Resident

We have seen that device drivers and interrupt handlers can be installed with DOS interrupt 27 hex. Function 31 hex performs a similar service, but with an added feature. This function also provides an error code that can be tested by including an ERRORLEVEL command in a batch file. Alternatively, the error code is obtained with function 4D hex, discussed in the next section.

As with interrupt 27 hex, we put the offset of the end of the resident program in the DX register. Then we set the AH register to 31 hex and execute interrupt 21 hex.

Function 35 Hex: Get Interrupt Vector

We have seen that it is possible to alter the operation of BIOS and DOS routines by changing the interrupt vectors at the beginning of memory. We can do this by copying the original vector into our program before changing the vector to point into our program. We can then branch from our program to the original address. As another example, we may want to restore an interrupt vector to its original value at some point. Then we should copy the original vector into a storage area before we change it. Once we have done so, we can easily restore the original from the stored value.

Place the interrupt number in the AL register, set the AH register to 35 hex and execute interrupt 21 hex. On return from the interrupt, the ES:BX registers will hold the requested vector. See function 25 hex for the complement.

■ Disk Files and File Handles

The next DOS functions manipulate files through the use of file handles. They can only be used with DOS versions 2 and larger. We can use handles to create, read, write, rename, and delete disk files.

A file specifier in DOS version 1 is limited to a disk drive, an eight-character primary name and a three-character extension, for example:

C:SORTFAST.ASM

DOS version 2 introduced the concept of subdirectories. Now, one or more subdirectory names, terminated with a backslash character, can also be included in the file specifier. Thus, a file reference under DOS version 2 might look like this:

C:\ASSEMBLER\SYSTEMS\SORTFAST.ASM

The idea of a file handle was introduced to simplify the reference to the longer path name. We place a zero at the end of the path name (this is called an ASCIIZ string), point the DS:DX registers to the beginning of the path name, set the CX register to the file attribute (normally zero), and execute the appropriate function. DOS returns either the assigned handle or an error code in the AX register. We can distinguish the two cases by the carry flag—it is set for an error condition. The file attributes are identified in Table 2.5. The standard error codes are given in Table 2.6.

The maximum number of file handles a program can use is initially set to eight. However, you can increase this number to 20 with the command

FILES = 20

Attribute	Meaning
0	Normal
I	Read only
2	Hidden
4	System

Table 2.5: *The file attributes.*

Hex Code	Meaning
I	Invalid function number
2	File not found
3	Path not found
4	No more handles
5	Access denied (hidden)
6	Invalid handle
7	Memory control blocks destroyed
8	Insufficient memory
9	Invalid memory address
A	Invalid environment
B	Invalid format
C	Invalid access code
D	Invalid data
F	Invalid drive
10	Trying to delete current directory
11	Not same device
12	No more files

Table 2.6: *The standard error codes for file handling.*

Furthermore, DOS automatically assigns five handles (0–4) to the three peripheral devices CON, AUX, and PRN (three handles are used by CON). However, your programs are charged for only three handles. This leaves a default of five handles, a number that can be increased to 17. The DOS handle assignments are shown in Table 2.7. Handles assigned to your files begin with 5.

Function 3C Hex: Create New File

Function 3C hex creates a new disk file according to the referenced path name. If a file with the same name already exists, it is destroyed. This is usually what we want. However, if you want to avoid deleting an existing file with the same name, you should check the directory first.

As we saw in the previous section, we place a zero at the end of the path name and point the DS:DX registers to the beginning of the path name. The CX register is set to zero, the file attribute. Regardless of the value in CX, DOS will automatically set the file attribute to zero since we are creating a new file. Set the AH register to 3C hex and execute interrupt 21 hex. On return, see if the carry flag is set, indicating an error. Because the error codes are the same for all file-handle access, you can create a standard error routine for all file-handling routines. If there is no error, save the file handle. It must be used in all further references to this file.

Function 3D Hex: Open Existing File

If we want to read an existing file, we must first open it, with function 3D hex. As before, we place a zero at the end of the path name and point the DS:DX registers to the beginning of the path name. We place in

Device	Handle	Use
CON	0	Standard input (normally keyboard)
CON	1	Standard output (normally video)
CON	2	Error output to video
AUX	3	Auxiliary input and output
PRN	4	Printer output (LPT1 or PRN)

Table 2.7: *The five handles assigned by DOS.*

the AL register one of the access modes listed in Table 2.8; this is normally a value of zero. Set the AH register to 3D hex and execute interrupt 21 hex. On return, see if the carry flag is set, indicating an error. If there is no error, save the file handle that is returned in the AX register.

Function 3E Hex: Close Disk File

After we have created a file with function 3C hex, and written data into it with function 40 hex, we must close the file or it will not be usable. Place the corresponding file handle in the BX register, set the AH register to 3E hex, and execute interrupt 21 hex. On return, see if the carry flag is set, indicating an error.

Function 3F Hex: Read File or Device

After a disk file has been created, written to, and then closed, we can read the data back into a program. Of course, we must first open the file again with function 3D hex to get an assigned file handle. We move the handle to the BX register and place in the CX register the number of bytes we want to read at a time. We can choose any number, but the larger the better. Furthermore, it should be a multiple of the sector size—512 or 1024 bytes for faster operation. The DS:DX register points to the location in memory where the data are to be copied. Set the AH register to 3F hex and execute interrupt 21 hex. On return, check to see if the carry flag is set, indicating an error. If there is no error, AX contains the number of bytes read from the disk. If this number is less than the number in the CX register, you have reached the end of the file. Otherwise, there are more bytes of data to be read. Therefore, after processing the current data, issue function 3F hex again. You do not have to close a file if you are only reading from it, although closing a file releases the assigned handle for another operation.

Mode	Meaning
0	Read only
1	Write only
2	Both read and write

Table 2.8: *The access modes for opening a file.*

Since DOS automatically assigns handles to the peripherals, you can use this function to read from the keyboard. In that case, the file handle in the BX register is zero.

Function 40 Hex: Write File or Device

After we have created a file with function 3C hex, we can write data to it with function 40 hex. This function is the complement of function 3F hex. The assigned file handle is placed in the BX register, the DS:DX registers point to the location of the data in memory, and the number of bytes to write from the memory buffer is placed in the CX register. Set the AH register to 40 hex and execute interrupt 21 hex. On return, see if the carry flag is set, indicating an error. If there is no error, AX contains the number of bytes written to the disk. If this number is less than the number in the CX register, you have reached the end of the file. Otherwise, there are more bytes of data to be written. Be sure to close the file with function 3E.

Since DOS automatically assigns handles to the peripherals, you can use this function to write to the video screen. In that case the file handle in the BX register is 1.

Function 41 Hex: Delete Disk File

Function 41 hex is used to delete an existing file; actually, it only marks the directory entry to indicate that the file is deleted. Therefore, it may be possible to recover an accidentally deleted file. We have seen that we need to delete an existing file when creating a new file of the same name. Function 3C hex automatically does this.

To use 41 hex, we place a zero at the end of the path name and point the DS:DX registers to the beginning of the path name. Set the AH register to 41 hex and execute interrupt 21 hex. On return, see if the carry flag is set, indicating an error. You cannot delete an open file or a read-only file.

Function 43 Hex: File Attributes

We use function 43 hex either to determine or to change the current value of the file attributes. We place a zero at the end of the path name and point the DS:DX registers to the beginning of the path name. To determine the attributes, set the AL register to zero, set the AH register to 43 hex, and execute interrupt 21 hex. On return, check to see if the carry flag is set, indicating an error. If there is no error, the attributes are found in the CX register. A value of FFFF hex in the AX register indicates no error for a hard disk.

Alternatively, we can change the attributes by setting the AL register to 1 and the CX register to the desired value. We can set any or all of the second, third, and fourth attributes. That is, a value of 7 will make a file read-only, hidden, and system, while a value of zero will clear these attributes back to normal.

Function 4A Hex: Change Size of Memory

When an executable program is started, it is allocated all of the remaining memory. Later in this book we will write a small program that will execute another program, using function 4B hex. When we do that, we must release the memory allocated to the first program to make room for the second. Function 4A hex is used for this purpose.

The ES register refers to the block to be changed; for our programs this will be the same as the CS register. The BX register contains the number of 16-byte paragraphs left after we reduce the allocated memory to the minimum amount needed by the first program. You can calculate the value by dividing the program length by 16 and incrementing the result. Set the AH register to 4A hex and execute interrupt 21 hex. On return, check to see if the carry flag is set, indicating an error. We are now ready to use this function for function 4B hex.

Function 4B Hex: Load and Execute a Program

Function 4B hex can perform two different services by copying a disk file into memory. We can load data into memory and then use it, or we can copy another program into memory and execute it. Before we can load another program, however, we must release some of the allocated memory using the previous function, 4A hex.

To load a program, we place a zero at the end of the corresponding path name and point the DS:DX registers to the beginning of the path name. The AL register contains the value zero if the new program is to be loaded and executed, or 3 if a file is to be loaded but not executed.

The ES:BX registers point to a parameter block containing information about the new program. Table 2.9 gives details of this parameter block for loading and executing a program. The parameter block contains seven words (14 bytes). The first word gives the segment address of the environment string; the value is located at address 2C hex in the program. The environment string defines the drive where the COMMAND module is located. It also defines the search path and prompt if these have been established.

The remaining three double words locate information to be passed to the new program. The first of these is the command line, and the other two are the first and second file-control blocks (FCBs). We can use either the command line or the FCB to pass parameters to the new programs. If subdirectories are included in the parameters, we must use the command line. Otherwise, we can use the FCB. We next set the AH register to 4B hex and execute interrupt 21 hex. On return, check to see if the carry flag is set, indicating an error.

If we want to copy a disk file into memory but not execute it, we use a different parameter block, only two words long. The first word is the segment where the file is to be loaded, and the second is the relocation factor needed when an EXE program is loaded. This gives the relative placement of the program in the segment. The parameter block for loading is shown in Table 2.10.

After the second program has terminated, control returns to the original program. Since the second program can change all the registers, we must save the original values of the stack-pointer and stack-segment registers

Address	Bytes	Meaning
0	2	Segment value of environment string
2	4	Location of command line
6	4	Location of first FCB
10	4	Location of second FCB

Table 2.9: *Parameter block for execution with function 4B hex.*

Address	Bytes	Meaning
0	2	Segment where file is loaded
2	2	Relocation factor for EXE programs

Table 2.10: *Parameter block for loading with function 4B hex.*

before executing function 4B hex. Then we restore these registers after returning from the second program.

We will use this function in two programs we write later in the book.

Function 4C Hex: Terminate Program

There are several ways to terminate a program and return to DOS. We will generally use interrupt 20 hex, but this function can only be used for COM files; it cannot be used to terminate an EXE program. However, a universal method for terminating both COM and EXE programs is function 4C hex.

This function also provides an error code that can be tested with an ERRORLEVEL command in a batch file. Alternatively, a subprogram loaded with function 4B hex can pass an error code to the parent program. Then the error code is obtained with function 4D hex. Set the AH register to 4C hex and execute interrupt 21 hex.

This function also closes any files that were opened with functions 3C hex and 3D hex.

Function 4D Hex: Determine Error Code

As noted earlier, an error code is available when a subprogram terminates with either function 31 or 4C hex. The code is determined by calling Function 4D hex and is returned in the AL register. The AH register identifies the nature of the termination, as shown in Table 2.11. Zero means normal termination, 1 means Ctrl-Break was pressed, 2 reports a critical device error, and 3 indicates that the program terminated with function 31 hex.

Value	Meaning
0	Normal termination
1	Terminated with Ctrl-Break
2	Critical device error
3	Terminated with function 31 hex

Table 2.11: *Termination modes for function 4D hex.*

■ Function 56 Hex: Rename File

You can change the name of an existing file with function 56 hex. However, the new name must not already exist. The new name and the original name may be in different directories on the same disk, but they cannot refer to different disks.

Before calling this function, place a binary zero at the end of each name. This points the DS:DX registers to the old name and the ES:DI registers to the new name. Set the AH register to 56 hex and execute interrupt 21 hex. On return, check the carry flag for error. The AL register has the value 3 if the two names are on different disks. A value of 5 means the new name already exits.

SUMMARY

In this chapter we have reviewed the organization and operation of the disk-operating system (DOS). We looked at four of the DOS interrupts: 20, 21, 23, and 27 hex, and we studied the details of the 27 functions available with interrupt 21 hex. In the next chapter we will learn how to configure DOS for your particular system.

3

Setting Up
Your Computer

INTRODUCTION

We learned about the hardware and the operating system for the IBM PC in the previous chapters. In this chapter we will write two batch files to set up your computer for the particular hardware that is present and to select the features you are interested in. We begin by setting up a hard disk. If you do not have a hard disk or your hard disk is already working, skip over this section.

SETTING UP A HARD DISK

A new hard disk must be partitioned and formatted before it can be used. This step may have been done by the dealer you purchased the computer from. However, if you purchased it by mail order or directly from IBM, the hard disk may not have been set up.

Boot the computer from drive A using a DOS system diskette. Insert the diskette into drive A and turn on the computer. If the computer is already on, insert the system disk and press the Ctrl, Alt, and Del keys simultaneously. Listen for the single beep and check the video screen for the report of maximum memory. Run the FDISK program by typing its name and pressing the Return key. Select option 1 to create a single partition. Then answer "Yes" to the next question, to devote the entire disk surface to DOS. At the completion of this step, you still have to format the disk surface.

If your hard disk holds 20 megabytes or more, be sure to have DOS version 3 or later. DOS version 2 will use a minimum of 8K bytes of space for each disk file no matter how small it may be. By contrast, version 3 will use only 2K bytes minimum. Execute the format program but be careful to give the correct drive name. Be careful not to format your system disk in drive A. Give the command

    FORMAT C:/S/V

The C: indicates that the hard disk, drive C, is to be formatted. This should be the only time you need to format your hard disk. Be careful later not to format your hard disk accidentally after you have copied many files there. The /S parameter adds a copy of the DOS system—that is, the three files IBMBIO.COM, IBMDOS.COM, and COMMAND.COM—to the hard disk. This allows you to boot directly from the hard disk, and so you do not need a floppy disk in drive A at boot time. You give your hard disk a unique name by including the /V (for volume name) parameter. Of course, such a name is more useful for removable media like diskettes, which can easily be mixed up.

After the formatting step has finished and you have assigned a name to the disk, the system will report the total disk size, the amount of space devoted to the system, the number of hidden files, and the number of bad sectors (if any). Record this information on paper for future reference. If a printer is attached, hold the Shift key and press the PrtSc key to obtain a printout of the information on the screen.

Note: It's a good idea to recheck the number of bad sectors over the first few weeks to see if it is increasing. This can indicate a bad disk. Use the CHKDSK program for this by giving the command

        CHKDSK C:

Now that the hard disk has been partitioned and formatted and we have placed a copy of DOS there, we are ready to establish our subdirectories.

■Establishing Subdirectories on the Hard Disk

Go to drive C with this command:

        C:\

The *root directory* of the hard disk now contains three disk files—IBMBIO.COM, IBMDOS.COM, and COMMAND.COM. As we have seen, the first two of these files are hidden while the third can be found with the DIR command.

A hard disk can hold many files. Therefore, we must establish a systematic way to locate the information we want. We will do this by setting up several subdirectories. Each subdirectory will contain files for a particular subject. For example, there can be one subdirectory for FORTRAN programs, another for assembly-language programs, a third for BASIC programs, yet another for correspondence, and so forth.

You create a subdirectory with the built-in DOS command MD (short for "make directory"). You can also use the longer command MKDIR. Subdirectories can be nested to any level. That is, it is possible to create a subdirectory of a subdirectory and, of course, a subdirectory of a subdirectory of a subdirectory. However, you will generally find it easier to have only a single level of subdirectory. When you give the MD command, the new directory is a subdirectory of the current directory. Therefore, if you want to have only one level of subdirectory, you must be certain that the root directory is current before giving the MD command. If, say, you give the MD command to create an assembly-language subdirectory while the FORTRAN subdirectory is current, the new directory will be a subdirectory of the FORTRAN subdirectory.

To ensure that the root directory is current, give the command

    **CD **

or

    CD C:

if drive C is not the current drive. Give the second command now. We next establish our first subdirectory.

Establishing a DOS Subdirectory

We will now establish a subdirectory to contain the programs found on the two original DOS diskettes and then copy the programs to the hard disk. Ensure that the root directory is current by giving the CD command. Create the subdirectory by giving this command:

    MD DOS

This command creates a subdirectory named DOS. Give the command

    DIR

and you will see the file name

    DOS <DIR>

in the directory listing. The <DIR> symbol in the listing indicates that the item is a subdirectory, not a file.

Make the new subdirectory current with the command

    CD DOS

You can also give this command as:

    CD\DOS

These two commands happen to perform the same operation at this time. However, they have different meanings. The first command refers to a subdirectory of the current directory. The second command refers to a subdirectory of the root directory. If a subdirectory named FORTRAN were current and we gave the first command, the system would try to find a subdirectory belonging to the FORTRAN subdirectory. On the other hand, the second command would first change to the root directory and then to the requested subdirectory.

Now that the subdirectory name DOS is current, let us see what it contains. Give the command

> **DIR**

and you will see two files that do not seem to have names. One name consists of only a single dot and the other a double dot. These two entries are always shown in the directory listing of a subdirectory. The double dot refers to the parent directory, while the single dot refers to the current directory. Therefore, the command

> **DIR . .**

displays a directory listing of the parent directory, while the command

> **CD . .**

makes the parent directory the default. Be especially careful with the command

> **DEL .**

which deletes all files from the current directory.

Give this command:

> **DIR **

and you will see a listing of the root directory instead of the current directory. Give the commands:

> **CD **
> **DIR**

and you will see that the root directory has been made current.

Let us see how to determine the name of the current directory.

■ Discovering the Name of the Current Subdirectory

The default prompt presents only the name of the current drive followed by the > symbol. It does not identify the current subdirectory name. We can determine the name by giving the CD command without a parameter. Thus the command

CD

will display the line

C:\

if the root directory is current, or the line

C:\DOS

if the DOS subdirectory is current. However, there is a better way to find the current subdirectory.

We can change the default prompt so as to include the directory name with this command:

PROMPT PG

Give the command and the prompt will appear as:

C:\>

if the root directory is current. Then enter the DOS subdirectory. The prompt now appears as:

C:\DOS>

We will now copy the auxiliary DOS programs from the two original floppy disks. Put the main DOS diskette in drive A, but be sure that subdirectory DOS on drive C is current. Give the command

COPY A:*.*

to copy all the files on the first diskette. After all the files have been copied, change to the auxiliary diskette and repeat the command, by pushing the F3 key.

Now let us set up another subdirectory.

Establishing a Directory for the Editor

We are next going to establish a subdirectory for the editor and related programs such as the spelling and syntax checkers. However, if we give the MD command now, the new directory will be a subdirectory of the DOS subdirectory. Instead we want the new directory to be a subdirectory of the root directory. Therefore return to the root directory with the command

**CD **

The prompt will now be

c:\\>

Establish your word-processing directory called EDIT by giving this command:

MD EDIT

Make this new directory current with the command

CD EDIT

The prompt now looks like this:

c:\\EDIT>

Place the diskette containing your word processing software into drive A. Copy the programs into the new subdirectory with this command:

COPY A:*.*

Give the DIR command to see the files that are present.
We need one more directory.

The Directory for Assembly Language

We must set up a third directory, for the assembly-language programs we are going to write. Give the command

CD

and then the command

    MD ASM

to establish the directory.

    We have now established three subdirectories on the hard disk. We will add more as time goes by. We also need to establish a means of communication between subdirectories. For example, we will want to create assembly-language programs in the ASM directory using the editor in the EDIT directory. Some editor programs can create and edit a file in a different directory; others cannot. The popular editor named WordStar cannot work on a file in another directory, because it needs access to its overlay files. Therefore, we have to provide for this limitation. One way is to create each file in the EDIT directory, and then copy it to the ASM directory. If we need to alter a program, however, we must go back to the EDIT subdirectory to make the changes. Then we must copy the new version to the ASM directory. Another possibility is to place copies of the overlay files in all the other directories. However, this solution wastes space. The best solution uses the DOS program named SUBST to establish a separate disk drive. Let us see how.

Establishing the Editing Subdirectory as Drive D

    The program SUBST.COM is available on the DOS version 3.1 diskette. (If you are using version 2 on a hard disk, you should upgrade to version 3.) SUBST can establish a dual path for a subdirectory. For example, the command

    SUBST D: C:\EDIT

makes the entire EDIT subdirectory appear as drive D. Give this command now. (Of course, the EDIT subdirectory is still accessible in the usual way.)
    Move to the ASM directory with the command

    CD \ASM

Then give the command

    DIR D:

and the directory listing for the EDIT subdirectory will appear. Move to drive D and start up WordStar. You can now create or alter files on the current subdirectory (EDIT in this example). Alternatively, you can run the WordStar installation program to configure it for drive D. Then you can run WordStar from any subdirectory on drive C.

Let us now create two auxiliary files.

TWO DOS CONFIGURATION FILES

If you skipped over the previous section because you did not have a hard disk, this is where you continue.

We learned previously that each time DOS is started, it looks for two disk files: CONFIG.SYS and AUTOEXEC.BAT. These files are used to configure DOS for your particular requirements. However, they are not required for the operation of DOS. In fact, they are not even supplied with DOS; you must create them yourself. Check to see if these files exist on your system diskette in drive A or on the root directory of the hard disk. If they are present, get a printed copy. Turn on your printer and give these commands:

```
COPY CONFIG.SYS PRN
COPY AUTOEXEC.BAT PRN
```

If the files are not present, we will create them now.

We will make one version for a hard-disk computer and another for a floppy-disk system. We begin with the CONFIG.SYS file.

Creating the CONFIG.SYS File for a Hard Disk

If you have a hard disk, make the root directory the current one. If the new drive D: is current, first give the command

```
C:
```

and then the command

```
CD\
```

We are first going to create the file CONFIG.SYS. If your editor is configured for drive D you can begin at this point. Otherwise, move to drive

D and create this file on drive C. For WordStar, be sure to use the N (nondocument) command rather than the D (document) command.

Enter these two lines:

```
BUFFERS = 16
FILES = 15
```

if you have a 10 megabyte (MB) hard disk. If you have a 20 or 30 MB disk, set the number of buffers to 32. This will increase the number of buffers from the default value of 2 for the PC or 3 for the AT and increase the number of available file handles from the default of eight. If you already have a CONFIG.SYS file and these commands are not present, use your editor to add them. If the commands are present and the values are smaller, use your editor to increase them to the values shown.

The BUFFERS command specifies how many 128-byte disk buffers will be established in memory. When information is read from disk, it is placed in memory buffers. Each time data is to be read from disk, the buffers are first checked to see if the information is already in memory. If so, it can be read more rapidly from the buffer than from the disk. A larger number of buffers will keep more data in memory from recently read disk files. However, there are two disadvantages to increasing the number of buffers.

A large number of buffers reduces the size of working memory. Furthermore, as the number of buffers increases, it takes longer to search the buffers for the desired data. You can experiment with your system to determine the optimum number of buffers, but you should start with the above values.

The FILES command sets the largest number of file handles that can be assigned to one program. The default value is eight. However, the system uses three of these for the peripherals, as discussed in Chapter 2.

■ Creating the CONFIG.SYS File for a Floppy-Disk System

With a floppy-disk system, use your editor to create the file CONFIG.SYS on the system diskette in drive A. Add these three lines:

```
BUFFERS = 4
FILES = 15
DEVICE = VDISK.SYS 345
```

if you have the full 640K bytes of memory. Reduce the number from 345 if you have less memory. Notice that the number of buffers is greatly reduced from the hard-disk value, but the number of files remains the same. Furthermore, a third line has been added.

The VDISK program creates a virtual disk in main memory that appears to be another disk. The advantage is that it operates many times faster than a floppy disk. It is even faster than a hard disk. Unlike other virtual disk programs, such as SuperDrv, it does not require changing switches within the computer system unit.

The VDISK program is found on the DOS disk for version 3. It is not provided with version 2 but it can be used with this version. The VDISK program can also be used with a hard-disk system, but it does not provide such a noticeable change, since hard disks are so much faster than floppy disks. An exception is the PC AT computer.

The manuals state that, for DOS versions 2 and 3, 640K is the upper limit to usable memory, even for the AT. However, this limitation is artificial, and in Chapter 9, we'll look at a method of expanding the available memory to 704K. Moreover, while the regular PC and XT are limited to 1 MB of memory, the AT can address 16 MB. DOS versions 2 and 3 can only use a maximum of 640K bytes, even on the AT. However, you can expand the memory by purchasing a memory board such as the AST Advantage. The memory on this board fills out the 512K bytes to 640K bytes and then adds more memory above 1MB. The VDISK program normally establishes its RAM disk in main memory below the 640K-byte limit. But on the AT computer, VDISK can establish the RAM disk entirely above 1MB, leaving a full 640K bytes of memory for DOS. With this arrangement, we should not use the SUBST program to set up our editor directory as a separate drive. Rather, we establish a RAM disk as drive D for the editing program.

Now let us consider the AUTOEXEC program.

■ Creating the AUTOEXEC.BAT File

We will now create the second file that DOS automatically reads each time the computer is turned on or reset. This is the AUTOEXEC.BAT file. We can place a list of commands in this file and DOS will perform the indicated operations. With your editor create a file called AUTOEXEC.-BAT and add these lines:

```
ECHO OFF
BREAK ON
```

```
VERIFY ON
PATH A:\ or PATH C:\DOS
```

The first line turns off the ECHO command. It reduces the amount of information displayed on the screen as the other commands are carried out.

You may want to terminate an executing program prematurely, perhaps because the command-line parameters are wrong or because the data are incorrect. Holding the Ctrl key and pressing the Break key will terminate a program only when there is keyboard input or screen output. But there may not be input or output during the beginning of a program. However, if BREAK is turned on, DOS will check for Ctrl-Break when any DOS function is executed. The default setting is OFF. Some people think that BREAK should be turned off when debugging a program; but I have not found this to be a problem.

Normally when DOS writes a disk file, it does not check to see if the information was correctly written. The third command turns on verification so that DOS will check that each file is correctly written. Of course, when VERIFY is on, it takes longer to write a disk file. However, the delay is not noticeable.

The fourth line establishes a search path for executable programs; it tells DOS where to look for a program when it cannot be found on the current disk. Use drive A for a floppy-disk system and drive C for a hard-disk system.

You will want to place other commands in the AUTOEXEC.BAT file. For example, if you have an AST battery-powered clock and a print spooler such as SUPERSPL, you should include the next two commands:

```
ASTCLOCK >NUL
SUPERSPL LPT1:/M = 18
```

The first line sets the system clock from the battery-powered clock. The >NUL command reduces the output on the screen.

The second command establishes an 18K-byte printer buffer or spooler in memory for the parallel printer. Normally, when you send a file to the printer or print the video screen with Shift-PrtSc, you have to wait until the printer has finished before you can do any other computing. When a print buffer has been established, however the buffer is rapidly filled and so control quickly returns to you. You can then perform your next operation while the printer works from the memory buffer.

You will want to copy your editor, assembler, linker, debugger, and related programs into a RAM disk if you have established one. We will add other files to this list as we develop them—our macro library, for example.

Here are the typical commands you will want to include in your AUTO-EXEC.BAT file at this point:

```
COPY A:WS*.*  C: >NUL          (Editor)
COPY A:MASM.EXE C: >NUL        (Assembler)
COPY A:LINK.EXE C: >NUL        (Linker)
COPY A:EXE2BIN.EXE C: >NUL     (COM converter)
COPY A:DEBUG.COM C: >NUL       (Debugger)
```

On the other hand, if you have a PC AT with a hard disk as drive C and a RAM disk as drive D, the corresponding commands might be these:

```
COPY C:\EDIT\WS*.* D: >NUL      (Editor)
COPY C:\DOS\MASM.EXE D: >NUL    (Assembler)
COPY C:\DOS\LINK.EXE D: >NUL    (Linker)
COPY C:\DOS\EXE2BIN.EXE D: >NUL (COM converter)
COPY C:\DOS\DEBUG.COM D: >NUL   (Debugger)
```

SUMMARY

In this chapter we have learned how to set up the computer so that it will be easy to use. We saw how to partition and then format a hard disk, how to increase the default number of disk buffers and file handles, and how to activate the BREAK command to terminate a program prematurely and the VERIFY command to ensure that disks files are properly written. We learned how to establish a RAM disk and a printer buffer to speed up the operation of our computer.

In the next chapter we briefly review assembly-language programming and learn several ways to write an executable program.

Assembly
Language

INTRODUCTION

In the previous chapters we studied the hardware and the operating system of the IBM PC. We also learned how to configure your computer for easy operation. In this chapter we review assembly-language programming, write a simple program, learn several ways to write executable programs, and then consider the use of macros.

A computer can only execute instructions that are written in binary code and located in the main memory. We could, in principle, program a computer by writing the desired instructions in binary, but there are easier ways. Computer languages such as BASIC, FORTRAN, and Pascal make it relatively easy to get a computer to do what you want. These languages are ideal for science and engineering problems. You write a *source program* containing expressions that specify how a particular problem is going to be solved. Then a translator program called a *compiler* or *interpreter* converts your source program into the binary code directly executable by the computer. Each line of the source program may produce several binary instructions for the computer. Unfortunately, these high-level languages produce relatively large binary programs. Therefore, they are not suitable for writing *systems programs,* which help make the computer run more efficiently.

Another approach to writing computer programs is assembly language. Here, also, a source program is written to specify the desired operation. A translator program, called an *assembler,* converts the source program to binary instructions. However, unlike FORTRAN, BASIC, and Pascal programs, assembly language is a low-level computer language. Each line of the source program corresponds to one machine-language instruction. Since there is a one-to-one correspondence between the source code and the resulting binary instructions, the code is small and runs fast. Therefore, assembly language is ideally suited to systems programs.

The disadvantage of assembly language is that it is more obtuse and requires a good knowledge of the CPU instruction set. Furthermore, it may require several instructions to perform a single task. For example, to display the string

Hello, world.

on the video screen, we must write six lines of instructions in addition to the string itself. Yet it is possible to simplify the operation with a *macro,* an assembler directive that defines a group of commands. In fact, we will write a macro for just this purpose. Then we can write a string with the simple statement

@write   'Hello, world.'

We will return to the subject of macros when we use them in a sample program later in this chapter. Let us first consider the form of an assembly-language program.

The Assembly-Language Source Program

The assembly-language source program is written with an ordinary text editor such as WordStar. But you must be careful to use the N, nondocument, mode rather than the D, document mode. Otherwise, some of the characters you enter into the source file will not be understandable by the assembler. (We will later write a program to convert such a WordStar document file into a form the assembler can understand.)

We arrange the source program in four columns, or *fields,* by using the Tab key. The assembler does not require this alignment, but it is conventional, and programs aligned in this way are easier to read.

The source program is composed of three types of lines—operation codes ("op codes" for short), assembler directives (pseudo-operation codes, or "psuedo ops"), and comments. The operation codes create instructions for the CPU; the other two types do not generate instructions. As the name suggests, assembler directives give instructions to the assembler (not the CPU). Alternatively, directives can create constants or establish data areas. Comments, of course, are for our benefit; they remind us of what the program is trying to accomplish.

The Operation Code

A source line containing an operation code can have the following four columns:

LABEL   MNEMONIC   OPERAND   COMMENT

The *label* is a symbolic reference to the memory location (called the *offset* in the code segment) where the next instruction, represented by the mnemonic, is located. It can be the target of a jump or subroutine call. The label can contain as many as 31 characters but is usually much shorter. The characters can be letters, digits, the underline, dollar sign, question mark, and the at-sign (@). The first character in the label cannot be a digit. A colon is placed at the end of the label to indicate that it will be referenced only within the current segment. To make our programs easier to read, we will try to place labels on separate lines from the instructions.

The *mnemonic* corresponds to a CPU instruction (the instruction set is summarized in Appendix C). Additional information can be obtained in the *IBM Technical Reference* manual and other programming books.[1] The *operand* modifies the operation of the instruction by providing one or two parameters. Consider this sample instruction:

```
no_par:    MOV AL,    [buf_cnt]    ;get buffer size
```

This line begins with the label *no_par,* which defines the location of the opcode—in this example, MOV. The colon indicates that the label will be referenced only within the code segment, the 64K-byte block that contains the op codes. The mnemonic is converted to a CPU instruction that moves a byte of data from a memory location, referenced by the symbol *buf_cnt,* into the CPU register known as AL. The comment reminds us of the action; it begins with a semicolon. This instruction demonstrates a style used throughout the book. Symbols, such as MOV and AL, that are defined within the assembler are given in uppercase letters. On the other hand, symbols that are defined by the programmer are given in lowercase letters. (In running text they appear in *italic* type.) However, this is only for clarity. The assembler does not distinguish between uppercase and lowercase letters in symbolic names.

■ The Assembler Directive

Assembler directives control the operation of the assembler. As an example, the directive

```
PAGE     ,132
```

tells the assembler to format each page of the listing with up to 132 columns rather than the standard 80 columns. The assembler directives are listed in Appendix D.

Directives can also be used to define constants. For example, suppose we want to load a register with an ASCII character such as the blank or period. If we use the ASCII character directly, as in this example:

```
MOV        AL,' '
```

---

[1] *IBM Technical Reference, IBM Personal Computer,* 6322507, Boca Raton. Fla.: 1984, and J. W. Coffron, *Programming the 8086/8088,* Berkeley, Calif.: SYBEX, 1983.

it may be misread in the listing. It would be clearer if we first defined a constant called BLANK, and then used that throughout the program. For example, the directive

```
blank        EQU           20h
```

defines the blank symbol, that is, a symbol having the ASCII value for a blank space, 20 hex or 32 decimal. Then the instruction

```
MOV          AL,blank
```

performs the same operation as the previous version, but it is easier to read. This technique is also useful for the unprintable ASCII characters, such as carriage return and line feed. For example, we can define these symbols:

```
cr          EQU           13            ;carriage return
lf          EQU           10            ;line feed
```

Then we can use the symbols directly. For example:

```
CMP          AL,cr
```

is clearer than the equivalent expression:

```
CMP          AL,13
```

Another reason for using symbolic constants is that changes can be made more easily. That is, only the definition needs to be altered.

We go through the steps of program development next.

ASSEMBLY AND EXECUTION OF A PROGRAM

Let us consider the steps needed to convert an assembly-language program to an executable program. We learned previously that there are two types of executable programs—those with the extension EXE and those with the extension COM. We will usually create only the COM file in this book, although we will write two EXE programs in this chapter to show their structure.

The assembly-language source program is written with an editor; it is given a file name that has the extension ASM. We generate a COM file from the ASM file in several steps. First we execute the macro assembler, MASM, to generate a file with the extension OBJ (for object). Then we run the linker, LINK, to create an EXE file. Finally, we convert the EXE file to a COM file with the EXE2BIN program. (As we shall see, not all EXE files are executable.)

Because each of these steps can require parameters to be specified, the assembly and linkage process can be complicated. Therefore, we will greatly simplify the operation with a batch file named EXEC. Then we can assemble a program named, say, KEYSWAP simply by giving this command:

EXEC   KEYSWAP

Our EXEC program will work with both a floppy-disk system and a hard-disk system if we have established a search path to the DOS subdirectory. (See Chapter 3 for ways to set up your computer.)

■ A Batch File for Assembling and Linking an ASM File

Set up subdirectories on your disk as outlined in the previous chapter. If you have a hard disk, your editor should be located in a directory named EDIT and cross-referenced as drive D by use of the SUBST program. Place the assembler MASM.EXE, the linker LINK.EXE, and the EXE2BIN.EXE program in the DOS subdirectory. Define the path to be

C:\DOS

so that you can access these files from any subdirectory. There should be a directory named ASM to hold the assembly-language source files.

If you have a floppy-disk system, set up your system disk as outlined in the previous chapter. If you have 640K bytes of memory, you can devote 350K bytes to a RAM disk. Then, under the direction of the AUTOEXEC-.BAT program, the system can copy the editor, assembler, and related programs from the system disk to the RAM disk each time you start your computer.

If your electricity is not dependable, you must be careful about losing source files stored on the RAM disk. If the electricity goes off, you will lose anything stored on the RAM disk (as well as information in main memory). Only the source file is irreplaceable; a copy of the system files remains on the diskette in drive A. Therefore, create and edit the source file shown in Figure 4.1 on floppy disk B, then place a copy on RAM disk C. Finally, run the batch file to compile, link, and run your program. Let us go through the code.

When you give the command

EXEC *fname*

where *fname* stands for the primary file name of your source program (do not include the ASM extension), the EXEC file performs all the necessary work. Throughout the file you see the symbol %1. This is a dummy parameter that is replaced by the file name you give as a parameter on the command line. The first line displays a message:

Assemble and link fname

on the video screen, reminding you of what is happening. Your file name is clearly shown. The second line checks to see that the file you want to assemble exists. If not, the program terminates with a branch to the label END at the end of the file. The next line erases the OBJ file from the previous assembly, if it exists. If it does not exist a nonfatal error message appears, telling you that such a file does not exist. The fourth line:

MASM %1,%1;

directs the assembler to create an OBJ file from your ASM file if no syntax errors are present. The fifth line checks to see that the OBJ file is

```
REM Assemble and link %1
IF NOT EXIST %1.ASM GOTO END
ERASE %1.OBJ
MASM %1,%1;
IF NOT EXIST %1.OBJ GOTO END
LINK %1,%1,NUL;
IF NOT EXIST %1.EXE GOTO END
IF NOT "A%2" == "A" GOTO RUN
EXE2BIN %1.EXE %1.COM
ERASE %1.EXE
:RUN
PAUSE   CTRL-BREAK TO TERMINATE OR
%1
:END
```

Figure 4.1: *EXEC, a batch file for assembling an ASM file.*

present. (The absence of an OBJ file indicates errors in your source program.) If an OBJ file does not exist, the batch file terminates with a branch to the label END.

The sixth line:

```
LINK %1,%1,NUL;
```

directs the linker to create an EXE file from the OBJ file. The NUL command prevents creation of the assembly listing. The following line checks to see if the linker completed its task. A branch to the end occurs if no EXE file can be found.

The line

```
IF NOT "A%2" == "A" GOTO RUN
```

checks to see if a second parameter was entered on the command line. If it was, A%2 will not equal A, and so the batch program branches to the label RUN. This step is used for EXE files. (Of course, we will not use a second parameter when we assemble a COM file.) The next step:

```
EXE2BIN %1.EXE %1.COM
```

converts the EXE file to a COM file. The following line deletes the EXE file since it is no longer needed. (As we learned earlier, the EXE form of a COM file cannot usually be executed.)

The PAUSE command gives you a choice of running the new program or terminating without running. It displays the line

```
CTRL-BREAK TO TERMINATE OR
```

on the screen. Then the PAUSE command automatically causes DOS to add the line

```
Press any key to continue
```

You can press Ctrl-Break to terminate the batch file or any other key to run the newly assembled and linked executable program. (The %1 command tells DOS to run your program.)

Let us see how to get a program listing.

■ A Batch File for an Assembly Listing

In the previous section we used a batch file to assemble and link our program into an EXE or COM file. However, this operation did not produce an assembly listing of our program, which would contain the corresponding addresses and code. If you want to alter a program, or try to find an error with the debugger, it helps to have an assembly listing. Let us create another batch file for this purpose. This version begins relatively simply. However, we will add several features to it later in the book.

Create a new file, named EXLIST.BAT, and add the lines shown in Figure 4.2. The first line of the batch file displays the line

Produce an assembly listing for <fname>

on the video screen. Of course, <fname> will be replaced by the name of your program. The second line:

MASM %1,NUL,%1.LST;

directs the assembler to create an assembly listing of your program and give it the extension LST. The NUL directive omits creation of the OBJ file. The third line:

IF "A%2" == "A" GOTO END

sends a copy of the listing to the printer if you entered a second parameter on the command line. It does not matter what symbol you use. If you did not include a second parameter, A%2 will equal A, and so the program will branch to the label END. The next-to-last line sends the assembly listing to the printer.

Now let us consider several examples of program organization.

```
REM Produce an assembly listing for %1
MASM %1,NUL,%1.LST;
IF "A%2" == "A" GOTO END
COPY %1.LST PRN
:END
```

Figure 4.2: *EXLIST, a batch file to print an assembly listing.*

EXAMPLES OF PROGRAM LAYOUT

As we have seen, DOS can execute two types of programs—those with the extension EXE and those with the extension COM. We must clearly distinguish between the two because they have different forms. The EXE program is a FAR procedure, called from another segment, and the COM program is a NEAR procedure, called from within the code segment. There is a further complication since COM programs have the extension EXE at some point in their creation. However, they cannot be executed in this form.

With the EXE program we can define four different segments—*code, data, extra,* and *stack*. This arrangement can be particularly convenient, as we can place the code in the *code* segment, the data in the *data* segment, and the stack in the *stack* segment. On the other hand, when we write a COM program we can only define a single code segment. Then we must place the data and the stack in that code segment. Nevertheless, except for sample programs in this chapter, we will always use the COM file since it creates smaller programs, which can be loaded faster.

Let us look at several different program layouts. Each will display the line

    Hello, world.

on the video screen. We begin with the EXE form.

A Sample EXE Program, Version 1

The assembly source program given in Figure 4.3 assembles to an executable EXE file. Three separate segments are defined: the stack segment, named *stack;* the data segment, named *data;* and the code segment, named code. The symbols *code, data,* and *stack* are arbitrary; any other symbol could have been used. Let us go through the program.

The first line is an assembler directive that sets the width of the printer listing to 132 characters. The next line is an assembler directive defining the title to be displayed at the top of each page of the listing. The third line begins a block of comments that continue over several lines. Two asterisks define the block.

The stack segment is defined next. We give it the symbolic name *stack.* The stack area is set to 16 times 8 bytes and is initially filled with the letters STACK followed by three blanks. The data segment is given the name *data* and contains the string we want to display. The string is terminated with a dollar sign, an end-of-string marker so that the print routine can determine the end.

The code segment follows the data segment; it is defined by the SEG-MENT and ENDS (end segment) directives:

```
code        SEGMENT
. . .
code        ENDS
```

This segment generates the instructions for the computer. It starts with the ASSUME directive, which tells the assembler that the symbols *code* and *data* will respectively define the code and data segments. Since the EXE file

```
            PAGE      ,132
            TITLE     HELLO1

COMMENT *
  Write Hello, world. on screen
  Program runs as EXE file
 *

stack   SEGMENT STACK
        DB        16 DUP('STACK    ')
stack   ENDS

data    SEGMENT
mes     DB        'Hello, world.$'
data    ENDS

code    SEGMENT
        ASSUME    CS:code, DS:data
main    PROC      FAR

strt:
        PUSH      DS              ;setup return
        XOR       AX,AX
        PUSH      AX
; set up DS
        MOV       AX,data
        MOV       DS,AX
; display message
        MOV       AH,9            ;DOS function
        MOV       DX, OFFSET mes  ;text
        INT       21h
        RET                       ;quit
main    ENDP

code    ENDS
        END       strt
```

Figure 4.3: *A sample EXE program.*

is a FAR procedure, we enclose the CPU instructions in a block defined by the two directives:

```
main      PROC        FAR
. . .
main      ENDP
```

When an EXE program begins execution, the CS register points to the beginning of the code segment. On the other hand, the DS and ES registers point to the address needed to return to DOS at the conclusion of the program. Since we must change the DS register to reference the data segment, our first task is to establish a return path before the information is replaced in the DS register. We do this with the first three instructions:

```
PUSH      DS
XOR       AX,AX
PUSH      AX
```

These instructions push the DS register onto the stack, set the AX register to zero (the offset of the Return instruction) with the XOR instruction, and then push this value of zero onto the stack. Now, a simple Return (RET) instruction will terminate the program and give control back to DOS. Of course, any other general-purpose register could have been used instead of AX. However, we cannot set a segment register to zero in this way.

The next step changes the DS register so that it refers to the data segment. This is done with two instructions. We move the location of the data segment into the AX register and then copy the AX register to the DS register. We must use the AX register since operations with segment registers are limited to transfers with other registers and with the contents of memory locations. Thus we cannot directly load DS with the offset of a memory location. Instead, we must use a register such as AX as an intermediate step. Again, any general-purpose register can be used in place of AX. The program can now terminate with a Return statement. The following six instructions, then, form the shell of the EXE program:

```
          PUSH      DS          ;setup return
          XOR       AX,AX
          PUSH      AX
; set up DS
          MOV       AX,data
          MOV       DS,AX
          . . .
          RET
```

They will always be needed when an EXE program terminates with a Return statement.

The next three instructions constitute the main part of the program. As we learned in Chapter 2, function 9 of DOS interrupt 21 hex displays a string of characters on the screen. We load the AH register with the function number, 9, and the DX register with the offset address of the string. Then we execute interrupt 21 hex, which displays the string on the screen. The program terminates with the Return statement.

Following the Return statement are three more assembler directives. The first (ENDP) closes the main procedure, the second (ENDS) closes the code segment, and the last (END) terminates the source program and designates the address *strt* as the starting point of the program at execution time.

If you want to try out this program, create a file named HELLO1.ASM that contains the lines shown in Figure 4.3. Then run the EXEC batch file (Figure 4.1). Give this command:

```
EXEC HELLO1 X
```

The second parameter, X, tells the batch file that this is an EXE file rather than a COM file. It can be replaced by any other letter or digit. It is just used as a flag. At the end of the assembly and linkage steps, you are given the choice of either running or not running the program. Your message:

```
CTRL-BREAK TO TERMINATE OR
```

is followed by the DOS message

```
strike a key when ready . . .
```

Press the Space bar to run the program and you will see the message

```
Hello, world.
```

on the video screen below your prompt. Alternatively, you can press Ctrl-Break to quit the batch file without running the newly created program. You would do this when you find an error message on the screen.

Let us look at a variation of the EXE program.

■ A Second Form of EXE Program

The previous sample EXE program runs on all versions of DOS. However, it is unnecessarily complicated. In this section we present a simpler version. The disadvantage is that the new version will only run on DOS version 2 or later. But since we assume throughout this book that you are running version 2 or later anyway, this restriction should not be a problem.

Our second version of the EXE program is given in Figure 4.4. Both versions are the same up to the beginning of the code segment. We still define the code segment block:

```
code        SEGMENT
. . .
code        ENDS
```

However, the new version does not use a procedure, and so there is no procedure block, nor is there a Return statement. Therefore, since we do not have to set up the stack for a Return statement, we do not have to push the return address, contained in DS, onto the stack. The instructions begin by establishing the data segment and end with a function call. Thus, the following four instructions:

```
; set up DS
            MOV         AX,data
            MOV         DS,AX
            . . .
            MOV         AH,4Ch
            INT         21h             ;quit
```

are common in this form of EXE file. The value 4C hex in the next-to-last line is a DOS function that terminates the program and returns control to DOS. The three lines that display a string constitute the main part of the program. As before, we close the code segment and finish with the END statement.

Copy the previous program, HELLO1, giving it the name HELLO2.ASM. Change it to look like Figure 4.4. Assemble, link, and run the program with the command

```
    EXEC        HELLO2        X
```

The result will be the same as before. Now let us look at COM files.

■ The COM Program

Because COM programs are smaller and load faster, we will use them for the programs we write in this book. Several forms can be used. We

will look at different versions that are commonly used in published programs before settling on a simple form.

A Sample COM Program, Version 1

The program shown in Figure 4.5 gives the same result as the previous
programs. However, it is a COM file rather than an EXE file. The first difference we can see is that there is only one segment. COM files begin execution with all four segment registers pointing to the termination address at
the beginning of the Program Segment Prefix (PSP). The executable code

```
             PAGE     ,132
             TITLE    HELLO2

COMMENT *
  December 15, 1985
  Write Hello, world. on screen
  Program runs as EXE file
  Three segments
  Terminate with INT 21h, Function 4Ch
  *

stack    SEGMENT STACK
         DB       16 DUP('STACK   ')
stack    ENDS

data     SEGMENT
mes      DB        'Hello, world.$'
data     ENDS

code     SEGMENT
         ASSUME   CS:code, DS:data

strt:
; set up DS
         MOV      AX,data
         MOV      DS,AX
; display message
         MOV      AH,9             ;DOS function
         MOV      DX, OFFSET mes   ;text
         INT      21h
         MOV      AH,4Ch
         INT      21h              ;quit

code     ENDS
         END      strt
```

Figure 4.4: *An EXE program for DOS version 2 and later.*

starts 100 hex (256 decimal) bytes into the code segment. Thus the ASSUME directive tells the assembler that the CS and DS registers are both set to the code segment. We are not allowed to define a separate stack segment when we create a COM program. Furthermore, we do not have to set these registers, since the linker does this for us. Of course, we can establish data and stack areas within the code segment if we need to.

The next directive:

ORG   100h

sets the instruction pointer to where the code must begin in the segment. We place such a statement at the beginning of each COM file; it is the distinguishing feature of COM files. You frequently see this statement at the beginning of published EXE files. However, it is unnecessary in an EXE file and therefore wastes 256 bytes of memory at the beginning of the code segment.

```
            PAGE      ,132
            TITLE     HELLO3

COMMENT *
  Write Hello, world. on screen
  Program runs as COM file, one segment
  Termination with RET statement
 *
code     SEGMENT
         ASSUME   CS:code, DS:code
         ORG      100h
main     PROC     near

strt:

; display message
         MOV      AH,9             ;DOS function
         MOV      DX, OFFSET mes   ;text
         INT      21h
         RET                       ;quit

; Data area

mes      DB       'Hello, world.$'
main     ENDP

code     ENDS
         END      strt
```

Figure 4.5: *A COM program that terminates with a Return.*

The procedure block:

```
main        PROC        NEAR
 . . .
main        ENDP
```

defines our statements. Notice that we have defined a NEAR procedure rather than a FAR procedure as in the first program. Programmers sometimes push the DS or ES register onto the stack and then push a zero, as in our first executable program. However, this step is unnecessary since DOS automatically sets up the stack for us. Thus, a simple Return is all that is needed to terminate the program.

The main part of the program is the same as before, except that we do not have to establish the DS register. As we have seen, DOS does this for us. Notice that the data—the string to be printed—is placed at the end of the code segment after the Return statement. Then we point the DX register to that location. The placement of the data in the code segment is problematical. If we place it at the beginning, we must branch over it, but if we place it at the end of the program, we must make a *forward reference,* that is, a reference to an instruction or data that has yet to be encountered by the assembler.

The assembler analyzes our source program twice. On the first pass, when our assembler encounters the statement

```
    MOV        DX,OFFSET mes              ;text
```

the meaning of the symbol *mes* is unknown. The assembler makes a guess and keeps going. Of course, the meaning of *mes* becomes clear when the data string is encountered at the end of the program. Then, on the second pass, the assembler can complete the above instruction. This is sometimes called "resolving" unknown references. The forward reference is interpreted correctly this time. However, in other cases it will cause errors. Therefore, we will frequently place our data at the beginning or middle of the code segment and then branch over it. This will avoid a forward-reference problem. We will consider this problem in more detail later.

If you want to try out this program, create a file with the name HELLO3.ASM Assemble, link, and run it with the EXEC batch file. Give the command

```
    EXEC       HELLO3
```

During the assembly operation, the linker issues this message:

Warning: no stack segment

Do not be alarmed, however. We have seen that we cannot define a stack segment for a COM program. Therefore, this is not an error message. In fact, it would be an error if we did define a stack segment. Unfortunately, this message will always appear during the linking of a COM file. Press the Space bar to run the program. The result will be the same as before.

We next see how to avoid using a Return statement.

A Sample COM Program, Version 2

In the previous example we terminated a COM program with a Return statement. This program was simpler than the previous ones, which created EXE files. Nevertheless, terminating a program with a Return statement requires careful control of the stack. We avoid this problem in our next example by not using a procedure and thus avoiding the Return statement. Instead, we terminate our program with interrupt 21 hex, function 4C hex. This is the same technique we used in the second version of our EXE program. In fact, this program can be run in its EXE form if we want to. However, there is no advantage to doing that. The program is shown in Figure 4.6. Let us go through the instructions.

```
              PAGE      ,132
              TITLE     HELLO4

COMMENT *
    Write Hello, world. on screen
    Program runs as COM file
    Terminate with INT 21, function 4C
  *
code    SEGMENT
        ASSUME  CS:code, DS:code
        ORG     100h
strt:

; display message
        MOV     AH,9            ;DOS function
        MOV     DX, OFFSET mes  ;text
        INT     21h
        MOV     AH,4Ch
        INT     21h             ;quit

; Data area

mes     DB      'Hello, world.$'

code    ENDS
        END     strt
```

Figure 4.6: A COM program terminating with INT 21h.

This second program looks much like the previous one, except that we omit the PROC and ENDP block. We still use three lines in the middle to print a string, and the string is placed at the end of the program. However, we change the Return instruction to

```
MOV        AH,4Ch
INT        21h                ;quit
```

for program termination. These two instructions can be used anywhere in our program when we want to terminate it. We do not have to be concerned about the status of the stack. If you want to run this program, make a copy of the previous file, giving it the name HELLO4.ASM. Change it to look like Figure 4.6.

Now let us look at our final version.

A Sample COM Program, Version 3

Our final version, shown in Figure 4.7, is almost the same as the previous one. As in the previous version, there is no procedure (subroutine) block. Therefore, we do not need to be concerned with the stack. The only difference between the two programs is that we use the two-byte instruction

```
INT        20h
```

to terminate the program. Remember, however, that this method can only be used to terminate a COM program, not for an EXE program. If you want to run this program, copy the previous version, using the file name HELLO5.ASM. Change the two instructions

```
MOV        AH,4Ch
INT        21h
```

to the one instruction

```
INT        20h
```

Assemble and execute as before with the command

```
EXEC       HELLO5
```

The programs we have been writing demonstrate several methods for creating assembly-language programs. We are going to use the last method as a template for the remaining programs in this book because it is compact, creates small code, and loads quickly. Nevertheless, it is possible to reduce the size of the assembly-language program even further. Let us see how.

BEGINNING A MACRO LIBRARY

Earlier in the chapter, we alluded to the concept of *macros*. A macro is an assembler directive that defines a collection of commands, instructions, general text, or other macros. A macro consists of two parts—the definition and one or more implementations called *expansions*. The macro name is associated with the text contained in the definition. Whenever a macro name appears in an assembly-language source program, the macro assembler substitutes the corresponding text. This replacement is known as the

```
            PAGE     ,132
            TITLE    HELLO5

COMMENT *
  Write Hello, world on screen
  Program runs as COM file, one segment
  Terminate with INT 20
  *
code     SEGMENT
         ASSUME  CS:code, DS:code
         ORG      100h
strt:

; display message
         MOV      AH,9            ;DOS function
         MOV      DX, OFFSET mes  ;text
         INT      21h
         INT      20h             ;quit

; Data area

mes      DB       'Hello, world.$'

code     ENDS
         END      strt
```

Figure 4.7: *A COM program terminating with INT 20h.*

macro expansion. Thus we can define a new kind of instruction that is a combination of regular instructions.

The macro definition can be placed either at the beginning of a program or in a separate disk file as a *macro library*. We will use the latter method. We are going to build a macro library that can be used by all the programs we write in this book. Before we are through, the library will contain over a dozen routines. Let us look at an elementary macro.

When the assembler encounters a macro name in the source program, it replaces the name with the corresponding text of the macro definition. Since the macro text is usually longer than the macro name, this step is commonly known as a macro expansion. As an example, consider the following four instructions:

```
PUSH      AX
PUSH      BX
PUSH      CX
PUSH      DX
```

We can define a macro called *@push_abcd* as follows:

```
@push_abcd   MACRO
             PUSH      AX
             PUSH      BX
             PUSH      CX
             PUSH      DX
             ENDM
```

That is, we add a header that defines the macro name, insert the desired instructions, and then close the macro with the ENDM directive. If we then use the macro name in our source program, like this:

```
@push_abcd
```

the assembler will substitute the four corresponding instructions as if we had placed them directly in the source program. Let us see how a macro can simplify our previous program (HELLO5, listed in Figure 4.7) by creating a library with two macros.

With your text editor, create a file named MYLIB.MAC. Add the lines given in Figure 4.8 to define our first two macros. Our library now contains two macros, *@go_dos* and *@write*. Macro names are formed like any other symbol. However, throughout this book we will begin all macro names with the at-sign. This will clearly indicate the presence of a macro implementation in our source program and avoid confusion with a label or definition. Notice that the macro library begins with a listing of the macros—the names, parameters if any, and a brief reminder of the purpose. Of course, a macro's name should be chosen to suggest its purpose.

Now that we have defined two macros, let us incorporate them into the previous program.

■ Adding Macros to Our Sample Program

Make a copy of the previous program and give it the name HEL-LO6.ASM. Change it to look like Figure 4.9. The first few lines are the same as the previous version, but just before the start of the code segment we add the following three lines:

```
IF 1
INCLUDE    mylib.mac
ENDIF
```

```
; Macro library for the IBM and Microsoft assemblers

; Macros in this library
;  @go_dos      MACRO              ;return to DOS by 20h
;  @write       MACRO     text?    ;write text on screen

@go_dos MACRO
;; Return to DOS
          INT     20h
          ENDM
@write    MACRO   text?
          LOCAL   around,mesg
;; Macro to embed version number
;; Usage:        @write  'title, date'
          PUSH    AX
          PUSH    DX
          MOV     AH,9               ;;write string
          MOV     DX,OFFSET mesg
          INT     21h
          POP     DX
          POP     AX
          JMP     SHORT around

mesg      DB      text?,'$'
around:                     ;;write
          ENDM
```

Figure 4.8: *The beginning of a macro library.*

The second line, the INCLUDE directive, tells the assembler to stop processing the lines of the current source program and continue with the source code in the library MYLIB.MAC. This directive has the same effect as inserting the entire library at this place in the source program. The INCLUDE directive greatly reduces the program size. Without a library file, we would have to place a copy of each macro definition at the beginning of each program. By placing the macro definitions in a common library, however, we can have each assembly-language program refer to a common library file.

The new first and third lines form a conditional block around the INCLUDE directive:

```
IF1
. . .
ENDIF
```

They tell the assembler to use the library only during the first pass of assembly. The assembler needs the macro definitions only during the first of the two passes. If you do not use this conditional block, the entire

```
            PAGE     ,132
            TITLE    HELLO6

COMMENT *
  Write Hello, world. on screen
  Program runs as COM file
  Terminate with INT 20
  With macro library
 *
            IF1
            INCLUDE mylib.mac
            ENDIF

code     SEGMENT
ASSUME   CS:code, DS:code
            ORG      100h
strt:
; display message
            @write   'Hello, world.'
            @go_dos           ;quit

code     ENDS
            END      strt
```

Figure 4.9: *Using macros with the HELLO program.*

library will be shown in the assembly listing as the assembler goes through the library the second time.

The next few lines are the same for both versions of our program. However, just after the label *strt* we find the two macro implementations:

```
@write      'Hello, world.'
@go_dos                     ;quit
```

Then the program concludes with the usual two statements, ENDS and END. Notice that the macro version of our source program is shorter than the previous version. Let us assemble the current version before we study the macros further.

Assemble the macro version with the EXLIST batch program rather than the usual EXEC file, so that we can study the assembly listing. The command is

```
EXLIST    HELLO6    X
```

The assembly listing should look like Figure 4.10. Notice that the listing is both wider and longer than the source file. The PAGE directive at the top of the program tells the assembler to allow for the wide lines; the macros increase the length.

The assembly listing shows our original source code on the right side of the page. The left side shows the corresponding addresses and the resulting code next to each instruction or data statement. Several lines contain a plus symbol. This identifies lines that were taken from the macro library rather than from your source program.

Let us look at the macro implementation of *@go_dos* in the assembly listing and compare it to the definition in the macro library. This macro is rather trivial. The first line of the definition contains two items, the symbolic name *@go_dos* and the MACRO assembler directive. A comment appears on the next line; it begins with two semicolons. This notation tells the assembler not to waste space by writing the comments into memory during assembly. The desired instruction follows. Finally, the directive ENDM concludes the macro definition. The ENDM directive must always be the last line of each macro definition. If you forget to include it at the end of a macro, the assembler can be confused and issue misleading error statements.

When we use the macro statement

```
@go_dos
```

in our source program, the assembler substitutes the corresponding instruction:

    INT   20h

It also adds the plus sign to remind us that the line was not present in the original source program. This macro does not save us much typing. However, it is easier to remember the name *@go_dos* than INT 20h. The other macro, *@write,* is more complicated. Let us consider its definition.
 The macro begins with the line

    @write **MACRO**   text?

which contains three parts. The first is the macro name, the second is the

```
                                    PAGE      ,132
                                    TITLE     HELLO6

                            COMMENT *
                                Write Hello, world. on screen
                                Program runs as COM file
                                Terminate with INT 20
                                With macro library
                                *
                                    ENDIF
0000                        code    SEGMENT
                            ASSUME CS:code, DS:code
0100                                ORG       100h
0100                        strt:
                            ; display message
                                    @write    'Hello, world.'
0100  50                    +       PUSH      AX
0101  52                    +       PUSH      DX
0102  B4 09                 +       MOV       AH,9
0104  BA 010D R             +       MOV       DX,OFFSET ??0001
0107  CD 21                 +       INT       21h
0109  5A                    +       POP       DX
010A  58                    +       POP       AX
010B  EB 0E                 +       JMP       SHORT ??0000
010D  48 65 6C 6C 6F 2C     + ??0001 DB       'Hello, world.','$'
011B                        + ??0000:
                                    @go_dos               ;quit
011B  CD 20                 +       INT       20h

011D                        code    ENDS
                                    END       strt
```

Figure 4.10: *Assembly listing for HELLO6.*

MACRO directive, and the third is a replaceable symbol known as a dummy parameter. The value can change from one use to the next. We terminate the dummy parameter with a question mark to designate the symbol as a macro parameter as clearly as possible. The second line begins with the LOCAL directive. It tells the assembler that the following two symbols, *around* and *mesg,* are local rather than global. That is, the symbols are not to be used literally. The assembler will create unique names to replace these symbols each time we use them. (The Microsoft and IBM assemblers choose ??0000 and ??0001, but other assemblers may use other symbols.) This will prevent a conflict of names if we use the macro more than once or if we use the symbols in another macro or elsewhere in the source program. If you use the LOCAL directive, it must be placed on the second line of the macro. Nothing can come between it and the first line, not even a comment. The next two lines are comments describing the macros.

The CPU instructions appear next. Here we add a feature that is not always needed, but does provide some safety: Whenever we alter a register in a macro, we will first save the contents by pushing them onto the stack. Then we restore the original information with the POP instruction before leaving the macro. Thus, we push the contents of the AX and DX registers at the beginning of the macro and pop them at the end.

The next three instructions are those we used in the previous program to display a string. We next pop the two registers we previously saved and then branch over the text to be printed. Notice that the dummy parameter for the text to be printed is placed at the end of the macro. However, there will be other instructions following the text, and so we must branch over the text to reach the other instructions. Let us look at the branching instruction.

We saw previously that a forward reference can cause trouble for the assembler on the first pass. Since this is a forward jump, the target of the jump is unknown on the first pass. The assembler guesses that a FAR jump will be needed, and so it codes a three-byte instruction. On the second pass, the assembler finds that a two-byte jump is needed instead. But it cannot now compress the code. Therefore, it places a dummy NOP instruction in the third byte. We can help the assembler by using the SHORT directive. Then the two-byte jump will be used on the first pass and the NOP instruction will not be needed. Notice that we never have to use the SHORT directive for a backwards jump, since the assembler will already know the meaning of the symbol. Now let us look at the implementation of this macro.

Our program uses this macro with the statement

```
@write      'Hello, world.'
```

It has two parts—the macro name and the parameter. Since the macro is defined at the beginning of the program (in the macro library), the macro symbol is known when the implementation is encountered. The assembler associates the dummy parameter *text?* in the macro definition with the actual parameter 'Hello, world.' in our source program.

Compared to the previous version, this macro makes it much easier to write a string of text on the video screen. We do not have to remember that function number 9 must be placed in the AH register and that register DX points to the string. Furthermore, we do not have to worry about where to place the string. We do not even have to remember to place a dollar sign at the end of the string, since the macro does that, too. We have only to give the command

```
@write      'Hello, world.'
```

and the assembler takes care of all the details, generating the corresponding code. Thus, our assembly-language program is beginning to look like a higher-level language such as FORTRAN or BASIC.

■ An Assembly-Language Template

Since we are going to adapt the layout of the previous program, we will create a template to avoid typing the same information over and over. But first we add a new macro to the macro library. Insert macro *@head*, given in Figure 4.11, to your macro library MYLIB.MAC. Place it between the other two macros to maintain alphabetical order. Also copy the first line of the macro to the beginning of the library. Insert a semicolon at the beginning of the line. Copy the source program given in Figure 4.9, giving it the name GENERIC.ASM. Insert the macro implementation:

```
@head      ' GENERIC, DATE '
```

just after the label *strt* in the generic program. The generic source program should look like Figure 4.12.

This new macro does not change the operation of the program, although the program will be a little larger. The purpose of macro *@head* is to identify the program name, version number or date, and perhaps a copyright notice. This information will normally be invisible, but it is a permanent part of each program. Later, we will write two programs that can display this information on the video screen or the printer. Also, as we shall see, the debugger can be used to display the header information.

Now let us consider how to reference information in memory.

```
@head    MACRO    num?
         LOCAL    around
;; Macro to embed version number
;; Usage:        @head    'title, date'

         JMP      SHORT around
         DB       num?
around:                           ;;head
         ENDM
```

Figure 4.11: *@head, a macro for creating a program header.*

```
         PAGE     ,132
         TITLE    GENERIC

COMMENT *
   Generic assembly language program
   Program runs as COM file
   Terminate with INT 20
   With macro library
 *
         IF1
         INCLUDE mylib.mac
         ENDIF

code     SEGMENT
ASSUME   CS:code, DS:code
         ORG      100h
strt:
         @head      ' GENERIC, DATE '

; your program goes here

         @go_dos            ;quit

code     ENDS
         END      strt
```

Figure 4.12: *A generic assembly-language program.*

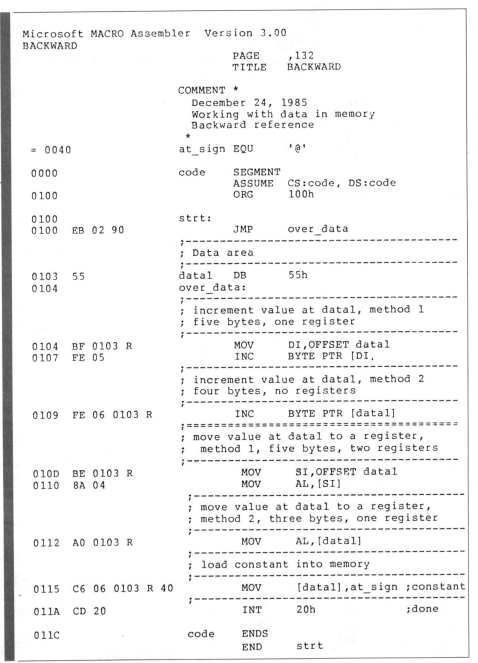

```
Microsoft MACRO Assembler  Version 3.00
BACKWARD
                              PAGE    ,132
                              TITLE   BACKWARD

                        COMMENT *
                          December 24, 1985
                          Working with data in memory
                          Backward reference
                          *
= 0040                  at_sign EQU    '@'

0000                    code    SEGMENT
                                ASSUME  CS:code, DS:code
0100                            ORG     100h

0100                    strt:
0100  EB 02 90                  JMP     over_data
                        ;-----------------------------------------------
                        ; Data area
                        ;-----------------------------------------------
0103  55                datal   DB      55h
0104                    over_data:
                        ;-----------------------------------------------
                        ; increment value at datal, method 1
                        ; five bytes, one register
                        ;-----------------------------------------------
0104  BF 0103 R                 MOV     DI,OFFSET datal
0107  FE 05                     INC     BYTE PTR [DI,
                        ;-----------------------------------------------
                        ; increment value at datal, method 2
                        ; four bytes, no registers
                        ;-----------------------------------------------
0109  FE 06 0103 R              INC     BYTE PTR [datal]
                        ;===============================================
                        ; move value at datal to a register,
                        ;   method 1, five bytes, two registers
                        ;-----------------------------------------------
010D  BE 0103 R                 MOV     SI,OFFSET datal
0110  8A 04                     MOV     AL,[SI]
                        ;-----------------------------------------------
                        ; move value at datal to a register,
                        ; method 2, three bytes, one register
                        ;-----------------------------------------------
0112  A0 0103 R                 MOV     AL,[datal]
                        ;-----------------------------------------------
                        ; load constant into memory
                        ;-----------------------------------------------
0115  C6 06 0103 R 40           MOV     [datal],at_sign ;constant
                        ;-----------------------------------------------
011A  CD 20                     INT     20h             ;done

011C                    code    ENDS
                                END     strt
```

Figure 4.13: *Assembly listing for a backward reference.*

REFERENCING INFORMATION IN MEMORY

In the programs we have been considering, we placed a string of text in memory and then referenced it through the DX register. We will frequently need to read or write information stored in memory. Therefore, let us consider how to reference such information.

The instructions for the 8088 CPU family allow no more than one memory reference per instruction. Thus it is possible to move information from a register to direct memory or from memory to a register, but not from one memory location to another in the same instruction. Of course, it is also possible to set a memory location or a register to a constant value. Let us begin with a backwards reference.

Backwards Reference

Consider the assembly listing given in Figure 4.13. This program performs no useful service, except to demonstrate how to access information in memory and use constants. Therefore you can create, assemble, and run it, but there will not be any output.

Near the beginning of the program we define a constant, the *at_sign* symbol, by using the EQU directive. This permanently defines the symbol for the duration of the program. We continue the program in the usual way, by defining the code segment and starting address for the instructions at 100 hex.

A memory location named *data1* is defined near the beginning of the program, using the DB directive. The DB directive (define byte) establishes data areas of memory. Its initial value is set to 55 hex. However, this value is not a constant; since it is stored in memory, we can change the value at any time. Since this memory location is in the path of the code, we must branch over it with the JMP instruction:

```
0100      EB 02 90    JMP         over_data
```

The value 0100 is the address of the instruction. The value EB 02 defines the jump instruction, and the value 90 is a NOP instruction. This is a forward-referenced branch to the label *over_data*, and so the assembler created a three-byte jump on the first pass. Then, on the second pass, the assembler changed the instruction to a two-byte short jump. However, it was too late to close up the program, since the assembler had already established later instructions. Therefore, a NOP instruction was placed in the third position, which was no longer needed. If the instruction had originally been written as

        JMP   SHORT   over_data

the assembler would have selected the two-byte jump on the first pass. We will use this improved form to help the assembler whenever we can. Look for the value 90 hex in your assembly listings. It usually means that you can shorten your code by better programming.

■ Incrementing Data in Memory

The next group of instructions shows how to increment data stored in a memory location. We will use two different methods. For the first method, we define the index register DI with the offset of the memory location. The OFFSET directive is used for this purpose:

        MOV   DI,OFFSET data1

The second operand is the offset of the label, not the contents of the corresponding memory location.

Next we increment the memory location with the instruction

        INC   BYTE PTR [DI]

using indexed addressing. The [DI] symbol refers to the contents of the referenced memory rather than the offset value. We use the two directives BYTE PTR to tell the assembler that we are interested in a byte-sized memory location rather than a word-sized location. This method is useful if we are going to access this location again. However, it requires a CPU register (DI) and uses five bytes for the two instructions. Let us look at an alternative method.

The second version is shorter:

        INC   BYTE PTR [data1]

This time we only need one instruction with four bytes; no register is needed. Again we use the BYTE PTR directives to indicate that a byte-sized location is wanted. The expression [data1] refers to the contents of location *data1*.

Other instructions are similar. For example, we can move the byte in memory to a register with either of two methods. In the first method:

```
MOV        SI,OFFSET data1
MOV        AL,[SI]
```

we load an index register as before with the offset value of the memory location. Then we move the value to the AL register. We did not need to use the BYTE PTR directives this time, since the AL register is byte-sized. At this point the SI register has the offset and the AL register has the contents of *data1*. These two instructions need five bytes and two registers.

Our second method is:

```
MOV        AL,[data1]
```

Again, the BYTE PTR directives are not needed, since the AL register dictates the size. With this method, only three bytes and one register are needed.

Our final example in this program refers to the at-sign. We defined the symbol *at_sign* to be a constant; it is not associated with a memory location. We can move it directly to a register or to a memory location. For example, this instruction:

```
MOV        [data1],at_sign
```

changes the value in *data1* from 57 hex (55 hex incremented twice by the previous instructions) to 40 hex, the ASCII value of the at-sign. Now we consider a forward reference.

◼ Forward Reference

Our second example demonstrates forward referencing of symbols. The listing for the Microsoft assembler is given in Figure 4.14. The instructions are similar to the previous example, but the referenced memory location is placed at the end of the instructions, after the return to DOS. No problem is apparent. But note that the *at_sign* symbol is also defined at the end of the program. The instruction

```
0111    B0 40 90    MOV     AL,at_sign ;get constant
```

shows the address of 111 hex and the code of B0 40. The third value, 90,

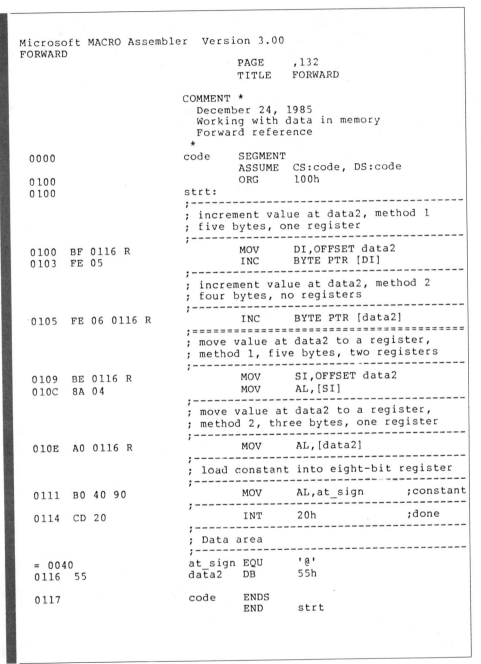

```
Microsoft MACRO Assembler   Version 3.00
FORWARD
                                  PAGE     ,132
                                  TITLE    FORWARD

                          COMMENT *
                            December 24, 1985
                            Working with data in memory
                            Forward reference
                            *
0000                      code   SEGMENT
                                  ASSUME  CS:code, DS:code
0100                             ORG     100h
0100                      strt:
                          ;-----------------------------------------
                          ; increment value at data2, method 1
                          ; five bytes, one register
                          ;-----------------------------------------
0100  BF 0116 R                   MOV     DI,OFFSET data2
0103  FE 05                       INC     BYTE PTR [DI]
                          ;-----------------------------------------
                          ; increment value at data2, method 2
                          ; four bytes, no registers
                          ;-----------------------------------------
0105  FE 06 0116 R                INC     BYTE PTR [data2]
                          ;=========================================
                          ; move value at data2 to a register,
                          ; method 1, five bytes, two registers
                          ;-----------------------------------------
0109  BE 0116 R                   MOV     SI,OFFSET data2
010C  8A 04                       MOV     AL,[SI]
                          ;-----------------------------------------
                          ; move value at data2 to a register,
                          ; method 2, three bytes, one register
                          ;-----------------------------------------
010E  A0 0116 R                   MOV     AL,[data2]
                          ;-----------------------------------------
                          ; load constant into eight-bit register
                          ;-----------------------------------------
0111  B0 40 90                    MOV     AL,at_sign        ;constant
                          ;-----------------------------------------
0114  CD 20                       INT     20h               ;done
                          ;-----------------------------------------
                          ; Data area
                          ;-----------------------------------------
= 0040                    at_sign EQU     '@'
0116  55                  data2   DB      55h

0117                      code    ENDS
                                  END     strt
```

Figure 4.14: *Assembly listing for a forward reference.*

is the NOP instruction. On the first pass, the assembler did not know what kind of symbol *at_sign* was going to be, a memory reference or a constant. It therefore left sufficient space for a memory reference. When *at_sign* turned out to be a constant, the NOP was placed in the third byte. Since the statement

    at_sign   EQU   '@'

is simply a definition, it can be placed anywhere in the program. The IBM macro assembler cannot correctly assemble the program unless the definition for *at_sign* is placed at the beginning of the program. Therefore, it is best to place such definitions at the very beginning of the program, as in the previous example. The exception occurs when you need to determine the length of the program itself. Then you must place the definition at the program end. Let us see how this works.

We will need to determine the length of several programs that we will write later. Alternatively, we may need the complement, the remaining space in the segment. Each case requires a forward reference to the program end. The assembly listing in Figure 4.15 shows how to do this. The

```
Microsoft MACRO Assembler   Version 3.00
PGMLEN
                        PAGE    ,132
                        TITLE   PGMLEN

                        COMMENT *
                          December 23, 1985
                          Working with data in memory
                          Forward reference
                        *
0000                    code    SEGMENT
                                ASSUME  CS:code, DS:code
0100                            ORG     100h
0100                    strt:
0100  BB 010C R                 MOV     BX,OFFSET pg_len
0103  BA FFF4                   MOV     DX,OFFSET strt-OFFSET pg_len
0106  BA FFF4 90                MOV     DX,pg_ln2       ;NOP

010A  CD 20                     INT     20h             ;done

=-000C                  pg_ln2  EQU     strt-$
010C                    pg_len  LABEL   BYTE

010C                    code    ENDS
                                END     strt
```

Figure 4.15: *Assembly listing for a forward reference, second example.*

last executable statement is INT 20h, generated by a macro. Following that is a constant, *pg_ln2*, defined as the difference between the program beginning and end. Then the label *pg_len* appears. Its offset is the program length; it is loaded into the BX register with this instruction:

```
MOV        BX,OFFSET pg_len
```

The next two instructions load the complement of the program length into the DX register:

```
MOV        DX,OFFSET strt–OFFSET pg_len
MOV        DX,pg_ln2
```

Both of these instructions determine the complement as FFF4 hex. The second version, however, includes the NOP instruction (90 hex) because of the forward reference. Therefore, as in the previous example, we should use a label rather than a constant for a forward reference. For our next example, we reference a different segment.

REFERENCING DATA IN ANOTHER SEGMENT

We have seen that a COM file must not define a separate data or stack segment. However, it is possible for such a program to reference information in other segments. The two most important segments we sometimes reference are the ROM BIOS at segment F000 hex and the interrupt vectors at segment zero. We will refer to other segments in several programs in this book, including the next example.

In the following example we reference the date and computer type coded into the ROM BIOS of your computer and move that information into the code segment of your executing program. As we have seen, the ROM BIOS is located in segment F000 hex. The ROM date, a kind of version number, appears near the end of that segment, at offset FFF5 hex. However, it is easier to use the equivalent address, FFFF:5. The date is coded in ASCII characters. The computer type is identified by a single byte at address FFFF:E. The possible dates and computer identifications are given in Table 4.1. The assembly-language source program given in Figure 4.16 will display the ROM date and identify the computer type. Let us go through the program.

We begin with the usual directives. The comment section identifies the dates and computer codes. After the reference to our libraries, we establish the ROM date segment with the AT directive and the SEGMENT-ENDS block:

```
romdate   SEGMENT   AT   OFFFFh
. . .
romdate   ENDS
```

In earlier programs we did not select the memory region where a segment was to be located; we let the linker do this for us. But in this example, we need to define the position of a fixed region. We therefore define the symbol *romdate* to have a segment value of FFFF hex.

Since the ROM date begins at offset 5, we establish this offset with the ORG directive:

```
ORG       5
```

Finally, we define the symbol *date* to be a FAR label in this segment, since it will be referenced from the code segment of our program, of course.

This first segment contains only assembler directives; it does not generate any instructions or data. Therefore, we can still create a COM file with the rest of the program.

Now we begin our main program in the usual manner, with the

```
code          SEGMENT
code          ENDS
```

block. The ASSUME directive in this program is a little different. We are going to reference the ROM BIOS segment with the DS register, and we

ROM date	Code	Meaning
04/24/81	FF	PC
10/19/81	FF	PC
10/27/82	FF	PC
11/08/82	FE	PC XT, portable
01/10/84	FC	PC AT, 20 MB
06/10/85	FC	PC AT, 30 MB

Table 4.1: *ROM BIOS dates and computer codes.*

```
              PAGE     ,132
              TITLE    ROMDATE

COMMENT *
  December 26, 1985
  Program to display ROM date

          ROM dates    Code     Meaning
          04/24/81     FF     PC
          10/19/81     FF     PC
          10/27/82     FF     PC
          11/08/82     FE     PC XT, portable
          01/10/84     FC     PC AT   20 MB
          06/10/85     FC     PC AT, 30 MB

  Macros: @go_dos, @head, @write, @write_r
     *
          IF1
          INCLUDE mylib.mac       ;macro library
          ENDIF


;-------------------------------------------
; ROM BIOS routines
;-------------------------------------------
romdate SEGMENT AT 0FFFFh
        ORG     5
date    LABEL   FAR             ;ROM date
romdate ENDS

code    SEGMENT
        ASSUME  CS:code, DS:romdate, ES:code
        ORG     100h

strt:
        @head    'ROMDATE,12.27.85 '
        MOV      AX,romdate
        ASSUME   DS:romdate
        MOV      DS,AX
        MOV      SI,OFFSET date   ;source
        MOV      DI,OFFSET r_date ;destination
        MOV      CX,OFFSET st_end-OFFSET r_date
;-------------------------------------------
; copy ROM date to this program
;-------------------------------------------
        REP      MOVSB
        ASSUME   DS:code
        MOV      AX,CS
        MOV      DS,AX            ;reset DS
; terminate string with dollar sign
        MOV      BYTE PTR [doll],'$'
;-------------------------------------------
; display ROM date
;-------------------------------------------
```

Figure 4.16: *ROMDATE: displaying ROM date and computer type.*

```
        @write_r <OFFSET p_ver>
;-------------------------------------------
; display computer type
;-------------------------------------------
        MOV     AL,[c_type]
        CMP     AL,0FCh             ;AT
        JNZ     not_at
        @write  ' A PC AT'
        JMP     SHORT done
not_at:
        CMP     AL,0FEh             ;XT
        JNZ     not_xt
        @write  ' A PC XT'
        JMP     SHORT done
not_xt:
        CMP     AL,0FFh             ;PC
        JNZ     not_pc
        @write  ' A regular PC'
        JMP     SHORT done
not_pc:
        @write  ' Not a PC'
done:
        @go_dos                     ;quit
;-------------------------------------------
; Data area
;-------------------------------------------
p_ver   DB      'ROM date: '
r_date  DB      'xx/xx/82'
doll    DB      '?'
c_type  DB      '?'
st_end  LABEL   BYTE

code    ENDS
        END     strt
```

Figure 4.16: *(continued).*

are also going to use the ES register. Therefore, we alert the assembler at
the beginning by referencing all three segment registers:

    ASSUME   CS:code, DS:romdate, ES:code

(Remember, we are not allowed to define the stack segment in a COM
program.) As usual, the ORG directive sets the address of the first instruction, and then we begin the instructions. We start with our *@head* macro
to encode the program name and date.

    We could in principle work directly with the information contained in
the ROM BIOS. However, it would be better to copy the information

from the ROM BIOS into the code section of our program first. We use one of the various instructions for operating on strings. These instructions make it easy to manipulate strings of characters. We will use several of them in later programs. We are now going to use the instruction for moving a string of characters from one memory location to another. We need one pointer to the original string (the source string) and another to the new location (the destination string).

The source string (in the ROM BIOS) is referenced with the DS:SI registers (SI means source index) and the destination string is referenced with the ES:DI registers (DI means destination index). We load the ROM BIOS segment value into DS in two steps—first to the AX register and then to the DS register. We convert the label *date* to a constant with the OFFSET directive and then move it into the SI register. The ES register is already pointing to our code segment. However, we still have to set the DI register to the location defined by *r_date* at the end of our program. The CX (count) register is given the length of the string. We can use the instruction

```
MOV        CX,10
```

but if we then want to change the length of the string to be moved, we must remember to change this constant, too. Therefore, we will let the assembler compute the length for us.

Since the string is located at the end of the program, we need a forward reference. We can define a constant:

```
st_len     EQU          $-r_date
```

at the end of the program and then load the CX register with the following instruction:

```
MOV        CX,st_len
```

This will place the value 10 (A hex) in the CX register. Because of the forward reference, however, there will be an extra NOP byte. The assembly listing for the line will look like this:

```
011E    B9 000A 90 MOV        CX,st_len ;length
```

Therefore we will use another technique. We place a label at the end of the program:

```
st_end     LABEL        BYTE
```

Then we define the CX register with this instruction:

MOV   CX,OFFSET st_end-OFFSET r_date

This method also loads CX with the value 10. However, there is not an extra NOP instruction. In fact, this method produces exactly the same code as directly loading the constant 10 into the CX register. The assembly listing shows this:

011E B9 000A   MOV CX,OFFSET st_end-OFFSET r_date

Now if we change the length of the string, the value loaded into the CX register will change accordingly.

In the next step we use the two instructions

REP   MOVSB

(repeat move-string-byte) to perform the string move. The DS, SI, ES, DI, and CX registers are required. The MOVSB instruction moves a byte from the source (the ROM BIOS) to the destination (our code segment). Then it increments both the SI and DI registers and decrements the CX register. The REP (repeat) instruction keeps executing the string-move instruction until the CX register reaches zero.

We now have both the date and the computer code in the data section at the end of our code segment. Since we want to display the date on the video screen, we will use the DOS string-display function. To do so, we must terminate the string with a dollar sign. (This is another reason for copying the date from the ROM BIOS to our program. We cannot, of course, write a dollar sign into the ROM.) Fortunately, there is an extra character between the end of the ROM date and the computer code. This is where we will place the dollar sign. We cannot directly display the computer code since, unlike the date, it is not in ASCII form.

We have identified the location of the dollar sign in our program with the label *doll*. The instruction:

MOV   [doll],'$'

places a dollar sign in the desired memory location. Notice that, although this is a forward reference, it does not cause a problem since we refer to a label.

Now we can display the words "ROM date:" followed by the date itself. We use the *@write_r* macro, a variation of our *@write* macro:

    @write_r <OFFSET p_ver>

This macro, shown in Figure 4.17, is similar to our *@write* macro in that both use DOS function 9 of interrupt 21 hex to display a string on the video screen. However, in this new version, the string to be displayed is not coded within the macro; it is located somewhere else. Of course, the macro parameter gives the location of the string rather than the string itself.

Notice that the single parameter of the macro implementation contains two words and is surrounded by angle brackets. The macro assembler interprets the space and comma symbols as delimiters marking the end of a parameter. The angle brackets therefore define a single parameter that contains a space or comma. Of course, a pair of quotation marks, like the angle brackets, also defines a single parameter. If we omitted the angle brackets, only the first word, OFFSET, would be used as the parameter, and this is not what we want. Add macro *@write_r* to your macro library; place it at the end, after *@write,* to maintain alphabetical order. Copy the first line to the top of the library.

The next section of our program decodes the computer type and displays the appropriate description. Since we are going to make several comparisons, we move the byte from location *c_type* into the AL register. (Use the AL or AX register whenever possible since the code is usually shorter compared to using other registers. That is, the AX register is designated as an accumulator or default register.) Then we make a comparison with each of the three types. (We assume that this program will not be run on a PC jr, which uses the byte code FD hex. You can add the extra

```
@write_r MACRO  addr?
;; display text at location addr?
;; text must end with $
;; Usage:   @write_r <OFFSET p_ver>

        PUSH    DX
        MOV     DX,addr?
        MOV     AH,9
        INT     21h
        POP     DX
        ENDM
```

Figure 4.17: *Macro @write_r for displaying a remote string.*

comparison for this purpose if you need it.) The program terminates in the usual fashion through a common exit.

Type up the program shown in Figure 4.16. Begin with the generic program given in Figure 4.12. Use the name ROMDATE.ASM for the new program. Assemble, link, and run the program using the EXEC batch file. Try out this program on as many different computers as you can. When you run ROMDATE on a regular PC, a line such as

```
ROM date: 10/27/82 A regular PC
```

appears on the video screen.

To look at the assembled code, create an assembly listing with the EXLIST batch file. Near the beginning of the code segment you will see this instruction:

```
0116 B8 — R        MOV AX,romdate
```

Notice that the address of the *romdate* segment is missing from the listing. Only four dashes are shown. Remember, this listing was generated by the assembler. But the assembler usually does not know where segments will be loaded at execution time. Since this task is performed by the linker, the missing value is filled in during the linking step. The final COM file will have the correct value.

SUMMARY

In this chapter we set up one batch file for assembling and linking an assembly-language source file and a second one for creating and printing an assembly listing. Then we learned several ways to create both EXE and COM files. We created a macro library and incorporated two macros into an assembly-language program. Finally, we wrote a program for displaying the ROM BIOS date and identifying the computer type. In the next chapter we see how to use the debugger.

The beginning of your macro library should now look like this:

```
; Macros in this library
;@go_dos     MACRO               ;return to DOS by 21h
;@head       MACRO     num?      ;header information
;@write      MACRO     text?     ;write text to screen
;@write_r    MACRO     addr?     ;display text at addr?
```

The Debugger

INTRODUCTION

In the previous chapter we learned how to write two types of assembly-language programs, EXE files and COM files. We also introduced the concept of macros. In this chapter we will learn to use the debugger, DEBUG.COM, to explore the computer's memory, to patch existing programs, to create simple executable programs, and to study EXE and COM files. We begin by exploring the memory.

DEBUG is a powerful program that can be used for many tasks. It can assemble or disassemble instructions, and it can display or create data areas. Furthermore, as the name implies, you can use DEBUG to run your programs one instruction at a time and thus, by watching the program as it executes, find and remove errors. This is known as *single-stepping* through a program. Alternatively, you can set stopping points, known as *breakpoints,* in your program. Having done so, you can start your program under control of DEBUG. When a breakpoint is reached, DEBUG takes over, so that you can explore what your program has done.

DEBUG.COM is included on the supplemental DOS diskette. However, if you have more than one version of DOS, you should be careful to match your version of DEBUG with the corresponding DOS version. Some versions of DEBUG will not run on the wrong DOS version; they will terminate and give an error message. On the other hand, DEBUG on DOS version 3, which has a feature not available on version 2, appears to run correctly with DOS version 2.

There are 19 DEBUG commands; they all begin with a single-letter mnemonic for the operation. One or more parameters may follow the command. The commands are discussed in the DOS manual and are briefly summarized in Table 5.1. The P command is not available with version 2. We will use the most important commands in this chapter.

EXPLORING THE MAIN MEMORY

Let us start up DEBUG and explore the main memory of the computer. Give the command DEBUG at the DOS prompt and you will see the DEBUG prompt, a minus sign. Type the letter R and press the Return key to see the current value of the registers. The result might look like this:

```
AX = 0000 BX = 0000 CX = 0000 DX = 0000 SP = FFEE BP = 0000 SI = 0000 DI = 0000
DS = 66C6 ES = 66C6 SS = 66C6 CS = 66C6 IP = 0100 NV UP DI PL NZ NA PO NC
66C6:0100 47 INC DI
```

The general-purpose registers appear on the top row, the segment registers and the instruction pointer on the next. The flags are identified near the end of the second line; they are described in Table 5.2. The third line of the display describes the current instruction, the one at CS:IP. Notice that all DEBUG numbers are given in hexadecimal notation, whereas decimal is the default for the assembler.

The ROM BIOS Date

In the previous chapter we read and then displayed the date and computer type coded in the ROM BIOS. We will now explore this area with the debugger. Give the command

   RES

Code	Meaning
A	Assemble a program
C	Compare two memory blocks
D	Display a portion of memory in hex and decimal
E	Enter into memory hex and ASCII characters
F	Fill a region of memory with specified values
G	Execute the program (go)
H	Hexadecimal arithmetic
I	Input and display from port
L	Load a program from disk to memory
M	Move a block of memory
N	Define file name to read or write
O	Output to a port
P	Proceed with (execute) subroutine or interrupt
Q	Quit DEBUG
R	Register display
S	Search memory for specified bytes
T	Trace program execution by single-stepping through code
U	Unassemble code
W	Write to disk

Table 5.1: *The DEBUG commands.*

to change the value in the ES register. DEBUG responds with the current value and then displays a colon prompt so that you can enter a new value. The screen might look like this:

ES 66C6

:

Type the value FFFF after the colon to change the ES register to FFFF hex, the value we will use for the ROM date. Give the R command without a parameter to see the results. The display will look something like this:

```
AX = 0000 BX = 0000 CX = 0000 DX = 0000 SP = FFEE BP = 0000 SI = 0000 DI = 0000
DS = 66C6 ES = FFFF SS = 66C6 CS = 66C6 IP = 0100 NV UP DI PL NZ NA PO NC
66C6:0100 47 INC DI
```

Give the command

DES:0 LF

This DEBUG command displays the memory range starting at address ES:0 and extending for 15 (F hex) bytes. When a DEBUG parameter describes a block of memory, there are two methods of giving the parameters. With one method you give the first and last addresses, separated by a space. The first address may include a segment register. For the alternative method, shown in this example, you give the starting address, the letter L (length), and then the number of bytes in the block.

Flag	Set	Clear	Meaning	
Overflow	OV	NV	Overflow	Not overflow
Direction	DN	UP	Decrement	Increment
Interrupt	EI	DI	Enable	Disable
Sign	NG	PL	Minus	Plus
Zero	ZR	NZ	Zero	Not zero
Aux carry	AC	NA	Carry	Not carry
Parity	PE	PO	Even	Odd
Carry	CY	NC	Carry	Not carry

Table 5.2: *The CPU flags.*

The result will look like this:

```
FFFF:0000 EA 5B E0 00 F0 31 30 2F-32 37 2F 38 32 FF FF  J['.p10/27/82..
```

This display has three parts: the first part is the address, the second is the hexadecimal representation of the data in memory, and the third is the ASCII representation of the same memory region. Dots are given if the ASCII values are not printable; that is, if they are below 32 or above 127.

The first five bytes of this display are the instruction for a branch to the reset routine in the ROM BIOS. This is the first address the CPU executes after a restart. The next eight bytes are the ROM date. We can see that the ASCII values are 10/27/82. The final byte, FF hex, is the code identifying a regular IBM PC.

The Interrupt Vectors

We next look at the interrupt vectors. As we have seen, the ROM BIOS vectors are located at the beginning of memory and are followed by the DOS interrupt vectors. However, we must be careful when we are using the debugger to explore the interrupt vectors. The debugger changes some of these vectors in order to control the computer operation. Therefore, we should not be surprised to see vectors pointing into the debugger rather than to their usual locations. (In the final chapter we will write a program to explore these vectors. Then we will see the correct values since our program will not change them.)

Give the DEBUG command

    DO:0 L70

to see the first 27 interrupts (INT 0–INT 1B). The result might look like

```
0000:0000 72 30 E3 00 47 01 70 00-C3 E2 00 F0 47 01 70 00
0000:0010 47 01 70 00 54 FF 00 F0-47 FF 00 F0 47 FF 00 F0
0000:0020 DF 01 17 5E 2F 01 F2 62-DD E6 00 F0 DD E6 00 F0
0000:0030 DD E6 00 F0 DD E6 00 F0-57 EF 00 F0 47 01 70 00
0000:0040 65 F0 00 F0 4D F8 00 F0-41 F8 00 F0 7E 01 61 06
0000:0050 39 E7 00 F0 59 F8 00 F0-2E E8 00 F0 48 01 0F 63
0000:0060 00 00 00 F6 F2 E6 00 F0-6E FE 00 F0 40 01 70 00
```

Figure 5.1: *Hexadecimal display of ROM BIOS interrupt vectors.*

Figure 5.1. We have omitted the ASCII representation in this display because no valid ASCII characters are present. We can see that the BIOS PrtSc interrupt 5, at address 14, points to address F000:FF54, its usual value. (The addresses appear to be written backward, because it is conventional to display memory addresses with the least-significant byte (LSB) first, followed by the most-significant byte (MSB). In a later program, we will display such addresses in their more natural form.) On the other hand, the BIOS keyboard interrupt 9, at address 24, points to 62F2:012F rather than its usual value of F000:E9A4 in the ROM BIOS. However, this value has not been changed by the debugger; it was changed by a routine that changes some of the keyboard scan codes. We shall write such a program in Chapter 9.

The ROM BIOS Data Area

As a final example, let us look at the ROM BIOS data area at 0:400. (This address is sometimes given as 40:0.) As we have seen, this region contains various pieces of information, such as the port addresses and the equipment list.

Display the data area with the command

```
D0:400 L20
```

and the response might be this:

```
0000:0400 F8 03 00 00 00 00 00 00-BC 03 78 03 00 00 00 00
0000:0410 BF 82 00 C0 02 40 02 00-00 00 34 00 34 00 44 20
```

We can see the serial port address, 3F8 hex, at location 400; the first parallel port address, 3BC hex, at address 408; and the second parallel port address, of 378 hex, at address 40A. (These port addresses also appear to be backward.)

The equipment flag is located at address 410. We will change this location when we write a program in Chapter 9 to switch between the monochrome and graphics screens.

PATCHING EXECUTABLE PROGRAMS

A second use for the debugger is to patch, or alter, existing programs. You would not do this with programs you write, because it would be much easier to rewrite your source program. But DEBUG is useful for altering programs written by others, especially if you know the patch points. As an example, consider the editor known as WordStar. Many of the patch points were published with the earliest CP/M versions and are generally the same in the IBM version. Let us consider several patches to WordStar.

■ Patching WordStar

As we have seen, the IBM monochrome screen can display information in several ways, including normal, bright, and reverse video. The IBM version of WordStar displays regular text with bright characters and marked blocks with dim characters. However, you may find it easier on the eyes to use normal characters for regular text and reverse video for marked text. This change is especially helpful in locating text in marked blocks because the spaces are highlighted.

The attribute for displaying regular text in WordStar is located at offset 28B, and the attribute for marked text is at offset 284. We will change the original attribute, F hex (bright), to 7 (normal) at address 28B. Then we will change the attribute 7 to 70 (reverse) at address 284.

Place a working copy of WordStar and one of DEBUG on a disk with sufficient space. A RAM disk is best, a hard disk is next best. However, the operation can also be performed with a floppy disk. Give the command

DEBUG WS.COM

to start DEBUG and copy WordStar into memory. Give the command

E28B

and press the Return key. DEBUG will display the address 28B and the current value at that address, something like:

XXXX:028B 0F

Then DEBUG waits for you to enter a value. (*XXXX* will be the segment DEBUG uses to store WordStar. But its value is of no consequence here.) Type the value 7 and press the Return key.

Now give the command

E284

and press the Return key. DEBUG will display the address 284 and show the current value (7). Type the value 70 and press the Return key again. These two commands are all that is needed to change the appearance on either the monochrome or the graphics screen.

If you have a color screen, WordStar will appear in black and white. Therefore, you may want to use the value 1E at location 28B, rather than the value 7, so that WordStar will present a blue background with yellow lettering. This combination will also work well with the monochrome screen. But if you use a black-and-white monitor attached to the graphics card, do not use the value 1E. The lettering will be illegible. These changes are summarized in Table 5.3.

Before we save the changes, let us consider some other options.

■Changing the Default Drive

WordStar frequently refers to two overlay files that have the extension OVR. WordStar first looks for these files on the current drive; if they are not there, it looks on drive A. However, if you have set up your Word-Star on drive C or D as described in Chapter 3, you should change WordStar accordingly. The number stored in address 2DC tells WordStar where to find the overlay files. This is normally the value 1 for drive A. If your overlay files are on drive C, you should change this value to 3. If you use drive D, the value should be 4.

To change this value, give the command

E2DC

and press the Return key. After DEBUG displays the address and original value, change it to the appropriate one and press the Return key again. Let us make another change.

Text	Address	Original	New	Color
Regular	28B	7	70	1E (yellow on blue)
Block	284	F	7	7

Table 5.3: *WordStar patches for video attributes.*

■ Protecting Against Accidental Loss of a Line

The WordStar commands are given as one or two Ctrl characters. Some of these commands move the cursor while others delete text. Three commands—Ctrl-G to delete a character, Ctrl-T to delete a word, and Ctrl-Y to delete a line—are very close together on the keyboard. If you accidentally press Ctrl-Y when you meant one of the others, you instantly lose an entire line. You can reduce the risk of this happening by patching WordStar so that Ctrl-Y must be struck twice before it takes effect. Then, if you accidentally strike Ctrl-Y once, you can press the Space bar to cancel the operation. But if you do want to delete an entire line, just press Ctrl-Y a second time.

Addresses 535 and 536 originally contain the values 19 (the ASCII value for Ctrl-Y) and zero. The zero in the second location means that the command consists of a single character. We will change the second value from zero to 19 to indicate a two-character command. Give this DEBUG command:

    E536

and press the Return key. Enter the value 19 and press the Return key again.

■ Fixing the Backspace and DEL Keys

There are four cursor-movement keys on the number pad. WordStar responds to these keys in the expected manner. For example, if you press the left arrow, the cursor moves to the left; if you press the up arrow, the cursor moves up to the previous line. The PgUp and PgDn keys also behave as expected, moving either to the next or the previous page. However, two keys in this region do not perform as expected.

The Backspace key, marked with a left-pointing arrow, is positioned next to the Num Lock key. When you press this key, DOS and most programs move the cursor to the left and delete the character there. WordStar, however, simply moves the cursor one position to the left. Thus, it behaves just like the left-cursor key. Similarly, the DEL key is different. This key usually deletes the character at the current cursor position, but in WordStar it moves the cursor to the left and deletes the character there. Let us fix these two keys.

We have to change four locations, two of them side by side. Give the DEBUG command

    E49B

and press the Return key. DEBUG will display the current value, 0D. Type the value AE and press the Space bar. DEBUG will show the current value of the next position, 7E. Type the value 83 and press Return. Give the command

    E6E6

and press Return. Change the current value from 8 (a backspace) to 13 (Ctrl-S, cursor left). Finally, give the command

    E71C

and press Return again. Change the value 7F (DEL) to 7 (Ctrl-G, delete character).

Our final patch will make WordStar start up faster because it changes the time the start-up message is displayed. Change the value at location 2D2 from 10 to 0.

We have made several changes to WordStar. However, we made them only to the memory image of the program. The next step is to write the changed version to disk.

■Saving the WordStar Changes

If you want to save the new version under the same name as the original (and delete the original), give the command W, for write. DEBUG will respond with a statement telling you how many bytes are being written. Alternatively, to use a new name, give the N command followed by the new file name. For example, the line

    NWSN.COM

will create a new file with the name WSN.COM. (But be sure there is room for both versions.) Then give the W command to save the new version. In either case, give the Q command to quit DEBUG and return to DOS.

You can make additional changes to WordStar by running the INSTALL program that is provided with it. This program lets you change printer routines, the initial help level, and other features. In addition, you can change the meaning of the ten function keys. Some versions of WordStar display a help line at the bottom of the video screen defining the ten function keys. Unfortunately, the original definitions are still displayed on the screen after you redefine the keys with the installation program. Let us see how to change the help line with the debugger.

The characters displayed on the bottom of the screen are stored in ASCII near the end of WordStar. You can find the location with the help of the debugger. Load WordStar with this command:

DEBUG WS.COM

Give the R command to inspect the registers. Note the value in the CX register, which is the length of the WordStar program. Then use the search command of DEBUG to locate one of the symbols. The task is complicated by the fact that the video attributes alternate with the characters. For example, if you want to find the letters HELP, you have to search for the string HpEpLpPp. The lowercase p's are the video attribute.

If the CX register has the value 5380 and you want to find the string SAVE, give the command

S100 L5380 'SpApVpEp'

DEBUG will begin searching at address 100 hex (the first parameter) and continue for 5380 bytes. When the string is found, the corresponding address will be displayed. Be careful not to use the F command, since this letter stands for "fill" and not "find." Then you will write over (fill) the entire program area with the string SpApVpEp.

If DEBUG returns a value of 5069, display 12 lines in this area with the command

D5060 LC0

Study the ASCII display at the right side of the screen. (Press Shift-PrtSc to get a printed listing.) You will see the numbers 1–10 down the middle. Next to these are the key identifications alternating with the video attributes. You can write new characters with DEBUG. For example, if you want to change the string HELP to Hide for function key 1, give the command

E5069 'Hpipdpep'

Notice that the reverse-video attribute, corresponding to the lowercase p, alternates with the letters we want. When you have finished making the changes, save them with the W command, and then give the Q command.

CREATING NEW PROGRAMS WITH DEBUG

In the previous chapter we created both EXE and COM files, using the assembler. We wrote programs using symbols and then let the assembler convert the symbols into the corresponding code. However, we included numerous directives to help the assembler with its task. While this is certainly the best way to create longer programs, it is sometimes more convenient to write short programs with the A command of the debugger. Let us look at two examples.

Changing the Printer Typeface, Version 1

The standard parallel printer for the IBM PC uses a dot matrix to generate the characters. Therefore, a variety of typefaces are available, including draft, italic, wide, compressed, bold, and perhaps letter-quality. The typeface can be changed through software by sending the appropriate bytes to the printer. In the final chapter we will write a program that can select any of these styles. In the meantime, let us make a very short version with the debugger. This version will set the printer for compressed typeface, which allows more characters per line and is therefore useful for assembly-language listings.

At the beginning of each of our assembly-language programs, we have included the statement

        PAGE ,132

This directive tells the assembler to allow for lines as long as 132 characters. However, the parallel printer is normally set for 80 characters on a line. Therefore, we also have to reprogram the printer for this width.

It may be necessary to send several characters to the printer to change the style. However, selecting compressed type is very simple. Only one character is needed, F hex. Our first version is extremely simple. Give the command

        DEBUG COMPRESS

DEBUG will give the error message

        File not found

indicating that the requested file could not be located. Just ignore the message. On the other hand, if DEBUG is already running, give this command:

    NCOMPRESS

Then give the R command and check that the DS, SS, and CS registers are all the same. If they are different, leave DEBUG and restart it again.
    Give the command

    E100

and press the Return key. Enter the value F, press the Space bar, enter the value 1A, and then press the Return key. This short program consists of two bytes: one for the printer and another to mark the end of the file.
    Next we change the CX register to show the program length. Give the command

    RCX

and press Return. After the colon prompt, type the value 2, the number of bytes in the program, and then press the Return key again. Give the W command to write the file to disk, and then give the Q command to quit DEBUG. Your simple program is ready to go. Give the command

    COPY COMPRESS PRN

to change the typeface. This line can be placed in the AUTOEXEC.BAT file for your assembler disk so that the printer will always be set for the assembly listing.
    You can reset the printer to regular type by turning it off and then back on again. Alternatively, you can write another short file, called NORMAL. Use the value 12 for the first byte instead of F. Let us try a better version.

■ Changing the Printer Typeface, Version 2

The second version of our program to change the printer style is a little longer than the first but is easier to use. Give the command

    DEBUG COMPRESS.COM

Again you will see the DEBUG error message

File not found

This time we will create a regular COM program using DEBUG's A (for assemble) command. Give the command

A100

and press the Return key. DEBUG will display the requested address and wait for your input. Enter this program:

MOV DL,F
MOV AH,5
INT 21
INT 20

in either upper- or lowercase letters. Do not put the letter h at the end of these numbers, since hexadecimal is the default. Give two consecutive Returns after the last line and the assembly phase will terminate. Give the command

U100 L8

and the listing should look like Figure 5.2. Of course, the segment address *XXXX* will change from computer to computer. Let us look over the listing.

Our second version sets the DL register to F hex, the byte that changes the printer to compressed type. Then the AH register is set to 5 and interrupt 21 hex is executed. As we saw in Chapter 2, this function sends the byte in the DL register to the printer. We terminate the program with the interrupt 20 hex instruction.

Set the program length in the CX register with the DEBUG command

RCX

```
XXXX:0100 B20F    MOV    DL,0F
XXXX:0102 B405    MOV    AH,05
XXXX:0104 CD21    INT    21
XXXX:0106 CD20    INT    20
```

Figure 5.2: *Program to set compressed type, version 2.*

and press Return. Enter a value of 8 and press the Return key again. Give the W command to write the program, and then terminate with the Q command.

With our second version, you can turn on compressed type with the command

COMPRESS

As is the case with the first version, you can place this command in your AUTOEXEC.BAT file.

MAKING FLOPPY DISKS RUN QUIETLY

There is a small bug in DOS versions 3.0 and 3.1. The floppy disks make an annoying grinding sound when reading or writing. The problem is that the step rate, the speed at which the disk head is moved, is incorrectly set on startup. This problem is not present in version 2. The correct step rate is already coded into DOS, but DOS does not use it. The solution is to perform a disk reset. The program required to reset the disks is short enough that it can easily be created with DEBUG. Let us do that.

Start DEBUG with the command

DEBUG DSKRST.COM

and enter the program given in Figure 5.3. Type only the instructions on the right side; do not enter the addresses and corresponding code on the left. When you have finished, give the command

U100 L6

and the output will look like Figure 5.3. Set the program size in the CX register. Give the command

RCX

and enter the value 6, the program length. Give the W and Q commands.

Let us go through the listing.

The first instruction is an efficient way to load a register with a value of zero. It uses only two bytes of code, while the more obvious expression:

MOV AX,0

requires three bytes. The interrupt 13 hex instruction resets the floppy disks when the value in the AX register is zero. The final interrupt 20 hex instruction terminates the program. If you are running DOS version 3.0 or 3.1, you should put this program on your system disk and include the command

    DSKRST

at the beginning of your AUTOEXEC file.

Now let us use DEBUG to study our Hello programs.

ANALYZING THE HELLO PROGRAMS

One of the most important features of DEBUG is the ability to analyze existing programs, especially programs written by others. Be careful, though, with your own programs. It may be more effective to study your own source listing than the output from DEBUG. Nevertheless, sometimes we can find a bug by analyzing the registers and data area of memory using DEBUG. Let us use two of our Hello programs from Chapter 4 for this purpose.

Analyzing the HELLO2.EXE Program

In this section we are going to study the HELLO2.EXE program. If you do not have it, please go back to the previous chapter and create it. The examples in this section were assembled with the Microsoft version 3 assembler. However, other assemblers place the parts in a different order.

Give the command

    DEBUG HELLO2.EXE par1 par2

```
XXXX:0100 31C0      XOR     AX,AX
XXXX:0102 CD13      INT     13
XXXX:0104 CD20      INT     20
```

Figure 5.3: *Program to reset the floppy disks.*

using lowercase letters. This instructs DEBUG to convert our HELLO2.EXE into executable form and then wait for further commands. We have added two parameters that are not needed by our program, but will teach us something new.

Give the R command to see the values in the registers. The result might look like this:

```
AX = 0000 BX = 0000 CX = 00A0 DX = 0000 SP = 0080 BP = 0000 SI = 0000 DI = 0000
DS = 66DB ES = 66DB SS = 66EB CS = 66F4 IP = 0000 NV UP DI PL NZ NA PO NC
66F4:0000 B8F366     MOV AX,66F3
```

We have seen that DOS begins a COM program by setting all four segment registers to the same value. But in an EXE program, while the DS and ES registers have the same value, the CS and SS registers are different. This is apparent in the register display.

Give the command

   DO 19F

and you will see a display similar to Figure 5.4 if you have a Microsoft version 3 assembler. Notice that the segment address for the display, 66DB, corresponds to the DS register. Both the D and E commands refer to the DS register. On the other hand, the U and A commands refer to the CS register.

Notice that the first two bytes of the display are CD and 20, the INT 20 instruction. Also notice that the first and second parameters we entered, PAR1 and PAR2, appear at offset addresses 5D and 6D hex. Our later programs will look for parameters in this region. Furthermore, if you entered the parameters in lowercase letters, DOS has converted them to uppercase. Look at address 80. That line, called the *command-line tail,* gives both parameters starting at 82 hex. But if you entered lowercase letters, DOS did not convert them to uppercase. The value at address 80, B hex or 11, gives the number of characters in the command-line tail. A carriage return, D hex, has been placed at the end of the tail but is not included in the count at location 80.

The word STACK appears over and over from 100 to 17F hex. Obviously, this is the stack region of our program. Although it is not so obvious, our program code begins at address 190 hex. However, different assemblers may place the parts in a different order. Let us look at the code.

Give the command

   UO L10

and you will see the disassembled instructions, as in Figure 5.5. The addresses and code are also shown. Notice that the segment address for the disassembly, 66F4, is the code segment. Your value may be different, but the offsets will be the same. The first two instructions for our program reset the DS register to the value 66F3; this will be used to reference the data in our program. Look at the ASCII characters at the right side of address 66DB:0180 in Figure 5.4:

    66DB:0180 48 65 . . . 72 6C 64 2E 24 00 00 Hello, world.$..

Clearly, this must be our data segment. Look at address 66DB:0190 on the next line:

    66DB:0190 B8 F3 66 8E D8 B4 09 BA–00 00 CD 21 B4 4C CD 21

Compare the data—B8, F3, 66—with the disassembly in Figure 5.5. This is our code segment. Thus, with reference to the original value in DS, the

```
66DB:0000 CD 20 00 B0 00 9A F0 FF-0D F0 42 02 D5 63 70 02  M .0..p..pB.Ucp.
66DB:0010 D5 63 E2 04 90 05 D5 63-01 03 01 00 02 FF FF FF  Ucb...Uc........
66DB:0020 FF FF FF FF FF FF FF FF-FF FF FF FF D7 66 C8 2A  ...........WfH*
66DB:0030 D5 63 00 00 00 00 00 00-00 00 00 00 00 00 00 00  Uc..............
66DB:0040 00 00 00 00 00 00 00 00-00 00 00 00 00 00 00 00  ................
66DB:0050 CD 21 CB 00 00 00 00 00-00 00 00 00 00 50 41 52  M!K.........PAR
66DB:0060 31 20 20 20 20 20 20 20-00 00 00 00 00 50 41 52  1      .....PAR
66DB:0070 32 20 20 20 20 20 20 20-00 00 00 00 00 00 00 00  2      ........
66DB:0080 0B 20 70 61 72 31 20 70-61 72 32 20 0D 00 00 00  . par1 par2 ....
66DB:0090 00 00 00 00 00 00 00 00-00 00 00 00 00 00 00 00  ................
66DB:00A0 00 00 00 00 00 00 00 00-00 00 00 00 00 00 00 00  ................
66DB:00B0 00 00 00 00 00 00 00 00-00 00 00 00 00 00 00 00  ................
66DB:00C0 00 00 00 00 00 00 00 00-00 00 00 00 00 00 00 00  ................
66DB:00D0 00 00 00 00 00 00 00 00-00 00 00 00 00 00 00 00  ................
66DB:00E0 00 00 00 00 00 00 00 00-00 00 00 00 00 00 00 00  ................
66DB:00F0 00 00 00 00 00 00 00 00-00 00 00 00 00 00 00 00  ................
66DB:0100 53 54 41 43 4B 20 20 20-53 54 41 43 4B 20 20 20  STACK   STACK
66DB:0110 53 54 41 43 4B 20 20 20-53 54 41 43 4B 20 20 20  STACK   STACK
66DB:0120 53 54 41 43 4B 20 20 20-53 54 41 43 4B 20 20 20  STACK   STACK
66DB:0130 53 54 41 43 4B 20 20 20-53 54 41 43 4B 20 20 20  STACK   STACK
66DB:0140 53 54 41 43 4B 20 20 20-53 54 41 43 4B 20 20 20  STACK   STACK
66DB:0150 53 54 41 43 4B 20 20 20-53 54 41 43 4B 20 20 20  STACK   STACK
66DB:0160 53 54 41 43 4B 20 20 20-53 54 41 43 4B 20 20 20  STACK   STACK
66DB:0170 53 54 41 43 4B 20 20 20-53 54 41 43 4B 20 00 00  STACK   STACK ..
66DB:0180 48 65 6C 6C 6F 2C 20 77-6F 72 6C 64 2E 24 00 00  Hello, world.$..
66DB:0190 B8 F3 66 8E D8 B4 09 BA-00 00 CD 21 B4 4C CD 21  8sf.X4.:..M!4LM!
```

Figure 5.4: *DEBUG display of program HELLO2.EXE created with the Microsoft version 3 assembler.*

stack runs between offset 100 and 17F, the data segment runs from 180 to 18D, and the code runs from 190 to 19F. In the next section we will see a very different layout for the COM file. Now let us single-step through our program.

Single-Stepping through the EXE File

Give the T (trace) command and DEBUG will execute the first instruction. Then it will display the registers again, along with the next instruction. The AX register now has the value 66F3, the data segment for our program. The instruction address is based on the CS register, since this is program code. Notice that the IP register matches the offset of the next instruction. Give the T command a second time, and we see that the value 66F3 has been moved into the DS register, too. Press T a third time to see that the next instruction:

```
66F4:0007   BA0000   MOV   DX,0000
```

moves the value zero into the DX register. Of course, the zero offset is relative to the DS register. We saw that the DS register starts 16 bytes ahead of the CS register. Press T a fourth time, and we find the next instruction to be

```
66F4:000A   CD21   INT 21
```

The registers are now established and we are ready to execute DOS interrupt 21 hex. However, we must be careful at this point not to give the T command again. If we do, we will single-step through DOS. Instead, we want to execute all the interrupt 21 instructions at once and then stop at the next instruction in our own program. We can do this in either of two

```
66F4:0000 B8F366      MOV      AX,66F3
66F4:0003 8ED8        MOV      DS,AX
66F4:0005 B409        MOV      AH,09
66F4:0007 BA0000      MOV      DX,0000
66F4:000A CD21        INT      21
66F4:000C B44C        MOV      AH,4C
66F4:000E CD21        INT      21
```

Figure 5.5: *Disassembled listing of program HELLO2.EXE.*

ways. One method works with both DOS versions 2 and 3. We will set a breakpoint at the following instruction when we issue the execute, G, command. The command is

    GC

This tells DEBUG to set a breakpoint at address C hex, the next instruction, and then to begin execution at full speed. With this method we must be careful to set the breakpoint at the right place. If we give an address that our program does not execute, we will not get control. Therefore, a better method is to use the P command, which tells DEBUG to execute the next statement in our program and set a breakpoint at the following instruction. But we do not have to specify the address. Clearly, this second method is better. However, the P command is not available in DOS version 2. In either case, interrupt 21 hex will be executed and the string in our data segment will be displayed on the screen. Then the program will stop at the next instruction. We will see the following display on the screen:

```
Hello, world.
AX = 0924 BX = 0000 CX = 00A0 DX = 0000 SP = 0080 BP = 0000 SI = 0000 DI = 0000
DS = 66F3 ES = 66DB SS = 66EB CS = 66F4 IP = 000C NV UP DI PL NZ NA PO NC
66F4:000C B44C MOV AH,4C
```

We can now give the G command without a parameter to complete the program and return control to DEBUG.

■ Analyzing the HELLO6.COM Program

In this section we are going to study the program HELLO6.COM, which we wrote in the previous chapter. If you do not have this program, please go back to Chapter 4 and create it.

Give the command:

    DEBUG HELLO6.COM par1 par2

using lowercase letters. This instructs DEBUG to load our HELLO6.COM program into memory and then wait for further commands. As in the previous example, we have added two parameters that are not needed by our program.

Give the R command to see the values in the registers. The result might look like this:

AX = 0000 BX = 0000 CX = 001B DX = 0000 SP = FFFE BP = 0000 SI = 0000 DI = 0000
DS = 66DB ES = 66DB SS = 66DB CS = 66DB IP = 0100 NV UP DI PL NZ NA PO NC
66DB:0100 50 PUSH AX

We can see that, in contrast to the EXE program, all four segment registers have the same value. Display the appropriate memory location with the command

DO 11F

The result is shown in Figure 5.6.

The first part of this display is similar to Figure 5.4. The first two bytes are CD 20, the instruction for interrupt 20. We can also see the two parameters at 5D, 6D, and 82 hex. Looking at the ASCII representation of the display, we can see our string:

Hello, world.

starting at offset 10B hex. The instructions are on both sides of the string. Give these commands:

U100 10A
U119 11A

```
0000 CD 20 00 B0 00 9A F0 FF-0D F0 42 02 D5 63 70 02 M .0..p..pB.Ucp.
0010 D5 63 E2 04 90 05 D5 63-01 03 01 00 02 FF FF FF Ucb...Uc........
0020 FF FF FF FF FF FF FF FF-FF FF FF FF D7 66 C8 2A .............WfH*
0030 D5 63 00 00 00 00 00 00-00 00 00 00 00 00 00 00 Uc..............
0040 00 00 00 00 00 00 00 00-00 00 00 00 00 00 00 00 ................
0050 CD 21 CB 00 00 00 00 00-00 00 00 00 00 50 41 52 M!K.........PAR
0060 31 20 20 20 20 20 20 20-00 00 00 00 00 50 41 52 1           .....PAR
0070 32 20 20 20 20 20 20 20-00 00 00 00 00 00 00 00 2        ........
0080 0B 20 70 61 72 31 20 70-61 72 32 20 0D 70 61 72 . parl par2 .par
0090 31 20 70 61 72 32 20 0D-0D 72 0D 6F 72 79 2C 20 1 par2 ..r.ory,
00A0 41 55 54 4F 20 32 0D 00-00 00 00 00 00 00 00 00 AUTO 2.........
00B0 00 00 00 00 00 00 00 00-00 00 00 00 00 00 00 00 ................
00C0 00 00 00 00 00 00 00 00-00 00 00 00 00 00 00 00 ................
00D0 00 00 00 00 00 00 00 00-00 00 00 00 00 00 00 00 ................
00E0 00 00 00 00 00 00 00 00-00 00 00 00 00 00 00 00 ................
00F0 00 00 00 00 00 00 00 00-00 00 00 00 00 00 00 00 ........M!Xk.Hello
0100 50 B4 09 BA 0B 01 CD 21-58 EB 0E 48 65 6C 6C 6F P4.:..M!Xk.Hello
0110 2C 20 77 6F 72 6C 64 2E-24 CD 20                , world.$
```

Figure 5.6: *DEBUG display of program HELLO6.COM.*

to see the disassembled code, listed in Figure 5.7. We have to give two U commands to skip over the data in the middle of our code. Notice that the segment address is the same for the D (display) and the U (disassembly) commands. You can single-step through this program using the T command just as you did with the EXE program. When you reach the end, control returns to DEBUG.

```
66DB:0100 50            PUSH    AX
66DB:0101 B409          MOV     AH,09
66DB:0103 BA0B01        MOV     DX,010B
66DB:0106 CD21          INT     21
66DB:0108 58            POP     AX
66DB:0109 EB0E          JMP     0119

66DB:0119 CD20          INT     20
```

Figure 5.7: *Disassembled listing of program HELLO6.COM.*

SUMMARY

In this chapter we learned how to use the debugger, DEBUG.COM. Using this software tool, we explored the main memory, patched Word-Star, wrote two short programs, and single-stepped through both an EXE and a COM program. In the next chapter we will add more macros to our library, create a new library, and write several short but useful programs.

Short but Useful Programs

INTRODUCTION

In the previous chapters we learned some of the ROM BIOS and DOS features and saw how to write assembly-language programs. In later chapters we will write complex and lengthy programs that read and write disk files. In this chapter we will write relatively short but useful programs to gain more familiarity with the computer and assembly language. We will also add four macros to our library. Our new programs will alter the operation of the computer to provide a new service, correct an error, or improve an inconvenient feature. The first program interchanges the two serial ports. The next programs reduce the memory size, designate the RAM disk as the system disk, and change the cursor size. The final two programs disable and restore the PrtSc function. Before we begin our programs, we need to create a library of constants.

A LIBRARY OF CONSTANTS

In the following programs we are going to need ASCII characters such as the carriage return, line feed, blank, period, and others. It will be convenient to define mnemonic symbols for these characters. Therefore, create a second library, named MYLIB.EQU, and enter the lines shown in Figure 6.1. These symbols will be available to any program that contains the directive

    INCLUDE mylib.equ

Although we do not use all these symbols in every program, it does no harm to have them available.

You might wonder why we cannot simply place these definitions in our macro library. If we do that, we you must then move the conditional statements:

    IF 1
    . . .
    ENDIF

that surround the reference to the macro library. The macro definitions are needed only during the first pass of the assembler, but the EQU definitions are needed during both passes. Therefore, if you combine the two libraries, you must move the conditional statements into the library, placing them around the macro definitions but not around the EQU statements. Now we look at a program to interchange the serial ports.

SWITCHING THE SERIAL PORTS COM1 AND COM2

We have seen that the IBM PC can be equipped with one or two serial ports, designated COM1 and COM2. One serial port can be used with a modem to communicate with another computer over a telephone line. Serial devices such as a daisy-wheel printer or plotter can be controlled through the other port.

Suppose you have a phone modem attached to COM1 and a printer connected to COM2. You can, in principle, communicate with each device by referring to the appropriate port, COM1 or COM2. However, if the software that runs these devices always expects to use COM1, you must either switch cords in the back of your computer or reprogram the ports. Let us consider the latter method.

We learned earlier that the addresses of the serial and parallel printer ports are stored in memory starting at address 400 hex. It should thus be possible to interchange two ports simply by switching the corresponding addresses. Unfortunately, this method will not always work. Some programs write directly to a particular port without using the addresses at 400 hex. Nevertheless, let us write a program to switch the two port addresses for COM1 and COM2.

Create a file named SWAPCOM.ASM and enter the lines shown in Figure 6.2. Assemble and link the program, but do not run it yet. If you have one or two serial ports, load the new program with the debugger. The command is

    DEBUG SWAPCOM.COM

Display the area of memory that has the port addresses with the command

    D0:400 LB

The result might look like this:

    0000:0400 F8 03 F8 02 00 00 00 00-BC 03 78 03

The two serial-port addresses 3F8 and 2F8 appear first. Then, after the

```
; equates from mylib.equ
blank    EQU      32       ;space
comma    EQU      44
cr       EQU      13       ;carriage return
eof      EQU      1Ah      ;end of file
esc      EQU      1Bh      ;escape
lf       EQU      10       ;line feed
period   EQU      46       ;decimal point
tab      EQU      9
```

Figure 6.1: *The symbol library MYLIB.EQU.*

```
            PAGE    ,132
            TITLE   SWAPCOM

COMMENT *
  December 31, 1985
  Program to swap ports COM1 and COM2
  Macros: @go_dos, @head, @write
 *
            INCLUDE mylib.equ
            IF1
            INCLUDE mylib.mac
            ENDIF

rom_data SEGMENT AT 40h
port1    DW      ?                   ;COM1
port2    DW      ?                   ;COM2
rom_data ENDS

code     SEGMENT
         ASSUME  CS:code, DS:code
         ORG     100h
strt:
         @head   ' SWAPCOM,12.31.85 '
         @write  <' COM1 and COM2 interchanged',cr,lf>
         ASSUME  DS:rom_data
         MOV     AX,rom_data
         MOV     DS,AX               ;set of DS
         MOV     AX,[port1]          ;get original
         MOV     BX,[port2]          ; data
         MOV     [port1],BX          ;switch
         MOV     [port2],AX          ; it
         @go_dos                     ;quit

code     ENDS
         END     strt
```

Figure 6.2: *Source program to switch the serial ports.*

hyphen, we see the two parallel ports, 3BC and 378. Run our new program under control of DEBUG with the G command (no parameters). When the message

Program terminated normally

appears, display the port addresses again. The result should now look like this:

0000:0400 F8 02 F8 03 00 00 00 00-BC 03 78 03

We can see that the addresses for COM1 and COM2 have been interchanged. Of course, if you run this program a second time, the addresses will be restored to their original positions. Let us go through the instructions of the program.

After the usual directives at the beginning, we establish an absolute segment:

rom_data SEGMENT AT 40h

. . .

rom_data ENDS

to define the ROM BIOS data area. The two 16-bit port addresses are defined with the labels *port1* and *port2*. Remember, we cannot define data or code in this segment. However, we can use the question mark after the DW (define-word) directive.

We begin the main program with the *@head* macro to code the title and date and the *@write* macro to tell the user what is happening. We inform the assembler with the ASSUME directive that we are about to change the value in the DS register. We then set the DS register to the ROM BIOS segment at 40 hex (40:0 hex is the same as address 0:400 hex). We copy the original address of COM1 into register AX and the original address of COM2 into register BX. The next two instructions change both ports. (Remember, we cannot move data directly from one memory location to another; we must use an intermediate register.) We terminate the program with our *@go_dos* macro.

■ Switching the Parallel Ports

We learned earlier that the IBM PC can have one, two, or three parallel ports. The first port, which may be part of the monochrome screen, is referenced as PRN or LPT1. The other two ports are called LPT2 and

LPT3. Suppose you have a dot-matrix printer attached to LPT1 and a daisy-wheel printer attached to LPT2. You can send a file to either printer with the DOS commands:

```
COPY f_name LPT1
COPY f_name LPT2
```

When printing a file from a text editor, however, you may not have a choice. The output goes to LPT1.

To interchange these two ports, we can write a program similar to the previous one to switch LPT1 and LPT2. We only have to change each location of COM to LPT in the source program. Also, the ORG 0 statement at the beginning of the *rom_data* segment must be changed to 8. After assembling and running the new version, we can use the debugger to see that the first and second parallel port addresses at locations 408 and 40A have been interchanged. However, the change will not have any effect. The Shift-PrtSc command always uses the original LPT1 port, as do WordStar and BASIC. Of course you can use the DOS commands

```
COPY F_NAME LPT1
```

and

```
COPY F_NAME LPT2
```

to send ASCII files to either printer.

Our next program reduces the memory size.

REDUCING THE MEMORY SIZE

We have seen that the 8088 CPU family can in principle address more than a megabyte of memory. However, DOS versions 2 and 3 are limited to 640K bytes for program execution. If you have this amount of memory, you will find many programs that can use all 640K of it. Unfortunately, there are several commercial programs that will not operate with 640K memory. Yet these programs run correctly with a smaller amount of memory, usually 512K bytes or less. Furthermore, if you attempt to run such a program with 640K memory, you get this confusing error message:

```
Insufficient memory
```

The solution to this problem is to reduce the effective size of memory temporarily, for these executable programs.

Of course, you can reduce the effective memory size by installing a RAM disk. If you have a PC AT, however, it would be better to install a RAM disk above the regular one-megabyte memory space. Then you still have 640K bytes for program execution.

We will reduce the memory size by another method—creating a resident program. We learned in Chapter 2 that DOS gives an executing program all the remaining memory space. Then, if that program terminates normally through interrupt 20 hex or function 4C of interrupt 21 hex, DOS recovers the allocated space for the next program. However, if a program terminates with DOS interrupt 27 hex, a portion of memory is permanently reserved. The effective memory is reduced accordingly. This technique is commonly used to install device drivers such as a print spooler or RAM disk, but in this case we will simply allocate a 64K block of memory. The computer will not execute any code in this space.

Our program is given in Figure 6.3. If you have 640K memory available, you will occasionally need to run this program. Even if you have less memory, you can try it out. Create a file named FILL.ASM and type up the program. Be sure to have the macro library we developed in Chapter 4, since the program uses macros @head and @write. You will also need the new library MYLIB.EQU, since the carriage return and line feed are needed.

Run the DOS program CHKDSK and record the amount of available memory. For example, with 640K bytes of memory you will see something like this:

```
655360 bytes total memory
618464 bytes free
```

Assemble and execute the program and you will see the expression

```
Memory reduced 64K bytes
```

on the screen. Run the CHKDSK program again and verify that the memory has been reduced. Now the results might look like this:

```
655360 bytes total memory
552912 bytes free
```

Let us go through the instructions.

We begin the program with the usual assembler directives and comments. We now have two INCLUDE directives, one for the macro library and one for the EQU library. Since this is a COM file, we set the instruction pointer to 100 hex with the ORG statement. The executable instructions begin with the *@head* macro, which encodes the program title and data. Then the *@write* macro displays a message telling the user that the memory has been reduced in size. Notice that the symbols *cr* and *lf* are used in the message; they are defined in our EQU library.

There are only two more CPU instructions:

```
MOV DX,OFFSET strt-OFFSET  pg_len
INT  27h                        ;done
```

One defines the length of the resident code in the DX register; the other

```
            PAGE      ,132
            TITLE     FILL part of memory

COMMENT *
  December 24, 1985
  Program to fill part of memory with
  resident program (some programs will
  not run when there is too much memory.
  Macros: @head, @write
  INT 27h
 *
            INCLUDE mylib.equ           ;equates
            IF1
            INCLUDE mylib.mac           ;macro library
            ENDIF

code        SEGMENT
            ASSUME  CS:code, DS:code
            ORG     100h

strt:
            @head   ' FILL,12.24.85 '
            @write  <cr,lf,' Memory reduced 64K bytes'>
;-----------------------------------------------
; quit and stay resident
;-----------------------------------------------
            MOV     DX,OFFSET strt-OFFSET pg_len
            INT     27h              ;done
pg_len      LABEL   BYTE

code        ENDS
            END     strt
```

Figure 6.3: *Source program for reducing the memory size.*

terminates the program with DOS interrupt 27 hex, leaving 64K bytes resident. The resident length is calculated by the assembler, using the labels *pg_len* and *strt*. This technique was discussed in Chapter 4. We need to add two macros for the next program.

TWO NEW MACROS FOR OUR LIBRARY

Add the two macros given in Figure 6.4 to your macro library. Be careful to place them in alphabetical order. Copy the first line to the top of the library to provide an easy reference. Let us look at these new macros.

Finding the DOS Version

Several different DOS versions are available; these include three from version 1, versions 2.0 and 2.1, and versions 3.0 and 3.1. The higher-numbered versions include features not available on the lower versions. If a program tries to use a feature that is not available, the results are unpredictable. Therefore, when you use a feature that is restricted to certain versions, you should check to see that the correct version is present. (All the programs in this book require DOS version 2 or higher. However, we do not check for this, since it is assumed that you are not running version 1.)

As we learned in Chapter 2, DOS function 30 hex, interrupt 21 hex returns the DOS version that is currently running. The major version—1, 2, or 3—is returned in the AL register, and the minor version (the part after the decimal point) is returned in the AH register. Since this function was not added until version 2, it does not return the correct number for

```
@dos_ver MACRO
;; return DOS version in AL
         MOV      AH,30h
         INT      21h
         ENDM
@get_vec MACRO   ?vec
;; return address of interrupt vector
;;   ?vec in ES:BX
         MOV      AL,?vec
         MOV      AH,35h
         INT      21h
         ENDM
```

Figure 6.4: *The macros @dos_ver and @get_vec.*

version 1; it simply returns the value zero. Thus, to determine the version number, add our new macro:

```
@dos_ver
```

and then check the AL register for 0, 2, or 3. (The difference between minor versions is so small that we will not be concerned with it.) We check interrupt vectors with the next macro.

■ Determining an Interrupt Vector

We have seen that the beginning of memory contains 32-bit pointers to routines in the ROM BIOS and DOS. These addresses are called interrupt vectors. Of course, we do not need to know the value of a vector if we just want to use it. As in the previous program, we just give the corresponding command, such as:

```
INT 20h
```

However, we are going to write programs that change these vectors. Then we will want to copy the original value before making the change. The original value tells us where to continue after we have performed our operations. Alternatively, we can restore the original value when we have finished our operations. A third reason for determining an interrupt vector is that we may need to reference information that is located relative to it.

To determine the value of an interrupt vector, use the @get_vec macro with the vector number as a parameter:

```
@get_vec 22h
```

Vector 22 hex is referenced in this example. As we learned in Chapter 2, function 35 hex, interrupt 21 determines the value of an interrupt vector. On return, the desired vector will appear in the ES:BX registers.

Now that we have added two macros, we are ready for our next program, which fixes a bug in DOS version 2.

■ READING COMMAND.COM FROM THE RAM DISK

We saw previously that the files IBMBIO, IBMDOS, and COMMAND are read from disk into memory each time DOS is started. The first two files stay in memory until the computer is turned off, and so they do not have to be available on any disk except the system disk. The third file, however, can be written over by large programs. Therefore, COMMAND occasionally has to be read again from disk into memory. DOS will normally look for COMMAND on the drive from which the system was booted, usually drive A for a floppy system and drive C for a hard disk. However, if you establish a RAM disk as drive C, it would be faster to read COMMAND from the RAM disk. With DOS version 3 you can do this by including the two commands

```
COPY A:COMMAND.COM C:
SET COMSPEC=C:\COMMAND.COM
```

in your AUTOEXEC.BAT file. However, these commands will not work with DOS version 2. The program given in Figure 6.5 corrects this bug. Of course, you only need this program for DOS version 2; it is not needed for version 3. If you want to see where your DOS expects to find COMMAND, give the command

SET

and DOS will respond with several lines of text. One of them will look something like this:

```
COMSPEC=C:\COMMAND.COM
```

The symbol C:\ means that DOS will look for COMMAND on drive C.

If you are running a RAM disk and DOS version 2.0 or 2.1, you should use the program shown in Figure 6.5. Create a file named COMSPC.ASM.

```
                PAGE    ,132
                TITLE   COMSPEC

COMMENT *
    January  3, 1986
    Fix bug in DOS Ver 2 to change
    location of A:\COMMAND.COM to another drive
    Commands in AUTOEXEC.BAT file are:

        COPY A:COMMAND.COM C:
        COMSPC C:
```

Figure 6.5: *Source program for making RAM disk C the system disk*

```
              SET COMSPEC=C:\COMMAND.COM
        Macros: @dos_ver, @get_vec, @go_dos,
        @head, @write, @write_r
        *

              INCLUDE mylib.equ
              IF1
              INCLUDE mylib.mac
              ENDIF

; next constant is start of A:\COMMAND.COM
dsk       EQU       939h

code      SEGMENT
          ASSUME    CS:code, DS:code
          ORG       5Ch
param     LABEL     BYTE                ;drive name

          ORG       100h
strt:
          @head     ' COMSPC, 01.03.86 '
          @dos_ver                      ;version
          CMP       AL,2                ;must be 2
          JNZ       bad_ver
;----------------------------------------
; find location of A:\COMMAND.COM
;----------------------------------------
          @get_vec  ?2h
; set up drive C for default
          MOV       AL,'C'
;----------------------------------------
; check for parameter on command line
;----------------------------------------
          MOV       AH,[param]
          OR        AH,AH
          JZ        no_parm
          MOV       AL,AH
          ADD       AL,'A'-1            ;to ASCII
;----------------------------------------
; change drive for COMMAND.COM location
;----------------------------------------
no_parm:
          MOV       ES:[dsk],AL
          MOV       [new_d],AL
          @write_r  <OFFSET mes_d>
          @go_dos
bad_ver:
          @write    ' DOS version must be 2 '
          @go_dos
mes_d     DB        ' COMMAND.COM now read from drive '
new_d     DB        'C$'
code      ENDS
          END       strt
```

Figure 6.5: (continued).

(Notice the slight change in spelling; COMSPEC is a DOS reserved word.) Enter the lines given in Figure 6.5. Make sure you have added the new macros @dos_ver and @get_vec to your library. Assemble and link the program but do not run it yet. Give the DOS command SET without parameters. Notice the value of the disk drive. Now, if your RAM disk is drive C and you are running DOS version 2, you can execute the new program with the C parameter:

```
COMSPC C:
```

(Do not forget the colon after the drive name.) Since we programmed drive C to be the default drive, you do not need to enter a parameter. Also give the command

```
SET COMSPEC = C:\COMMAND.COM
```

to change the response from the SET command. (Notice the slight difference in spelling.) Of course, if your RAM disk has another letter, use that letter instead. Also change the default in the middle of the program. If you only have two floppy disks you can try out this program just for fun. Give the commands:

```
COMSPC B:
SET COMSPEC = B:\COMMAND.COM
```

In either case, give the SET command again to see that DOS is ready to read COMMAND from the desired disk. Run a program that overlays the command processor, like Turbo Pascal. When you quit, the system will try to read COMMAND.COM from the disk you specified in the COMPSPEC command.

You can freely change the drive from which COMMAND is read by running our COMSPC program more than once. However, if you do not also give the SET COMSPEC = command, the SET command without parameters will not show the correct drive. Let us go through the source program.

We begin the program as usual. However, we include the constant:

```
dsk             EQU             939h
```

to locate the offset where the disk drive name is stored. After the SEGMENT and ASSUME directives we find the usual ORG directive. However, the value is not 100 hex but 5C hex. As we saw in the previous chapter, this is one of the two places where parameters entered on the command line appear. If the first parameter begins with a drive name followed by a colon, it will be identified at this location. The value 1 means that drive A was given, while the value 3 refers to drive C. If no drive name was given, the value is zero.

Our program begins at 100 hex in the usual way. The @head macro identifies the program and date. We then check the version number with the new macro @dos_ver. If the version is not 2, we branch to an error message and terminate the program. We locate interrupt vector 22 hex in the next step. This vector will help us find the drive location we are look-ing for. The segment of the vector is returned in the ES register. We do not need the offset returned in the BX register; we will use the value of the symbol *dsk* (at 939 hex) instead.

The next step sets up the new drive for C. That is, if no parameter was entered, we choose drive C as the default. We place an ASCII letter C into the AL register. Then we move the value from location *param* (5C hex) to the AH register and check for a value of zero with the OR state-ment. If we find it, we know that no parameter was entered. Otherwise, we move the value from the AH register to the AL register. Then we convert the drive number to the corresponding ASCII character by adding an ASCII A minus 1. We move the parameter into the appropriate location with the instruction

```
MOV ES:[dsk],AL
```

We then send a message identifying the new disk drive using the @write_r macro and terminate the program with the @go_dos macro.

This is a fairly simple program, at least when using macros. You might want to add further checking. For example, you can limit the range of acceptable drive letters to A, B, or C. However, you will not normally execute this program from the keyboard. Instead, you will place the three appropriate commands in your AUTOEXEC batch file, where they will be issued automatically.

Before we leave this program, let us explore the command-line tail. We saw in the previous chapter that the command-line tail could be found in two places—5C hex and 80 hex. The version at 80 hex appears exactly as it was typed, whereas the version at 5C hex is edited. In particular, if a drive letter and colon are entered, DOS changes the letter to a number (A = 1, C = 3) and removes the colon. Therefore, the commands

```
COMSPC C
COMSPC C:
```

and

```
COMSPC C:\
```

will appear differently at 5C. Let us use the debugger to explore this difference.

Give the command

DEBUG COMSPC   C

and then give this DEBUG command:

D50 8F

The results should look like Figure 6.6. Notice the value zero at location 5C, which indicates that no colon (drive name) was entered. The next byte, 43 hex, is the uppercase letter C, also visible in the ASCII representation, that was entered as the parameter. By contrast, the value 2 at location 80 hex indicates that one character was entered. (Remember, the space in front of the parameter is included in the count.) Now let us repeat the process.

Leave DEBUG with the Q command and begin it again. (Press the F3 key to repeat the last command.) Add a colon this time, so that the command looks like this:

DEBUG COMSPC   C:

Again, display memory with the command

D50 8F

and the result will look like Figure 6.7. Now there is no letter C visible in the ASCII display. The value at location 5C hex is 3, indicating that drive C was specified. The remainder of this part is blank (20 hex). By contrast, the value 3 at location 80 hex indicates that two characters were entered. Both the lowercase C and the colon are visible in the ASCII representation. Compare the value at location 82 hex in Figures 6.6 and 6.7. Then compare the region around 5C hex. You can see that it is easier in this case to use the 80 hex region.

Although it is not specifically stated, it is common practice to allow more than one blank when only a single blank is required. Then, a variation of the previous command is this:

DEBUG COMSPC   C:

where two spaces are placed between COMSPEC and C:. Give this command

and display the region between 50 and 8F hex. The resulting display should look like Figure 6.8. The drive letter C is coded as the value 3 at 5C hex, just as it was with the previous example. However, the character count at 80 hex is one larger, reflecting the extra space. Furthermore, there are blanks at locations 81 and 82. The letter C begins at address 83, rather than 82 as in the previous example. (In Chapter 7 we will write a routine to remove leading blanks from parameters.)

Give the DEBUG command:

DEBUG COMSPC C:

and observe the results. You will find the information at location 5C hex to be the same as in the previous two examples. However, it will be different at 80 hex.

We add another macro next.

```
0050 CD 21 CB 00 00 00 00 00-00 00 00 00 00 43 20 20   .!...........C
0060 20 20 20 20 20 20 20 20-00 00 00 00 00 20 20 20              .....
0070 20 20 20 20 20 20 20 20-00 00 00 00 00 00 00 00            ........
0080 02 20 63 0D 00 00 00 00-00 00 00 00 00 00 00 00   . c...........
```

Figure 6.6: *DEBUG display for command DEBUG COMSPC.COM C:.*

```
0050 CD 21 CB 00 00 00 00 00-00 00 00 00 03 20 20 20   .!...........
0060 20 20 20 20 20 20 20 20-00 00 00 00 00 20 20 20              .....
0070 20 20 20 20 20 20 20 20-00 00 00 00 00 00 00 00            ........
0080 03 20 63 3A 0D 00 00 00-00 00 00 00 00 00 00 00   . c:..........
```

Figure 6.7: *DEBUG display for command DEBUG COMSPC.COM C:.*

```
0050 CD 21 CB 00 00 00 00 00-00 00 00 00 03 20 20 20   .!...........
0060 20 20 20 20 20 20 20 20-00 00 00 00 00 20 20 20              .....
0070 20 20 20 20 20 20 20 20-00 00 00 00 00 00 00 00            ........
0080 04 20 20 63 3A 0D 00 00-00 00 00 00 00 00 00 00   .  c:..........
```

Figure 6.8: *DEBUG display for command DEBUG COMSPC.COM C:.*

DETERMINING THE SCREEN MODE

We have seen that the IBM computer can be fitted with either a monochrome screen, a color graphics screen, or both. Furthermore, the graphics screen can be set to any of seven different modes. Before we can make changes to the screen, then, we must determine the current mode. We will use the macro *@screen_mode,* shown in Figure 6.9, for this purpose. This macro uses function F hex of ROM BIOS interrupt 10 hex. As we saw in Chapter 1, this interrupt can perform many different services; the value in the AH register selects the desired function. The video mode is returned in the AL register. Add this macro to your library in alphabetical order. As usual, copy the first line to the beginning of the library.

We look at cursor size next.

CHANGING THE CURSOR SIZE

The cursor is a blinking marker on the video screen that indicates where the next character will appear. The cursor shape is normally an underline made from two lines at the bottom of a character position. As we learned in Chapter 1, characters are created on the monochrome screen within a matrix of 14 by 9 dots. On the other hand, characters on the graphics screen are formed in a matrix of 8 by 8 dots.

However, not all rows and columns are used for creating the regular characters. The top and bottom rows are used for ascenders and descenders and the last columns are used to separate adjacent characters.

Each row of dots is known as a scan line. There are 14 scan lines (numbered 0–13) for the monochrome screen and eight scan lines (numbered 0–7) for the graphics screen.

```
@screen_mode  MACRO
;; Macro to determine screen mode
;; Number in AL is mode:
;;
        MOV     AH,0Fh   ;;read mode
        INT     10h
        ENDM
```

Figure 6.9: *Macro @screen_mode, for determining the screen mode.*

We learned in Chapter 1 that function 1 of ROM BIOS interrupt 10 hex can be used to change the cursor appearance. You specify the starting scan line with the CH register and the ending line with the CL register. The default values are:

```
CX = 0607    monochrome
CX = 0B0C    graphics
```

You can make the cursor a solid block in several ways. One way is to set CH to zero and CL to either 7 or C hex. However, our program will use another method. If the ending scan line is a smaller number than the beginning scan line, the cursor wraps around, making two blocks that touch each other. Thus the value

```
CX = 0605
```

will create a solid cursor (with two touching blocks) for either the monochrome or the graphics screen. We will also create a cursor shape that consists of two separate blocks, one at the top and the other at the bottom of the character position.

The program shown in Figure 6.10 will create cursors of three different shapes: normal, solid block, and split. Create a file named CURSOR.ASM and type up the program. Be sure to add the *@screen_mode* macro to your library. Assemble and run the program. Nothing should change. Press the F3 key and add the L (large) parameter:

```
CURSOR L
```

and run it again. The cursor will change to a solid block. Press F3 again and use the M (medium) parameter. Now the cursor is a split block. This shape is very easy to find when working with a text editor. Run CURSOR again, giving a number for the parameter, and see the different shapes that are available. If you find a shape you like, put the corresponding command in your AUTOEXEC file. Let us go through the program code.

Near the beginning of the program we define two constants, *maxm* and *maxg*. These set the maximum scan lines for the monochrome and the graphics screen, respectively. After the SEGMENT and ASSUME directives, we define the labels *param1* and *param2* at locations 5D and 6D hex. We saw in the last section that this region is one of the places where the first and second parameters appear.

The regular code begins at location 100 hex with the *@head* macro. We set the BL register to the maximum scan line for the monochrome screen. Then we determine the current screen type with the *@screen_mode*

```
              PAGE     ,132
              TITLE    CURSOR-- set size

COMMENT   *
  December 29, 1985
         Usage:
              CURSOR
              CURSOR param1
              CURSOR param1   param2
   where param1 is:
         no parameter = reset to normal (B,C/ 6,7)
         L - large, solid block
         M - medium, split blocks
         X - where X = stop line number (1,C / 1,7)
    For two parameters:
         param1 = start line
         param2 = srop line

   Macros: @go_dos, @head, @screen_mode
   Int 10h
 *
         INCLUDE mylib.equ
         IF1
         INCLUDE mylib.mac
         ENDIF

maxm     EQU      0Ch            ;max line for monochrome
maxg     EQU      7              ;max line for graphics

code     SEGMENT
         ASSUME   CS:code, DS:code
         ORG      5Dh
param1   LABEL    BYTE           ;first parameter
         ORG      6Dh
param2   LABEL    BYTE           ;first parameter

         ORG      100h
start:
         @head    ' CURSOR, 12.29.85 '
         MOV      BL,maxm        ;set for mono
; determine screen type
         @screen_mode
         CMP      AL,7           ;monochrome?
         JE       monoc          ;yes
; reset maximum line for graphics
         MOV      BL,maxg
monoc:
         MOV      BH,BL
         DEC      BH
; get first parameter
         MOV      AL,[param1]
         CMP      AL,blank       ;anything?
         JZ       norm           ;no
```

Figure 6.10: *Source program to change the cursor size.*

Short but Useful Programs

```
            CMP     AL,'A'          ;letter?
            JB      notal
            CMP     AL,'M'          ;medium
            JNE     notmed
; cursor is two blocks
            MOV     CH,BH
            MOV     CL,2
            JMP     SHORT rest
notmed:
            CMP     AL,'L'          ;large
            JNE     norm
; cursor is large block
            MOV     CX,0605h
            JMP     SHORT rest
notal:
            AND     AL,0Fh          ;right 4 bits
            MOV     CH,AL           ;start line
; get second parameter
            MOV     AL,[param2]
            CMP     AL,blank        ;anything?
            JE      nopar2          ;no
            AND     AL,0Fh          ;4 bits
            MOV     CL,AL           ;stop
            JMP     SHORT rest
nopar2:
            MOV     CL,CH
            MOV     CH,BH           ;start
            JMP     SHORT rest
norm:
; normal cursor is two lines
            MOV     CX,BX
rest:
            MOV     AH,1            ;set cursor
            INT     10h             ;screen operation
            @go_dos                 ;done

code        ENDS
            END     start
```

Figure 6.10: *(continued)*

macro. If the value returned in the AL register is 7, the monochrome screen is current. Otherwise, we reset the BL register to the maximum scan line for the graphics screen. We move the maximum value to the BH register and decrement the value. Now the BX register is set for the standard cursor, the bottom two lines regardless of the screen type.

We move the value at location 5D hex to the AL register so that we can see whether a parameter was entered on the command line. If no parameter was entered, there will be a blank at 5D hex and now in the AL register. If that is the case, we skip over the next instructions and set the cursor to its normal appearance. If a parameter was entered, however, we check to see if it is a letter. Remember, any letters entered as parameters are automatically converted to uppercase in this region. If the parameter is smaller than (below) the letter A, we can expect a number. Otherwise, we check for the letter M (medium, split block) or L (large block) and set the cursor size accordingly.

If the parameter is not a letter, we select the right four bits by performing a logical AND with F hex. The result becomes the ending row of the cursor. The starting row is the next-to-last line. Therefore, a numeric parameter will create a two-part cursor.

If two parameters are entered, they become the beginning and ending rows. You can see that this program allows you to create a variety of cursor shapes. The command:

    CURSOR 1 2

creates an upside-down cursor that shows just the top two lines.

Now let us see how to change an interrupt vector.

CHANGING AN INTERRUPT VECTOR

In the previous chapter we briefly explored the interrupt vectors at the beginning of memory. We could, in principle, change an interrupt vector using the debugger. But this method can be disastrous if an interrupt occurs during the change. Therefore, DOS function 25 hex, interrupt 21 is provided for this purpose. We place the new interrupt vector in the ES:DX registers and the vector number to be changed in the AL register, and then execute the function. We can simplify the operation with a macro. Add macro @set_vec, given in Figure 6.11, to your library. We will use it in the next program.

```
@set_vec MACRO   ?vec
;; set interrupt vector to address ES:DX
;; Usage:  @set_vec  9
         MOV     AL,?vec
         MOV     AH,25h
         INT     21h
         ENDM
```

Figure 6.11: *Macro @set_vec to change an interrupt vector.*

We next consider the PrtSc interrupt.

DISABLING THE PrtSc COMMAND

The PrtSc command is a convenient feature of the IBM PC. Whenever you want a permanent copy of information on the video screen, you can hold a Shift key and press the PrtSc key. The information then appears at the printer. However, there are two cases where problems can arise. If there is no printer attached to your computer and you activate the PrtSc key, the computer will lock up. And even if a printer is attached to your computer, it can be inconvenient to press the Shift-PrtSc combination accidentally when you meant something else. Therefore, let us see how easy it is to disable the PrtSc command.

As we learned in Chapter 1, the ROM BIOS interrupt 5 activates the PrtSc operation. We can disable this function by changing the vector. We could, of course, write a resident interrupt handler to intercept the vector. However, there is an easier way. When we execute an interrupt instruction, INT, we call a subroutine somewhere in the memory. The final instruction for this routine is the return-from-interrupt instruction, IRET. Therefore, we can disable an interrupt simply by changing it to point to an IRET instruction. Frequently, the instruction located just before an interrupt routine is an IRET instruction for the previous routine. Let us see if this is so for interrupt 5.

Start DEBUG and give the command

    D0:0 L20

to display the first eight interrupt vectors. The results should look like this:

    0000 72 30 E3 00 47 01 70 00-C3 E2 00 F0 47 01 70 00
    0010 47 01 70 00 54 FF 00 F0-47 FF 00 F0 47 FF 00 F0

We can see that the address of vector 5 at 14 hex is F000:FF54 (reading backwards). Set the ES register with the command

    RES

to F000. Then give the command

    UES:FF53 L3

Notice that the starting offset address, FF53, is one less than the interrupt vector. The result should be this:

```
F000:FF53   CF   IRET
F000:FF54   FB   STI
F000:FF55   1E   PUSH DS
```

As expected, we have found an IRET instruction just before the interrupt routine. Therefore, we only have to decrement the vector to inactivate the routine.

The program shown in Figure 6.12 will disable the PrtSc function. Let us go through the instructions. After the opening directives, we establish the ROM BIOS segment at 0F000 hex. We define two labels. The first is the IRET instruction, and the second is the normal INT 5 entry point. We begin the main program with the @head macro and continue with the @get_vec macro to check the vector at interrupt 5. If it does not match the correct offset for label old_e, we terminate the program with an error message. This would happen if you ran this program twice.

We make another safety check to ensure that there is an IRET instruction at location new_e in the ROM BIOS. If not, we terminate with an error message. But if all is well, we change the interrupt vector using function 25 of DOS interrupt 21. Also, we write a message on the screen reminding the user that we have made the change. We terminate the program with our @go_dos macro.

Create a file named NOPRINT.ASM and type up the program given in Figure 6.12. Assemble and run it. Press Shift-PrtSc and see if this function is disabled. Of course, you can still use the printer in the usual way. Run this program a second time to get an error message.

Now we have to restore the function.

RESTORING THE PrtSc FUNCTION

In the previous section we disabled the Shift-PrtSc function by changing interrupt 5. In this section we write a similar program to restore the function. This program will be much simpler. We will restore the original vector without making any checks. You can run this program a second time without any problem.

Create a file named REPRINT.ASM and type up the program listed in Figure 6.13. Assemble and run it. Try the Shift-PrtSc function to be sure it works again. Let us briefly go through the code.

```
        PAGE    ,132
        TITLE   NOPRINT

COMMENT *
  December 29, 1985
  Disable Shift PrtSc by changing INT 5 to IRET
  Macros: @get_vec, @go_dos, @head, @set_vec, @write
 *
        INCLUDE mylib.equ
        IF1
        INCLUDE mylib.mac
        ENDIF

; ROM BIOS routines
rombios SEGMENT AT 0F000h
        ORG     0FF53h
new_e   DB      ?
old_e   LABEL   FAR
rombios ENDS

code    SEGMENT
        ASSUME  CS:code, DS:code
        ORG     100h
strt:
        @head   'NOPRINT,12.29.85 '
;--------------------------------------------
; check if already changed
;--------------------------------------------
        @get_vec 5
;--------------------------------------------
; original BIOS vector is F000:FF54
; ES:BX has current vector 5
;--------------------------------------------
        CMP     BX,OFFSET old_e
        JNZ     gotit           ;not original
;--------------------------------------------
; see if IRET is at F000:FF53
;--------------------------------------------
        CMP     BYTE PTR ES:[new_e],0CFh
        JNZ     no_ret          ;no IRET
;--------------------------------------------
; change INT 5 to IRET before PrtSc routine
; DS:DX has new vector 5
;--------------------------------------------
        @write  'PrtSc disabled'
        ASSUME  DS:rombios
        MOV     AX,rombios
        MOV     DS,AX           ;segment
        MOV     DX,OFFSET new_e ;offset
        @set_vec 5
        @go_dos                 ;done
;--------------------------------------------
; PrtSc already changed
```

Figure 6.12: *Source program to disable the PrtSc function.*

```
        ;--------------------------------------------
                ASSUME  DS:code
        gotit:
                @write  'PrtSc already changed'
                @go_dos                    ;quit
        ;--------------------------------------------
        ; IRET not in place
        ;--------------------------------------------
        no_ret:
                @write  'IRET not in place'
                @go_dos

        code    ENDS
                END     strt
```

Figure 6.12: *(continued)*

```
                PAGE    ,132
                TITLE   REPRINT

        COMMENT *
          December 29, 1985
          Restore printer with INT 5
          Macros: @go_dos, @head, @set_vec, @write
          *
                INCLUDE mylib.equ
                IF1
                INCLUDE mylib.mac
                ENDIF

        ; ROM BIOS routines
        rombios SEGMENT AT 0F000h
                ORG     0FF54h
        old_e   LABEL   FAR
        rombios ENDS

        code    SEGMENT
                ASSUME  CS:code, DS:rombios
                ORG     100h
        strt:
                @head   'REPRINT,12.29.85 '

                MOV     AX,SEG rombios
                MOV     DS,AX              ;segment
                MOV     DX,OFFSET old_e ;offset
        ;--------------------------------------------
        ; reset INT 5 with address DS:DX
        ;--------------------------------------------
```

Figure 6.13: *Source program to restore the PrtSc function.*

```
                @set_vec 5                  ;change vector
                ASSUME   DS:code
                MOV      AX,CS
                MOV      DS,AX               ;restore DS
                @write   'PrtSc restored'
                @go_dos                      ;done

       code     ENDS
                END      strt
```

Figure 6.13: *(continued)*

As in the previous program, we establish the ROM BIOS segment. This time, however, we define only one label, the normal entry point to the routine. After the *@head* macro, we point the DS:DX register to the ROM BIOS entry point. Then we use macro *@set_vec* to restore the vector. We display a short message to the user and terminate the program with our *@go_dos* macro.

SUMMARY

In this chapter we introduced four new macros to make our programming easier. We also wrote six short programs: to switch serial ports, to reduce the memory size, to change the cursor shape, to change the drive from which COMMAND.COM is read, and to disable and restore the PrtSc function. In the next chapter we consider more complex programs.

The beginning of your macro library should now look like this:

```
; Macros in this library
; @dos_ver        MACRO              ;get version
; @get_vec        MACRO              ?vec ;interrupt vector
; @go_dos         MACRO              ;return to DOS by 21h
; @head           MACRO num?         ;header information
; @screen_mode    MACRO              ;find screen type
; @set_vec        MACRO              ?vec ;change interr vector
; @write          MACRO text?        ;write text on screen
; @write_r        MACRO addr?        ;display text at addr?
```

Reading
Disk Files

INTRODUCTION

In the previous chapters we wrote assembly-language programs that simply displayed information on the video screen, or required input of only one or two characters from the user. In this chapter we will write several useful programs for displaying disk files and running hidden programs. These programs are more complicated, in that they require the user to type a complete file name or path name. They then read the requested file from disk. We will also add several new macros to our library and create a library of subroutines.

EXPLORING THE COMMAND-LINE TAIL

We've seen that when a program is executed, it is possible to give one or more parameters on the command line. For example, this command:

TYPEW   FILE1   FILE2

tells DOS to execute the program TYPEW and make available the two parameters *FILE1* and *FILE2*. These parameters are known collectively as the command-line tail.

We've also seen that the command-line tail can be found at location 82 hex. Text of the parameters may also appear starting at locations 5D and 6D hex. However, the parameter at 82 hex changes depending on the form of the input. By contrast, the form at 5D hex is more consistent. Blanks entered in front of the parameter are removed, and lowercase letters are converted to uppercase. Therefore, when we wrote the COM-SPC program we looked for a drive name at location 5C hex. We also found one or two parameters for the CURSOR program at 5D and 6D hex. It is convenient to use the 5C and 6C hex areas when we are only looking for a single letter. In the programs we write in this chapter, however, we will read an entire file name or path name, and so we will use the information in the 80 hex region.

The disadvantage of reading the command-line tail at 80 hex is that we must perform all the processing of the line. We must remove leading blanks, determine how many parameters have been entered, and convert lowercase to upper- if necessary. Nevertheless, we will write a set of routines to process the command-line tail so that we can use it in our programs. But before we write these routines, let us further explore the command-line tail.

As we have seen, a file name can contain as many as eight characters, a dot, and then three more characters. Thus we must expect a parameter such as

NEWSORT.TXT

when the file is on the current drive and directory. If we want to reference a file on another drive, however, we must include the drive name. Thus, if our file is on drive D, we use a specifier such as this:

D:NEWSORT.TXT

A further complication occurs if we have a hard disk. It is convenient to partition the hard disk into subdirectories, so that we can keep related files grouped together under appropriate names. Thus, when referencing a file in another directory, we must give the name of the subdirectory as well as the file name. For example, if the current directory is named EDIT and we want to reference a file named OLDSORT.TXT in the SORT subdirectory, we would use a name such as:

\SORT\OLDSORT.TXT

or

C:\SORT\OLDSORT.TXT

if drive C is not current. Of course, it is possible to have subdirectories of subdirectories. Then the name becomes even longer, for example:

C:\GEORGE\SORT\OLDSORT.TXT

References that contain subdirectory names are known as *path names*. When a directory name appears in a file name, the drive specifier appears as usual at 5C and 6C hex, but the file name and extension are not given there. We must then use location 82 hex exclusively. Let us use the debugger to explore this area again. As we saw in Chapter 5, the debugger is designed to run another program, including that program's usual parameters. Therefore, DEBUG can have three parameters. The first is the program it is to run, and the next two are parameters for the program we are studying. Let us run DEBUG with *debug* as a parameter. Give the command

debug debug.com file1.txt

(in lowercase letters). Of course, you can substitute any other COM file name for the first parameter. Then give this DEBUG command:

    D50 8F

and the result will look like Figure 7.1. Notice that the first parameter, *debug.com,* is not shown.

DEBUG has changed the information at both 5C and 80 hex so that the second parameter becomes the first parameter. If another parameter had been included, it would appear as the second parameter. Notice that the parameter at 5C has been edited. The lowercase letters are converted to uppercase, blanks fill out the first part of the name, and the dot has been removed. The value of zero at location 5C hex indicates that no drive was specified. The value at 80 hex gives the number of characters entered; the blank at 81 hex is included in the count. We have already seen what happens when we add extra spaces. Let us check the command-line tail again. Leave DEBUG with the Q command. Then give the command

    debug debug.com   file1.txt

being careful to add exactly two spaces between the first and second parameter. Your results will look like Figure 7.2. The results at 5C hex are the same as before. At 80 hex, however, the count is one larger and there are two spaces at the beginning (81 and 82 hex). Let us consider a third example.

```
0050 CD 21 CB 00 00 00 00 00-00 00 00 00 00 46 49 4C   .!...........FIL
0060 45 31 20 20 20 54 58 54-00 00 00 00 00 20 20 20   E1   TXT.....
0070 20 20 20 20 20 20 20 20-00 00 00 00 00 00 00 00      ........
0080 0A 20 66 69 6C 65 31 2E-74 78 74 0D 00 00 00 00   . file1.txt.....
```

Figure 7.1: *The file name at both 5C and 80 hex regions.*

```
-d50 8f
0050 CD 21 CB 00 00 00 00 00-00 00 00 00 00 46 49 4C   .!...........FIL
0060 45 31 20 20 20 54 58 54-00 00 00 00 00 20 20 20   E1   TXT.....
0070 20 20 20 20 20 20 20 20-00 00 00 00 00 00 00 00      ........
0080 0B 20 20 66 69 6C 65 31-2E 74 78 74 0D 00 00 00   . file1.txt....
```

Figure 7.2: *Extra spaces in front of the parameter.*

Leave DEBUG with the Q command. Then give the command

debug cursor.com c:\sort\file1.txt

(Press the F3 key to save some typing.) Then give the command

D50 9F

and the result will look like Figure 7.3. The path name entered as the last parameter is again available at 80 hex. You can see the drive name and sub-directory name there. However, the region starting at 5D hex is filled with blanks. Thus, when we expect a file name or path name, we must be careful to use the region at 80 hex.

We need five new macros before we write our next program, as well as a group of subroutines. We begin with a macro to display single characters.

MACRO @d_char TO DISPLAY A SINGLE CHARACTER

We previously wrote two macros to display strings of text on the video screen using function 9 of interrupt 21 hex. We are now going to write a macro to display a single character on the video screen using function 2 of interrupt 21 hex. Add macro @d_char, shown in Figure 7.4, to your macro library. This macro can display either a constant or the contents of a register. For example, the expression

    @d_char '*'

will display an asterisk on the screen. However, the line

    @d_char AL

will display the contents of the AL register. There is also a third method.

```
0050 CD 21 CB 00 00 00 00 00-00 00 00 00 00 03 20 20 20    .!...........
0060 20 20 20 20 20 20 20 20-00 00 00 00 00 20 20 20        .....
0070 20 20 20 20 20 20 20 20-00 00 00 00 00 00 00 00        ........
0080 12 20 63 3A 5C 73 6F 72-74 5C 66 69 6C 65 31 2E    . c:\sort\file1.
0090 74 78 74 0D 00 00 00 00-00 00 00 00 00 00 00 00    txt............
```

Figure 7.3: *File name at only the 80 hex region when a path name is present.*

Without a parameter:

>   @d_char

the macro displays the character already loaded into the DL register. The first instruction:

>   IFNB <par?>

tells the assembler to include the next two instructions (PUSH and MOV) if the parameter corresponding to *par?* is present (that is, not blank). Other-wise, these instructions are omitted. The first of these instructions saves the previous contents of the DX register on the stack, and the other moves the parameter to be displayed into the DL register. Near the end of the macro another conditional expression restores the original contents of DX if the parameter was present.

Our next macro reads a string of characters from the keyboard.

MACRO @read_bf
TO READ A STRING OF CHARACTERS FROM THE KEYBOARD

The programs we are going to write in this chapter and the next need one or two file names or path names. We have seen that the path name entered as a parameter appears in the command-line tail at location 80

```
@d_char MACRO    par?
;; display par? on video screen
;; Usage:   @d_char  AL          ;;from register
;;          @d_char  '*'         ;;constant
;;          @d_char              ;;value in DL
         IFNB    <par?>
         PUSH    DX
         MOV     DL,par?
         ENDIF
         MOV     AH,2
         INT     21h
         IFNB    <par?>
         POP     DX
         ENDIF
         ENDM
```

Figure 7.4: *Macro @d_char to display a single character.*

hex. But if a parameter was not entered on the command line, our program must ask for one from the user. Our next macro, *@read_bf,* will perform this service. It will read characters typed by the user and place them in the keyboard buffer. We will not use the buffer at 80 hex for this purpose; instead, we will establish a separate location in memory.

Copy the macro given in Figure 7.5 into your macro library. This macro loads into the DX the location of a buffer already allocated in memory. The dummy parameter, *loc?,* could be a fixed location. However, we will use the DI register as a pointer when we reference this macro. The macro sets up a call to DOS function A hex of interrupt 21 hex.

When text is entered in this way, all the usual DOS editing keys are available to the user: the left and right arrow keys, the backspace, Ins, and Del keys. We will look at the details of this function when we use it in our first program later in this chapter. Let us now see how to establish an input buffer.

ESTABLISHING THE INPUT BUFFER WITH MACRO @mak_buff

The previous macro sets up code for reading the input buffer after our programs have begun operation. Before we can read keyboard input with function A hex, we must set aside a portion of memory for the buffer to store the keystrokes. The buffer consists of four parts. The first byte determines the maximum number of allowed characters. The next byte is filled in by DOS; it gives the number of characters actually typed by the user. The remaining space holds the characters typed at the keyboard. Finally, an extra byte must be allocated for the carriage return at the end of the line. The maximum memory used by the buffer, then, is the maximum number of allowable characters plus three.

```
@read_bf MACRO  loc?
;; read keyboard buffer at loc? in DS
;; Usage:   @read_bf <OFFSET nambuff>
        PUSH    DX
        MOV     DX,loc?
        MOV     AH,0Ah
        INT     21h
        POP     DX
        ENDM                    ;;read_bf
```

Figure 7.5: *Macro @read_bf to read a line of text from the keyboard.*

Copy macro *@mak_buff*, given in Figure 7.6, into your macro library. This macro takes two parameters. The first is the symbolic name of the buffer and the second is the maximum number of characters that can be accepted. When we use the macro the first parameter becomes the symbolic reference to the buffer.

Our next two macros are needed to read data from a disk file.

OPENING A DISK FILE WITH THE @open MACRO

If you want to read information from an existing disk file, you must first execute DOS function 3D hex to open the file. Before using this function, however, you must place the path name of the file in memory and terminate the name with a binary zero. As we've seen, this construction is known as an ASCIIZ string. You must also set the DX register to point to the beginning of the name. On return from function 3D hex, there is a file handle, a 16-bit number, located in the AX register. (We saw previously that disk file handles begin with the number 5, since lower numbers are assigned to peripheral devices.) We must use the handle for all further operations on this file. Another function, F hex, can be used to open files, but it cannot process file names that contain subdirectory names. Consequently, we shall not use it in this book.

Copy macro *@open*, given in Figure 7.7, into your macro library. This macro has two parameters. The first points to the beginning of the path name. The second parameter is optional; it tells where to go if an error occurs. The macro generates code to save the DX register on the stack, and then to move the pointer given as the first parameter into the DX register. The parameter can be a direct memory reference, such as this:

```
@open <OFFSET buffer>
```

where the file name begins at the label *buffer*. Alternatively, the parameter

```
@mak_buf MACRO   name?, len?
;; establish a console input buffer
name?    DB      len?              ;maximum
         DB      ?                 ;actual
         DB      len? DUP(?)       ;buffer
         DB      cr                ;end
         ENDM
```

Figure 7.6: *Macro @mak_buff to establish a keyboard buffer.*

can be the name of a register that points to the file name:

@open SI

We set the AL register to zero, indicating a read-only operation. Other options are AL = 1 for write-only and AL = 2 for read or write. However, we shall not use these latter two options. We set the AL register to zero and the AH register to 3D hex. Then we execute interrupt 21 hex.

On return from the interrupt, the carry flag is set if an error occurred. In that case the error code is found in the AX register. But if there was no error, the AX register contains the assigned file handle. Our macro moves the value in the AX register to the BX register for safekeeping. If the optional second parameter is given, the macro generates a conditional jump instruction. We jump to the address of the second parameter, normally an error routine.

The only meaningful error we expect is "file not found," which happens if the user types the file name incorrectly or gives the wrong disk drive. Other errors, such as "invalid handle," are programming rather than operational errors, and so our programs will not test for them. Now we need to read information from the file.

READING A DISK FILE WITH THE @d_read MACRO

After we have opened a disk file with function 3D hex, we can read data from it. We will use macro @d_read for this purpose. Copy this

```
@open   MACRO   pointr?, where?
;; macro to open a disk file for reading only
;; pointr? is location of pathname
;; terminated with a zero
;; if error, branch to optional label where?
;; assigned handle or error code in BX
;; carry set if error
        PUSH    DX
        MOV     DX,pointr?
        MOV     AL,0            ;;read
        MOV     AH,3Dh          ;;function
        INT     21h
        MOV     BX,AX           ;handle
        POP     DX
        IFNB    <where?>
        JC      where?
        ENDIF
        ENDM
```

Figure 7.7: *Macro @open to open a disk file.*

macro, shown in Figure 7.8, to your macro library. We must read the information from a disk file into a buffer in memory. The DX register points to this buffer. The CX register specifies how many bytes are to be read from the disk, and the BX register has the assigned handle for the disk file.

Our macro is designed for two parameters; the file handle and the buffer pointer. However, the first parameter is optional. We generally place this macro right after the @open macro, and so the file handle will already be located in the BX register. When we use this macro with only the second parameter, we must be careful to include a comma in front of the parameter to indicate the missing first parameter. For example, we might use the expression

> **@d_read ,<OFFSET datbuff>**

This macro does not define the byte count in the CX register. Therefore, you must be sure it is correctly set before issuing the macro. Let us consider this value.

For a character device such as the keyboard or printer, we transfer one byte at a time because that is how the computer communicates with these devices. With disk transfers, however, information is transferred in groups called blocks. Therefore, it is most efficient to use a multiple of the block size.

The more sectors we read at one time, the faster the operation. On the other hand, we need to reserve a larger memory buffer to read more sectors. If the value of CX is set to one, it will take a very long time to read a disk file on this byte-by-byte transfer. A value of 256 will be faster by a

```
@d_read MACRO    handle?,pointr?
;; Read from disk with assigned handle?
;; pointr? is location of buffer
;; CX has bytes to read
;; carry set if error
        PUSH     DX
        MOV      DX,pointr?
        IFNB     <handle?>
        MOV      BX,handle?
        ENDIF
        MOV      AH,3Fh          ;;function
        INT      21h
        POP      DX
        ENDM
```

Figure 7.8: *Macro @d_read to read a disk file.*

factor of 100. However, we will use a value of 20 times 512 bytes or 10,240 bytes to speed up the program by another factor of four. (These differences in speed were determined by personal experimentation. We will consider this subject again in the next chapter when we discuss filters.)

On return from function 3F hex, the AX register has the number of bytes actually read. If the returned value in AX is less than the original value in CX, you have reached the end of the file. Otherwise, there is more data to be read.

We create a subroutine library next.

A SUBROUTINE LIBRARY FOR GETTING A FILE NAME

We created our macro library MYLIB.MAC to avoid placing copies of the same macros in each program. We place the INCLUDE directive at the beginning of the main program to tell the assembler where to look for the macros. We will take a similar approach with some of our subroutines. We place a group of subroutines in a library and then reference these routines from each program by using the INCLUDE directive. There is one major difference, however. The macro library does not contain any executable code, only macro definitions. Therefore the placement of the INCLUDE directive is not critical. Our subroutine library, however, contains regular instructions, and so we must be careful to place the INCLUDE directive exactly where we want the routines to appear.

Our first subroutine library contains three procedures and a buffer. Since the library is used to process a file name entered at the keyboard, we give it the name GET_ONE.LIB. By placing these routines in a separate library, we reduce the program size by more than half.

Create a file named GET_ONE.LIB and enter the lines given in Figure 7.9. We will discuss the routines as they are used by the calling program. Now let us look at a program to display files on the video screen.

DISPLAYING A WORDSTAR FILE ON THE VIDEO SCREEN

The ASCII character set uses only seven bits to display 128 numbers, letters, and other symbols. Therefore, the eighth bit is sometimes used for other purposes. Commonly, this bit is used to check parity during transfer of information from one computer to another. Consequently, this eighth bit

```
;**********************************************
; Form path name either from command line
; at 80 hex or by asking user. Zero placed
; at end of name.
; Auxiliary buffer follows this procedure.
; Procedures required: get_name, scan_pa
; Output:        DI = points to first character
;**********************************************
get_path          PROC
;----------------------------------------------
; check for parameter on command line
;----------------------------------------------
        MOV       DI,OFFSET buffer ;command tail
        MOV       CL,[DI-1]        ;count
        MOV       CH,0
        OR        CX,CX            ;zero?
        JNZ       ck_par           ;no
;----------------------------------------------
; get path name from keyboard
;----------------------------------------------
no_parm:
        @write    <cr,lf,'Source path name: '>
        MOV       DI,OFFSET buff_in ;pointer
        CALL      get_name
;----------------------------------------------
; check path name referenced by DI
; carry flag set if invalid name
;----------------------------------------------
ck_par:
        CALL      scan_pa
        JC        no_parm
        RET
get_path          ENDP
;******** End of procedure get_path ********
;----------------------------------------------
; auxiliary input buffer
;----------------------------------------------
handl   DW        ?                ;source handle
        @mak_buf buff_in, 45
;**********************************************
; Get path name from keyboard
; Buffer is ahead of this routine
; Input:         DI = buffer head
; Output:        DI = points to first character
;               CX = character count
;**********************************************
get_name          PROC
; read keyboard buffer
        @read_bf DI
        @write    <cr,lf>
        INC       DI               ;skip max
        MOV       CL,[DI]          ;count
        MOV       CH,0
```

Figure 7.9: *Subroutine library GET_ONE.LIB to process a file name entered at the keyboard.*

```
        INC     DI                      ;first input
        RET
get_name        ENDP
;******** End of procedure get_name ********
;*****************************************
; Establish path name, remove leading blanks,
; put zero at end of name
; Input:          DI = buffer pointer
;                 CX = number of characters
; Output:         SI = points to first character
;                 DI = points to zero at end
;                 Carry flag set if invalid name
;*****************************************
scan_pa PROC
        MOV     AL,blank
;----------------------------------------------
; move pointer past blanks
;----------------------------------------------
        REPE    SCASB                   ;find nonblank
        DEC     DI                      ;start name
        INC     CX                      ;count
;----------------------------------------------
; make SI register point to first nonblank
;----------------------------------------------
        MOV     SI,DI                   ;save position
        CMP     AL,[SI]
        JZ      no_parms                ;only blanks
;----------------------------------------------
; find end of path name: blank or cr
; AL is still set to a blank
; but CX will be zero at the carriage return
;----------------------------------------------
        REPNE   SCASB
        JNZ     sdi                     ;cr
        DEC     DI                      ;blank
sdi:
;----------------------------------------------
; put zero at end of path name (CH)
;----------------------------------------------
        MOV     [DI],CH                 ;CH has a zero
        INC     DI                      ;next name
        CLC                             ;reset carry
        RET
;----------------------------------------------
; set carry flag for invalid path name
;----------------------------------------------
no_parms:
        STC
        RET
scan_pa ENDP
;******** End of procedure scan_pa ********
```

Figure 7.9: (continued)

is sometimes called the "parity" bit. WordStar uses this bit for a different purpose; to help format a file for printing. The parity bit is set for the last character of each word, for spaces added by WordStar to provide justification, and for the carriage return at the end of each line within a paragraph. By contrast, the IBM PC uses an extended ASCII character set, containing all eight bits, to provide 256 characters. This makes available graphics characters, Greek letters, mathematical symbols, and other characters.

When WordStar displays a file on the video screen, the appearance is correct. But when such a file is displayed with the DOS command TYPE, the text is difficult to read. The characters with parity bits turned on are shown as extended ASCII characters, rather than their correct form. There are Greek letters and other mysterious symbols on the screen. Furthermore, while the carriage returns with the parity bit set are misinterpreted as graphics symbols, the line feeds are correctly shown. Let us see how to fix this problem.

■ Displaying a WordStar File With the TYPEW Program

The program shown in Figure 7.10 can display a WordStar file (or any ASCII file) on the video screen in the expected form because it resets the parity bit. It is a rather long program; however, we have broken it into two parts. Three of the subroutines and the input buffer are located in the separate file that we wrote in the previous section. Furthermore, by making small changes to this program, we can use most of it for other purposes. We will also use the library for other programs in this book.

The new program performs several tasks:

- get file name from user
- check for proper file name
- open the file
- read the file into memory
- change the file
- display the file on the video screen

Create a new file named TYPEW.ASM (type WordStar) and copy the listing given in Figure 7.10. Be sure to have library GET_ONE.LIB, created in the previous section, as well as our macro and equate libraries. Let us go through the program.

We begin with the usual directives, including comments on how to use the program. The block size, the number of bytes we read at one time, is

```
          PAGE     ,132
          TITLE    TYPEW

COMMENT *
  January 10, 1986
  Display WordStar characters as ASCII
  Usage:
          TYPEW
          TYPEW fname
          TYPEW \pathname\fname
  Macros: @d_char, @d_read, @go_dos, @head,
          @mak_buf, @open, @read_bf, @write
  Librarys: mylib.equ, mylib.mac, get_one.lib
  *
          INCLUDE mylib.equ
          IF1
          INCLUDE mylib.mac
          ENDIF
blk_siz EQU      512*20

code    SEGMENT
        ASSUME   CS:code, DS:code
        ORG      80h
buf_cnt DB       ?                   ;buffer length
buffer  LABEL    BYTE                ;buffer

        ORG      100h
strt:
        @head    ' TYPEW, 01.10.86 '
;-----------------------------------------------
; get path name for disk file
; pointer returned in SI
;-----------------------------------------------
        CALL     get_path
        @open    SI, error
;-----------------------------------------------
; read file, handle is in BX
;-----------------------------------------------
newbuff:
        MOV      CX,blk_siz      ;bytes to read
        @d_read  ,<OFFSET datbuff>
        JC       error
;-----------------------------------------------
; AX has bytes read, done if zero
;-----------------------------------------------
        OR       AX,AX           ;zero?
        JZ       exit            ;done
;-----------------------------------------------
; display buffer
;-----------------------------------------------
```

Figure 7.10: *Program TYPEW to display a WordStar file.*

```
             MOV      CX,AX           ;number of char
             MOV      SI,OFFSET datbuff ;pointer
             CALL     do_char         ;process char
             JMP      newbuff         ;next buffer
exit:
             @go_dos                  ;to DOS
error:
             @write   'Error:'
             CMP      AX,2
             JNZ      e2
             @write   ' File not found'
e2:
             @go_dos                  ;to DOS
;----------------------------------------
; procedures get_path, get_name, scan_pa
; and the auxiliary input buffer
;----------------------------------------
             INCLUDE get_one.lib
;********************************************
; Procedure to process each byte of file
; Terminate if end of file found
; Input:       SI = buffer pointer
;              CX = remaining characters
;********************************************
do_char PROC
newchar:
             MOV      DL,[SI]         ;get char
;----------------------------------------
; convert to ASCII by resetting bit 7
;----------------------------------------
             AND      DL,7Fh
             CMP      DL,eof          ;done?
             JE       done            ;yes
             @d_char                  ;display char
             INC      SI              ;next char
             LOOP     newchar
             RET
done:
             POP      AX              ;restore stack
             @go_dos
do_char ENDP
;********* End of procedure do_char *********
; buffer for disk data
datbuff LABEL    BYTE                 ;data buffer

code    ENDS
             END      strt
```

Figure 7.10: *(continued)*

defined with the symbol *blk_siz* to be 512×20. Then, after establishing the code segment, we define two labels—*buf_cnt* (buffer count) at 80 hex and *buffer* starting at 81 hex. We are careful not to define code in this region. As we have seen, this is the location where our program can read the parameter entered by the user.

We start the code at 100 hex with our *@head* macro to define the program name and the date. We call subroutine *get_path,* located in our subroutine library, to process the path name (that is, the parameter) entered by the user. Looking at this subroutine in Figure 7.9, we see that it begins by checking the 80 hex region. The DI pointer is set to 81 hex, the blank that follows the buffer count. Then we move the character count, referenced by DI minus 1, into the CL register. If this value is not zero, it means that a parameter was entered on the command. We then branch to label *ck_par* (check parameter) to process the name.

If no parameter was entered, we request one from the user. We write a message on the screen with the *@write* macro and then call subroutine *get_name* to read the input.

Between procedures *get_path* and *get_name* we place macro *@mak_buf.* This macro generates the four lines of data:

```
buff_in    DB      45
           DB      ?
           DB      45 DUP(?)
           DB      cr
```

needed for an input buffer to read the user response.

The first two lines are header bytes. The first is the maximum buffer length (45); the second is filled in by DOS with the actual number of characters typed by the user. The buffer begins with the third line. The fourth line provides space for the carriage return when the maximum number of characters is entered. Notice that the construction is a little different from the buffer at 80 hex. There, the actual number of characters at address 80 is always followed by at least one blank. With our new buffer, the character count is found in the second position, and the first character of the buffer is not a blank unless the user begins input by pressing the Space bar.

Reading Keyboard Characters

Subroutine *get_name* in Figure 7.9 begins with macro *@read_bf* that sets the DI register to the head of the buffer, *buff_in.* Notice that this is the maximum character count. Our macro *@read_bf* with parameter DI then reads a line from the keyboard. As we have seen, the user can correct mistakes with the usual editing keys during input. Then, when the Return key is pressed, the line is accepted. We use the *@write* macro to put a carriage return and line feed on the video screen to complete the line entered by the user.

We increment DI to the actual length of the input text (the file name character count) and move the value from there into the CL register using DI as a pointer. We also set the upper half of the CX register, CH, to zero. The DI register is incremented a second time so that it points to the start of the text in the buffer. Then we return to subroutine *get_path*.

We have now arrived at label *ck_par* in procedure *get_path*. The procedure branches here directly when a parameter is given on the command line. Subroutine *scan_pa* is called to process the parameter. The CX register contains the number of characters that were entered, and the DI register points to the beginning of the text. The address is either 81 hex, if a parameter was entered on the command line, or the label *buff_n + 2,* if our program had to ask for a file name. The first task that procedure *scan_pa* performs is the removal of leading blanks.

Removing Leading Blanks

We learned previously that parameters are separated by blanks, and when a blank is required, more than one blank may be entered. Therefore, we must first remove leading blanks. We use the SCASB (scan string byte) instruction to find the first nonblank character. We set the AL register to a blank, the character we are looking for. The CX register has a count of the number of characters to check, and the ES:DI registers point to the string. DOS originally sets the ES register to the code segment, and we have not changed it. We have previously set the CX and DI registers. Therefore the double command

REPE SCASB

checks the character at ES:DI against the blank in register AL. The DI register is incremented, and the CX register is decremented. The REPE (repeat while equal) command repeats the string operation each time a blank is found or until CX reaches zero.

The scanning process stops when a character is not a blank. This should be the first character of the path name. Since the DI register is automatically incremented after each step, it now points to the second character of the path name. Therefore, we must decrement DI to point to the first character of the path name. We increment CX to reflect the correct number of remaining characters since we decremented DI. We move the value in DI to SI, our pointer to the path name.

If the path name is valid, SI now points to the beginning of the name. However, another possibility is a line of blank characters. If that was encountered, scanning stopped because the CX register was decremented to zero. Now, SI is pointing to a blank. We test for this condition with the expression

    CMP AL,[SI]

because AL still contains the blank character. If the comparison is true, we have an invalid input. We therefore branch to label *no_parms,* where we set the carry flag to indicate an invalid name and return to the calling program. On the other hand, if the input is acceptable, we must find the end of the name and place a zero there.

Finding the End of the Name

At this point, the end of the file name will be marked with either a carriage return or a blank. (The blank appears if the user enters a second parameter or simply presses the Space bar before pressing the Return key. Otherwise, a carriage return appears.) We use the SCASB instruction a second time to locate the end of the name. The AL register still has a blank, DI and SI point to the beginning of the name, and CX has the number of remaining characters. This time, however, we want to *stop* scanning when a blank is found. Therefore we use the line

    REPNE SCASB

in which the REPNE command (repeat while not equal) keeps going until a blank is found or until CX has become zero.

When scanning stops this time, we must check the zero flag to distinguish between a carriage return and a blank. If the zero flag is set, we have found a blank. However, DI points to the next character after the blank. Therefore, we must decrement DI first. On the other hand, if the zero flag is reset, the DI register points to the carriage return at the end of the name. This is where we want it. In either case, we put a zero at the end of the name referenced by DI. We could use this instruction:

    MOV   BYTE PTR [DI],0

Instead, we use the faster and shorter (but more cryptic) instruction

    MOV [DI],CH

since the CH register still has the value zero. We reset the carry flag to
indicate that we have a valid path name and then return to the calling routine, *get_path*.

If we return to routine *get_path* with the carry flag set, we branch to
the label *no_parm* in that routine to get another parameter. But if the
parameter is valid, we return to the beginning of the main program and
open the requested file. The macro:

    @open SI

opens the file referenced by SI. As we saw previously, this instruction executes DOS function 3D hex. On returning from this function, the carry
flag is set if there was an error. If so, we branch to our error routine.
The only error we expect is "file not found," error code 2. We therefore
display this message if appropriate.

If the carry flag is reset on return from function 3D hex, we expect the
assigned file handle to be available in the AX register. Our macro moves
the value to the BX register.

Reading the File

In preparation for reading the file, we set the CX register to 512×20,
the value defined by the symbol *blk_siz*. This is the number of bytes that
will be read each time we execute function 3F hex. We use our *@d_read*
macro for setting up the code. On return from this function we check the
carry flag for error. But since the possible errors relate to faulty programming, not to execution, we do not expect a problem here. It is important,
however, to check the value in the AX register. This value will be zero
when there are no more characters to read. We check this value with a
logical OR instruction and terminate the program with our *@go_dos*
macro if we find it.

Displaying the File

If AX is not zero, it contains the number of characters that are to be displayed. We move this value to the CX register, set the SI pointer to the
buffer containing the data, and call subroutine *do_char*. This short routine

retrieves each character from the buffer, alters it if necessary, sends it to the video screen, and then increments the DI pointer. (The LOOP instruction automatically decrements the CX pointer.) Using the DI pointer, we move a character to the DL register and check to see if it is an end-of-file marker. If so, we terminate the program. Since we are in a subroutine, we POP the stack into the AX register and terminate with our @go_dos macro.

If the character is not an end-of-file marker, we perform a logical AND with the value 7F hex to reset bit 7, the parity bit. (Recall that WordStar often sets this bit as an internal marker.) Then we display the character with macro @d_char. We use the LOOP instruction to control the correct number of bytes to process, according to the value in the CX register. At the completion of this step we return to the main program. Looping continues back to label *newbuff,* where we reset the count in the CX register and read more data from the disk.

Assemble this program with the EXEC batch file. Use our new program to look at a WordStar file if you have one. Of course, you can also display any ASCII file including the assembler source file. Give the command

TYPEW fname

with the filename parameter (*fname*) on the command line. Display the file TYPEW.ASM if you have nothing else. Then try the command without a parameter:

TYPEW

and enter a file name at the prompt. Try a different disk drive name and add a subdirectory if you have a hard disk. Finally, give a fictitious file name and look for the error message:

Error: File not found

Let us see how to convert a WordStar file to an ASCII file.

■ Converting a WordStar File to an ASCII File

The program we have just written converts a WordStar file to ASCII and displays the result on the video screen. Sometimes, however, we need to convert a WordStar disk file to an ASCII disk file. This can happen if we edit an assembly-language file with WordStar and accidentally press the Ctrl-B formatting key. Then the assembler will not be able to read the program, because WordStar sets the parity bit of some of the characters. The same thing can happen with a BASIC program. In the next chapter we will write a program that can efficiently convert a WordStar file to ASCII. In the meantime, however, let us look at another, cruder method.

The redirection feature of DOS can divert text headed for the video screen to a disk file. Thus we can recover an assembly-language file that was scrambled by WordStar with the command

    TYPEW FILE.ASM >FILEOK.ASM

The symbol > tells DOS to create a file named FILEOK.ASM and place the output from the program TYPEW into it, rather than send it to the video screen. This method works reasonably well. However, you must be careful not to use the same names for the source and destination files. If you do, the file will be lost as the contents are emptied.

The major problem with this technique is its slow execution. The redirection feature creates a disk file from a character device, rather than a block device. Therefore, characters are handled one at a time instead of in blocks. In the next chapter we will write a program that will also unscramble WordStar files. The corresponding command will be:

    TOASCII FILE.ASM FILEOK.ASM

But that program creates the target file by transmitting blocks of characters. Therefore it can perform its task many times faster than the present method.

A minor disadvantage of the redirection method is that the resulting file contains binary zeros at the end. These can cause trouble the next time you edit the file. Nevertheless, if you scramble your assemby-language or BASIC file with WordStar, the redirection method can save it.

Let us look at a variation of our TYPEW program that we can use with executable files.

DISPLAYING THE ASCII CHARACTERS IN AN EXECUTABLE PROGRAM

The previous program, TYPEW, is designed to display ASCII files or files that are nearly in ASCII form. Our next program is for binary files—that is, files that contain executable code. If you try to examine either a COM or an EXE program with our TYPEW program or with the DOS command TYPE, you find the video screen is largely unreadable. The problem is that the video screen is an ASCII device, but programs are written in binary code. Of course, we have studied both COM and EXE files using the U and D commands of DEBUG. In particular, the D command gives us both a hexadecimal and an ASCII representation. But this is a slow method for looking through the file.

Because most of the bytes in executable programs consist of operation codes, the TYPE command is not much help. Nevertheless, such programs usually contain some meaningful ASCII information, such as the version number, date, copyright, and vendor names. In fact, we wrote macro *@head* to encode such information at the beginning of our own programs.

By making a few changes to our previous program, we can display the ASCII information in any disk file. Make a copy of the previous program, calling the new version TYPEB.ASM (type binary). Change the file to look like the listing shown in Figure 7.11. Only a few lines at the beginning and end are different. Let us go through the code.

The executable portion of both programs is identical up to the point of processing the text. Both need to perform the tasks outlined previously, in particular, getting and analyzing the file name. The difference is in the last routine, *do_char*. Therefore let us look at that.

As in the previous program, we use the SI pointer to work our way through the buffer and the CX register to count the remaining characters in the buffer. We move each character referenced by DI to the DL register. Then we check to see if the character is less than a blank, indicating a control character. If so, we skip over the character. Then we check to see if the character is greater than the tilde character. If so, it is above the regular ASCII character set and we skip it. If the character is in the printable range, however, we display it with the *@d_char* macro.

Assemble and run this program the same way we did the previous program. Be sure to have the new subroutine library GET_ONE.LIB on the disk. Give the command

    TYPEB TYPEB.COM

to have the program look at itself. You should see the information given in the *@head* macro. It might look like this:

    TYPEA, O1.11.86 \ = !r)?!rt) Pl!XError:$ = uP'!X File not found$ Mu!P!XEnter pathname: $5Tr–R!ZP!X$GG OA:tuO– r˜wt!FX

Of course, you can display ASCII files with this program. But since the carriage returns and line feeds are removed, all the lines are run together.

```
              PAGE     ,132
              TITLE    TYPEB

COMMENT *
  January 10, 1986
  Display ASCII characters in binary file
  Usage:
          TYPEB
          TYPEB fname
          TYPEB \pathname\fname
  Macros: @d_char, @d_read, @go_dos, @head,
          @mak_buf, @open, @read_bf, @write
  Librarys: mylib.equ, mylib.mac, get_one.lib
  *
          INCLUDE mylib.equ
          IF1
          INCLUDE mylib.mac
          ENDIF
blk_siz EQU       512*20

code    SEGMENT
        ASSUME   CS:code, DS:code
        ORG      80h
buf_cnt DB       ?                  ;buffer length
buffer  LABEL    BYTE               ;buffer

        ORG      100h
strt:
        @head    ' TYPEB, 01.10.86 '
;----------------------------------------------
; get path name for disk file
; pointer returned in SI
;----------------------------------------------
        CALL     get_path
        @open    SI, error
;----------------------------------------------
; read file, handle is in BX
;----------------------------------------------
newbuff:
        MOV      CX,blk_siz       ;bytes to read
        @d_read ,<OFFSET datbuff>
        JC       error
;----------------------------------------------
; AX has bytes read, done if zero
;----------------------------------------------
        OR       AX,AX            ;zero?
        JZ       exit             ;done
```

Figure 7.11: *Program TYPEB to display ASCII characters in a binary file.*

```
;----------------------------------------------
; display buffer
;----------------------------------------------
        MOV     CX,AX           ;number of char
        MOV     SI,OFFSET datbuff ;pointer
        CALL    do_char         ;process char
        JMP     newbuff         ;next buffer
  exit:
        @go_dos                 ;to DOS
  error:
        @write  'Error:'
        CMP     AX,2
        JNZ     e2
        @write  ' File not found'
  e2:
        @go_dos                 ;to DOS
;----------------------------------------
; procedures get_path, get_name, scan_pa
; and the auxiliary input buffer
;----------------------------------------
        INCLUDE get_one.lib
;*********************************************
; Procedure to process each byte of file
; Terminate if end of file found
; Input:       SI = buffer pointer
;              CX = remaining characters
;*********************************************
do_char PROC
newchar:
        MOV     DL,[SI]         ;get char
        CMP     DL,blank
        JB      skip
        CMP     DL,'~'          ;tilde
        JA      skip
        CMP     DL,eof          ;done?
        JE      done            ;yes
        @d_char                 ;display char
  skip:
        INC     SI              ;next char
        LOOP    newchar
        RET
  done:
        POP     AX              ;restore stack
        @go_dos
do_char ENDP
;********** End of procedure do_char **********

; buffer for disk data
datbuff LABEL   BYTE            ;data buffer

code    ENDS
        END     strt
```

Figure 7.11: (continued)

If you look at the two lines we obtained from our TYPEB.COM program, you can see meaningless characters among the useful strings. The problem is that many of the regular operation codes happen to have the same value as ASCII characters. Since such characters will not always appear in pairs (and single meaningful characters are difficult to decipher), we can improve our TYPEB program by not displaying single ASCII characters. That is, we can change procedure *do_char* so that an ASCII character is not displayed unless there is another one on either side. This improvement is left as an exercise for the reader.

We study file attributes next.

THE FILE ATTRIBUTES—READ-ONLY, HIDDEN, AND SYSTEM

We learned previously that disk files can be marked as read-only, hidden, or system; these features are known as *file attributes*. We also saw previously that the DOS files IBMBIO.COM and IBMDOS.COM are designated read-only, hidden, and system files. However, these file attributes are not frequently used otherwise. When a file is marked with one or more of these three attributes, it cannot be altered, renamed, or deleted. However, a file so marked can be displayed on the video screen with the DOS command TYPE.

When the read-only attribute is set, but not the hidden or system attributes, a file is visible in the directory listing and can be duplicated with the DOS command COPY. But when either the hidden or system attribute is set, the file name does not appear in the directory and cannot be copied.

When an executable program is marked as a system file, you cannot run it by typing its name. The properties of a hidden file depend on the DOS version. A hidden file can be executed under DOS version 3 but not version 2. We have seen that the two DOS files IBMBIO and IBMDOS are read from the system disk when the computer is first turned on. These files are both marked with all three attributes—read-only, hidden, and system.

DOS version 3 includes a separate program, called ATTRIB, that allows you to change the read-only attribute of a file. However, this program cannot change the other attributes. The Norton Utilities package includes a program for displaying and changing all three of these attributes. However, it is a fairly large program. You might want to designate all the executable programs on your system disk as read-only to prevent their being accidentally erased. Of course, programs you are likely to change should not be marked in this way.

Since you cannot execute system files (or hidden files under version 2), they might seem to be a useless feature. However, in the next section we will write two programs that can execute system and hidden files. But first we need a program that can identify and change these three file attributes. The advantage of our program is that it is very small, less than 600 bytes. Our program will also be able to display the attributes of hidden and system files.

Create a new file, named ATTR.ASM, and copy the program given in Figure 7.12. The beginning lines, along with procedure *scan_pa* (in our library GET_ONE), are the same as in the previous program, and so you can copy these parts. In addition, procedure *get_pa* is like procedure *get_path* except for three lines of code that have been removed. Assemble the program and run it. Let us go through the code.

The program begins by calling routine *get_pa* for a file name. (The name has been shortened to remind you that three lines of code have been removed.) This subroutine checks the default buffer at 80 hex for a parameter entered on the command line. If a valid parameter was entered, *scan_pa* points the SI register to the beginning of the name and places a zero at the end. If no parameter was entered, the carry flag is set and control returns to the main program. In our previous programs, we repeatedly asked the user for input until a valid file name was entered; here we do not.

On returning to the main program, we check the carry flag for valid input. If the carry flag is set, indicating that no parameter was entered, we branch to the label *help2* and display a help message. (We also show the help message if a question mark is given for a parameter.) There are two jump instructions in a row at this point, because conditional branches such as JZ are limited to a jump of 127 bytes. Since the help routine is farther away than that, we must reverse the logic. We make a two-byte NEAR jump to the help routine and branch around this jump instruction with a short conditional branch:

```
              JNZ      param
help2:
              JMP      help
param:
```

We check the second parameter next. The valid entries are N for normal, R for read-only, H for hidden, B for both read-only and hidden, and A for all three: read-only, hidden, and system. The attributes respectively correspond to the first three bits of the attribute byte, as shown in Table 7.1. If one of these letters is entered, we change the corresponding attribute. If no second parameter is provided, or an incorrect one is entered, we determine and display the current file attributes.

```
            PAGE    ,132
TITLE     ATTR - Change file attributes

COMMENT *
  January 11, 1986
  Usage:
          ATTR  FNAME X
          where FNAME is file name and
          X is file an attribute
            N = none, resets attributes to 0
            R = read only, 1
            H = hidden, 2
            B = both, 3
            blank returns current value
  Macros: @go_dos, @head, @write, @write_r, IRPC
  INT 21h function 43h
  *
          INCLUDE mylib.equ
          IF1
          INCLUDE mylib.mac
          ENDIF

code      SEGMENT
          ASSUME  CS:code,DS:code
          ORG     6Dh
param2    LABEL   BYTE              ;second parameter
          ORG     80h
buf_cnt   DB      ?                 ;buffer length
buffer    LABEL   BYTE              ;buffer


          ORG     100h
start:
          @head   ' ATTR, 01.11.86 '
;--------------------------------------------
; check for first parameter
;--------------------------------------------
          CALL    get_pa
          JC      help2
          CMP     BYTE PTR [SI],'?' ;help?
          JNZ     param             ;ok
help2:
          JMP     help              ;no parameter
param:
;--------------------------------------------
; check for second parameter
;--------------------------------------------
          CMP     [param2],blank
          JNE     par2
          JMP     no_par2
par2:
          XOR     CX,CX             ;zero
;--------------------------------------------
; convert second parameter to attribute code
```

Figure 7.12: *Program to identify and change file attributes.*

```
; N = none, R = read only, H = hidden,
; B = both read only and hidden
;----------------------------------------
        MOV     AL,[param2]
        IRPC    p?,NRHB
        CMP     AL,'&p?'
        JZ      set_at
        INC     CX
        ENDM
        MOV     CL,7
        CMP     AL,'A'          ;all three
        JZ      set_at
        JMP     bad_par         ;wrong parameter
set_at:
        MOV     DX,SI           ;file name
        MOV     AH,43h          ;attr
        MOV     AL,1            ;make change
        INT     21h             ;do it
        JC      no_file         ;error
        @write  <cr,lf,'Setting '>
        JMP     show            ;display attr
no_file:
        @write  <cr,lf,'ERROR: '>
        CMP     AL,2
        JNZ     no_f2
        @write  'File not found'
no_f2:
        @go_dos
;----------------------------------------
; no second parameter, display file attributes
;----------------------------------------
no_par2:
        MOV     DX,SI           ;file name
        MOV     AH,43h          ;attr
        MOV     AL,0            ;get value
        INT     21h             ;do it
        JC      no_file         ;error
        @write  <cr,lf>
show:
        TEST    CL,7
        JNZ     not_z
        @write  'Normal attribute'
        @go_dos
not_z:
        TEST    CL,1
        JZ      not_ro
        @write  'Read only '
not_ro:
        TEST    CL,2
        JZ      not_hi
        @write  ' Hidden '
not_hi:
        TEST    CL,4
```

Figure 7.12: *(continued)*

```
                JZ        done
                @write    ' System '
        done:
                @go_dos
        bad_par:
                @write    <cr,lf,'Bad parameter 2'>
        help:
                @write_r  <OFFSET h_msg>
                @go_dos
        ;*************************************************
        ; Form path name from command line at 80 hex
        ; Zero placed at end of name
        ; Procedure required: scan_pa
        ; Output:       DI = points to first character
        ;               Carry set for no name
        ;*************************************************
        get_pa  PROC
        ;-----------------------------------------------
        ; check for parameter on command line
        ;-----------------------------------------------
                MOV       DI,OFFSET buffer ;command tail
                MOV       CL,[DI-1]        ;count
                MOV       CH,0
                JCXZ      no_parm          ;no
        ;-----------------------------------------------
        ; check pathname referenced by DI
        ; carry flag set if invalid name
        ;-----------------------------------------------
                CALL      scan_pa
                JC        no_parm
                RET
        no_parm:
                STC
                RET
        get_pa  ENDP
        ;********* End of procedure get_pa **********
        ;*************************************************
        ; Establish path name, remove leading blanks,
        ; put zero at end of name
        ; Input:        DI = buffer pointer
        ;               CX = number of characters
        ; Output:       SI = points to first character
        ;               DI = points to zero at end
        ;               Carry flag set if invalid name
        ;*************************************************
        scan_pa PROC
                MOV       AL,blank
        ;-----------------------------------------------
        ; move pointer past blanks
        ;-----------------------------------------------
                REPE      SCASB            ;find nonblank
                DEC       DI               ;start name
                INC       CX               ;count
```

Figure 7.12: *(continued)*

```
;-----------------------------------------------
; make SI register point to first nonblank
;-----------------------------------------------
        MOV     SI,DI           ;save position
        CMP     AL,[SI]
        JZ      no_parms        ;only blanks
;-----------------------------------------------
; find end of path name: blank or cr
; AL is still set to a blank
; but CX will be zero at the carriage return
;-----------------------------------------------
        REPNE   SCASB
        JNZ     sdi             ;cr
        DEC     DI              ;blank
sdi:
;-----------------------------------------------
; put zero at end of path name (CH)
;-----------------------------------------------
        MOV     [DI],CH
        CLC                     ;reset carry
        RET
;-----------------------------------------------
; set carry flag for invalid path name
;-----------------------------------------------
no_parms:
        STC
        RET
scan_pa ENDP
;******** End of procedure scan_pa ********
;-----------------------------------------------
; Help message
;-----------------------------------------------
h_msg   DB      cr,lf,'First parameter is file name'
        DB      cr,lf,'Second parameter is attribute:'
        DB      cr,lf,' N = none, resets attributes'
        DB      cr,lf,' H = hidden'
        DB      cr,lf,' R = read only'
        DB      cr,lf,' B = both read only and hidden'
        DB      cr,lf,' A = All -- read only, hidden, system'
        DB      cr,lf,' no parameter displays current value$'

code    ENDS
        END     start
```

Figure 7.12: *(continued)*

We begin the next part by checking location 6D hex. As we have seen, there will be a blank character here if a second parameter was not entered on the command line. We use the expression:

```
CMP   [param2],blank
```

to determine this. If no second parameter was entered, we branch to the label *no_par2*. Otherwise, we analyze the entry. We use one of the three indefinite-repeat macros (IRPC) for this. Let us take a look at these macros.

The Repeat Macros

The three repeat macros REPT, IRP, and IRPC are quite different from the macros we have been using. Previously, we placed the macro definition, consisting of several lines, in a macro library. Then we used the macro by giving its name and perhaps a parameter or two in a one-line implementation. By contrast, the repeat macros appear in only one place. They are defined and used as we need them in our programs. They begin with the name REPT, IRP, or IRPC, and they terminate with the ENDM statement. There is no symbolic name associated with this type of macro.

The REPT macro is the simplest of the three. It directs the assembler to repeat the lines within the macro definition a given number of times, as specified by its parameter. Of course, we can use the DUP directive to repeat simple expressions. But the REPT macro is better for repeating several lines of code. For example, consider the following five lines:

```
p? =      10h
REPT      5
p? =      p? + 10h
DB        p?
ENDM
```

The first and third lines define and redefine the value assigned to the *p?* symbol. The REPT macro generates the DB expression five times. However, the value of *p?* changes each time. The result is five bytes ranging

Value	Meaning
0	Normal
1	Read-only
2	Hidden
4	System
20	Archive

Table 7.1: *The hidden and read-only bits of the attribute byte.*

from 20 to 60 hex. The assembly listing looks like this:

```
0200 20 + DB p?
0201 30 + DB p?
0202 40 + DB p?
0203 50 + DB p?
0204 60 + DB p?
```

The first column is the address, the second column is the corresponding data created by the macro, the plus symbol indicates a line generated by a macro, and the next two columns are our source statements.

The other two repeat macros require two parameters. The first is a dummy parameter, and the second is a list of symbols that may be enclosed in angle brackets. Each time the statements in the macro are repeated, a different symbol is substituted for the dummy parameter. For example, the macro

```
IRP par?,<one, two, three, four>
  (source statements)
ENDM
```

will repeat the included source statements four times. However, the symbol *one* will be substituted for the dummy parameter *par?* in those statements the first time. The second time, the symbol *two* will be substituted for *par?*, and so on.

Our program uses the IRPC macro, which means "indefinite-repeat character." The first parameter is a dummy symbol as in the previous example; the second is a list of ASCII characters. Again, the assembler repeats the macro statements once for each character. Furthermore, it replaces the dummy symbol with the appropriate character. The five lines we use in our program are

```
IRPC    p?,NRHB
CMP     AL,'&p?'
JZ      set_at
INC     CX
ENDM
```

The first line of this macro contains the dummy parameter *p?* and four characters—*N, R, H,* and *B.* The three lines of source code in the macro, therefore, are converted into 12 lines in our program. Thus, an assembly listing will contain the following lines:

```
CMP     AL,'N'
JZ      set_at
INC     CX
CMP     AL,'R'
JZ      set_at
INC     CX
CMP     AL,'H'
JZ      set_at
INC     CX
CMP     AL,'B'
JZ      set_at
INC     CX
```

The assembler replaces the dummy parameter with each of the four characters. Notice that when a dummy parameter appears within a quoted string, we must include the ampersand character. The second and third lines of text do not include the dummy variable, and so they are always the same. By using the IRPC macro we reduce the source program from 12 lines to five. Furthermore, if we wanted to add another parameter, say S for system file, we could simply add the letter S to the end of the second parameter of the IRPC macro. Then our five-line macro would generate 15 lines of instructions.

The code created by macro IRPC checks for a match between the second parameter and the four symbols—N, R, H, and B. We do not have to check the lowercase form of these letters, since DOS automatically changes the parameter to uppercase. Our four symbols are arranged in a particular order, corresponding to the values 0–3 for the desired attributes. That is why we increment CX at each point. When we reach label *set_at*, the value of CX corresponds to the desired attribute. If the second parameter does not match one of the four letters, we set CX to a value of 7 and check for the letter A. This corresponds to a setting of all three of the attributes. If the parameter entered by the user does not match any of the above letters, we display first an error message and then the help message.

When we find a valid second command-line parameter, the CX register has the corresponding number. The SI register still points to the path name, the first parameter. We set the AL register to unity to request a change by issuing function 43 hex of interrupt 21 hex. On return we check the carry flag for error. The error number is found in the AL register. However, the only error we expect is 2, indicating that the requested file name or path name could not be found. Therefore we check for this value and display our usual error message if we find it. If there is no error, we display a message on the screen indicating which attributes are being set. We branch to label *show* for this purpose. Then we terminate the program.

If a valid path is entered but a second parameter is not given, we determine the current attribute for the requested file. We issue function 43 hex again, but this time we set the AL register to zero to request status. (Notice that we use the MOV instruction:

```
    MOV   CH,O
```

to set an 8-bit register to zero, but we use the XOR command:

```
    XOR   CX,CX
```

to set a 16-bit register to zero. Both of these operation codes generate two bytes of code. However, the instruction

```
    MOV   CX,O
```

creates three bytes of code.)

The SI register still points to the path name. Therefore, we move the pointer to the DX register. On return from function 43 hex we first check for error message 2, "file not found," in the AL register. We then issue the appropriate message and terminate the program. Otherwise, the value in the CX register has one of the meanings shown in Table 7.1. Since we are not concerned here with the archive bit (discussed in the next section), we exclude it from our analysis by using the instruction

```
    TEST   CL,7
```

This instruction performs a logical AND with the value 7 and the CL register. That is, we only consider the first three bits. The appropriate flags are set, but the result of the operation is not saved. If all three of the bits—hidden, read-only, and system—are reset, the result will be zero. We then display the message

```
    Normal attribute
```

Then we check the read-only attribute by using the TEST instruction to perform a logical AND with the value 1. We show the message

```
    Read only
```

if the result is not zero. Similarly, we check the hidden-attribute bit by performing a logical AND with the value 2. We display the message

Hidden

if the result is not zero. Then we check the system attribute, performing an AND with the value 4. We show the message

system

if the result is not zero. One, two, or three messages will appear, depending on how many attribute bits are set. We then terminate the program.

■ The Archive Bit

From Table 7.1 we can see that the bit corresponding to the mask 20 hex is the archive bit. If you have a backup program for your hard disk, it should use this bit. Each time you alter a file with the editor or the debugger, the archive bit is set. Then, each time you back up the hard disk, it is only necessary to copy those files that were changed since the last backup. That is, only those files that have the archive bit set need to be copied. Then the copying program should reset the archive bit for those programs it backs up. Our program does not specifically address the archive bit. However, each time you run the ATTR program it will reset the archive bit. Of course, you can set the archive bit by changing the file with your editor or the debugger.

We look at file security next.

▌EXECUTING HIDDEN FILES

If you share a computer with others, you can keep your personal programs in your own subdirectory of the hard disk. But since DOS does not provide password protection, anyone else can run or even copy the programs shown in your subdirectory.

You can set the hidden and system attributes for your programs using the ATTR program we wrote in the previous section. Then your programs cannot be seen with the DIR command and they cannot be copied or run. As we saw in the previous section, hidden programs can be run under

DOS version 3 but not version 2. System programs cannot be run with either version of DOS.

You can, of course, use the ATTR program to change the attribute of a hidden or system program temporarily to normal so that you can run or copy it. However, let us consider an easier way, a program that can directly execute hidden and system programs. We learned in Chapter 2 that DOS function 4B hex, interrupt 21 hex can load and execute another program. This function is normally used to chain from one program to another or to load overlay files into memory. However, we can also use it to execute a hidden file.

Create a file named RUN.ASM and copy the lines shown in Figure 7.13. Notice that the beginning and end are similar to those of program TYPEW. You can save some typing by starting with a copy of that program. Furthermore, we look for three routines and the auxiliary input buffer in our library GET_ONE.LIB. Assemble the program with the EXEC batch file. Run the program, giving the name of your editor or another COM file as a parameter. The program automatically adds the COM extension, and so you can give a command in this form:

    RUN WS

You can also give one parameter:

    RUN WS fname.txt

But do not include a subdirectory name, since we read the parameter at 6C hex. Let us check our new program.

Change the attribute of a COM file to read-only, hidden, and system using the ATTR program we wrote earlier in this chapter. Use the A (for all) parameter. Give the DIR command to ensure that the file name does not appear in the listing. Try to run the program in the usual way. DOS should not find it. Now execute the hidden program with our RUN command:

    RUN WS

to see that it works. Let us go through the program.

We begin as usual, except that we define the label *env_seg* at address 2C hex. The segment address at this location points to the strings that describe such items as the search path and the location of the COMMAND.COM file. Let us explore this feature with DEBUG.

Start the debugger and include the name of another COM file such as RUN or ATTR. Do not forget to include the extension. For example, we

```
              PAGE     ,132
              TITLE    RUN files with DOS function 4Bh

     COMMENT *
       January 21, 1986
       Load and execute any file included hidden files
       Usage:  RUN   fname
               RUN   fname parameter
       Macros: @go_dos, @mak_buf, @read_bf, @write
       INT 21 functions 4Ah, 4B, 4Ch
     *
              INCLUDE  mylib.equ
              IF1
              INCLUDE  mylib.mac
              ENDIF

     code     SEGMENT
              ASSUME   CS:code,DS:code
              ORG      2Ch
     env_seg LABEL     WORD                 ;environment seg
              ORG      6Ch
     param2  LABEL     BYTE                 ;parameter
              ORG      80h
     buf_cnt DB        ?                    ;buffer length
     buffer  LABEL     BYTE                 ;command tail

              ORG      100h
     strt:
              JMP      SHORT over_data
              DB       ' RUN, 01.21.86 '
     ;-------------------------------------------
     ; no parameter is default
     ;-------------------------------------------
     fcb2    DB        0,11 DUP(' ')
     stk_ptr DW        0                    ;save stack
     stk_seg DW        0                    ;save stack
     extn    DB        '.COM',0
     par_blk DW        0                    ;environ string
     c0      DW        ?                    ;path name
     c1      DW        ?                    ;SEG cmd_line
             DW        OFFSET param2        ;first param
     c2      DW        ?                    ;SEG fcb1
             DW        OFFSET fcb2
     c3      DW        ?                    ;SEG fcb2

     over_data:
              CALL     get_path
              MOV      c0,SI                ;path-name start
              DEC      DI                   ;name end
     ;-------------------------------------------
     ; move '.COM',0 to end of path name
     ; DI still points to zero at end of name
     ;-------------------------------------------
```

Figure 7.13: *Program to execute hidden files.*

```
            MOV     CX,5              ;characters
            MOV     SI,OFFSET extn   ;COM
            REP     MOVSB
;-------------------------------------------------
; set up segments for parameter block
;-------------------------------------------------
            MOV     AX,[env_seg]
            MOV     par_blk,AX
            MOV     [c1],DS           ;cmd line
            MOV     [c2],DS           ;FCB1
            MOV     [c3],DS           ;FCB2
;-------------------------------------------------
; release memory to new program
;-------------------------------------------------
            MOV     BX,(OFFSET pg_len-OFFSET code)/16+1
            MOV     AH,4Ah
            INT     21h
            JC      no_reduc
;-------------------------------------------------
; save stack before executing program
;-------------------------------------------------
            MOV     [stk_ptr],SP
            MOV     [stk_seg],SS
;-------------------------------------------------
; load and execute program
;-------------------------------------------------
            MOV     DX,[c0]           ;path pointer
            MOV     BX,OFFSET par_blk
            MOV     AL,0
            MOV     AH,4Bh
            INT     21h
;-------------------------------------------------
; restore stack after executing program
; use CS to be sure of location
;-------------------------------------------------
            MOV     SP,CS:[stk_ptr]  ;restore stack
            MOV     SS,CS:[stk_seg]
            MOV     AH,4Ch
            INT     21h              ;quit
;-------------------------------------------------
; error message
;-------------------------------------------------
no_reduc:
            @write  ' Memory reduction failed'
            @go_dos
;-------------------------------------------------
; procedures get_path, get_name, scan_pa
; and the auxiliary input buffer
;-------------------------------------------------
            INCLUDE get_one.lib
pg_len  LABEL   BYTE      ;program length

code    ENDS
        END     strt
```

Figure 7.13: *(continued)*

could give this command:

DEBUG   ATTR.COM

Of course you can have DEBUG load another copy of itself. Give this DEBUG command:

D20 LF

and the result might look like this:

67BD:0020   FF FF FF FF FF FF FF FF—FF FF FF FF B9 67 66 00

Find the address given at location 2C hex. Set the ES register to this value (67B9 hex in this example). Give the command

RES

and press the Return key. Then enter the corresponding value (67B9 in this example). Now give the command

DES:0 L40

and the display will look like Figure 7.14. We have removed the middle portion of the display since we are only interested in the ASCII part. Three different items are visible in this example: the path, the location of COMMAND.COM, and the module name of the last resident program. Each item is separated by a dot in the ASCII listing although there is actually a zero at this location. We need to pass this information along to the program we execute.

We place several storage areas and parameter blocks near the beginning of the code. Therefore we do not need our *@head* macro; we can just enter the usual information at the beginning of the data area. We branch over the data area with a JMP SHORT instruction. We include storage space for the stack pointer and stack segment of the present program. We

```
67B9:0000 50 41 . 48 -00 43 4F 4D 53 50 45 43    PATH=A:\.COMSPEC
67B9:0010 3D 43 . 5C -41 4E 44 2E 43 4F 4D 00    =C:\COMMAND.COM.
67B9:0020 4D 4F . 4E -6E 65 78 74 70 72 00 00    MODNAME=nextpr..
```

Figure 7.14: *The environment referenced by the segment at location 2C hex.*

also prepare a parameter block for the new program. In this way we can pass along a command line and one parameter at 6C hex. (Since the program we want to run is the first parameter of the current program, the second parameter of the current program can be the first parameter of the program we execute.)

We begin the program in the usual way with routine *get_path* analyzing the command line. On return from this routine, the SI register points to the name of the program we want to execute. We then store this address at label *c0* in the parameter block. The DI register conveniently points to the end of this name.

We next use the string-move instruction to place the five characters—a dot, the letters COM, and a zero—at the end of the name. In this way we can run WordStar with the command

RUN WS *FNAME*

rather than the longer command:

RUN WS.COM *FNAME*

We have already written the required five characters into memory at the label *extn,* using the DB directive. Therefore we set the SI register to this location. We set the count register, CX, to five, the number of characters to move. We then issue the string command

REP MOVSB

to move the five characters into place. This double instruction moves the string pointed to by DS:SI to the location referenced by ES:DI.

The next instruction sets up more of the parameter block. We move the segment address for the environment from its location at 2C hex to the label *par_blk.* Since a memory-to-memory transfer is not allowed, we must use an intermediate register. We also copy the segment address of the current program into the locations *c1, c2,* and *c3.*

We have seen that DOS allocates all the available memory to an executing program. Therefore, we must release some of it for the new program. We do this with function 4A hex of interrupt 21 hex. We previously learned an effective way to calculate program length. This example is a little different in detail, although it uses the same technique. We divide the program length by 16 and increment the value. Notice that we are using the assembler to perform the division at assembly time, not the computer at execution time. On return from function 4A hex we check the carry flag to see if there is an error.

When the other program terminates, control is returned to the current program. However, the other program can change all registers. Therefore we must save the stack pointer and stack segment registers in memory before giving up control. We are now ready to execute the other program. We point the DX register to the name of the program we want to run and set the BX register to the parameter block, label c0 in our program. We set the AL register to zero to indicate to DOS that we actually want to run the program. (If we only want to load data or an overlay file, we set the AL register to unity.) Then we execute function 4B hex of interrupt 21 hex. Our program should now start up as if we had executed it directly. The advantage of our new method is that we can run hidden programs.

When the executing program terminates, control returns to us. We can expect only the CS and IP registers to be valid. Therefore, we reload the stack pointer and stack segment registers using the CS override. (The DS register would normally be used but it may have been changed by the other program.) Then we terminate our program with function 4C hex of interrupt 21 hex. Alternatively, if we wanted to perform some other operation at this point, we would have pushed all the other registers onto the stack before executing the other program. Then we could restore them after resetting the stack.

Let us look at an alternate method of running hidden files.

RUNNING A HIDDEN PROGRAM, METHOD 2

In the previous section we wrote a program to run hidden files. To use this method, however, the user must enter the names of two programs. Furthermore, only one parameter can be given for the second program. Let us look at an alternative method. In our second version only one name must be given, and it will be possible to include two parameters.

In this section, let us refer to the program we want to protect as the target program, and the program that runs our target program as the driver program. Both will be executable COM files. We are going to rename our target program and then give its original name to the driver program. Once we've done so, the execution will appear to be the same as before we made it complicated. For example, we can rename our target program from WS.COM to HIDEW.COM. Then we rename the driver program from RUNH.COM to WS.COM. To complete the task we change the attribute of the target program to hidden and then change the attribute of the driver program to read-only.

The driver program is shown in Figure 7.15. It is similar to the previous program except that we do not analyze the command line for a file name. Instead, we program the desired name directly into the driver program. Make a copy of the previous program, giving it the temporary name RUNH.ASM. Change it to look like Figure 7.15. Make the name of the target program match the name given at label *pgm_name*. It is shown as HIDEW.COM in our example, but of course you can change it to something else. Moreover, after you have assembled this program, you can make additional copies with different driver names. Then you can use the debugger to change the embedded target name to something else. There is space in the program to expand the target name with 20 additional characters. Of course, the target name in this version can include a drive name and a subdirectory name.

Assemble the program and link it. Change the name of the target program to match the one you chose at label *pgm_name*. Run the driver program with no parameters and see that the target program starts up. Then run the driver program with one or two parameters; the parameters should be passed along to the target program. Let us go through the code.

The program is similar to the previous one. However, we define both parameter areas at 5C and 6C hex because we can now easily transfer two parameters to the target program. Also, there is no code to look for a file name on the command line. We have removed routines *get_path* and *scan_pa*.

As before, the parameter block has space for saving the stack-pointer and stack-segment registers. We confuse the issue by entering extra characters at the label *dummy*. They will appear just before the file name of the target program. The name of the target program appears next; it is terminated with a zero. Let us look at that area with the debugger. Change the attribute of the target program, RUNH, back to normal and then give the command

```
DEBUG   RUNH.COM
```

unless you have renamed the driver program. If so, use the new name. Display the beginning of the program with the command

```
D100 14F
```

The result should look like Figure 7.16. Look at the ASCII display at the right side. It begins with the program title and date from macro *@head*. Notice the letters HIDEW.COM on lines 110 and 120. The extra letters XRDQN are also visible, ahead of the file name.

```
                PAGE    ,132
                TITLE   RUNH, run hidden program

COMMENT *
     January 8, 1986
     Load and execute hidden file
     File name is coded at pgm_name
     One parameter may be entered
     Example: to hide WS.COM
            rename WS.COM to HWS.COM
            encode HWS.COM at pgm_name
            rename this program WS.COM
     Usage:  WS
        or   WS fname
     Macros: @go_dos, @write
*
                INCLUDE mylib.equ
                IF1
                INCLUDE mylib.mac
                ENDIF
blk_siz EQU     512*20

code    SEGMENT
                ASSUME  CS:code,DS:code
                ORG     2Ch
env_seg LABEL   WORD                    ;environment seg
                ORG     5Ch
param1  LABEL   BYTE                    ;parameter 1
                ORG     6Ch
param2  LABEL   BYTE                    ;parameter 2
                ORG     80h
buf_cnt LABEL   BYTE                    ;buffer length
                ORG     82h
buffer  LABEL   BYTE                    ;command tail

                ORG     100h
strt:
                JMP     SHORT over_data
                DB      ' RUNH, 01.08.86 '
stk_ptr DW      0                       ;save stack
stk_seg DW      0                       ;save stack
dummy   DB      'XRDQN'                 ;confusion
;--------------------------------------------
; name of hidden file is next
;--------------------------------------------
pgm_name DB     'HIDEW.COM',0
                DB      20 DUP(0)        ;room to grow
par_blk DW      0                       ;use default
c0      DW      OFFSET buffer
c1      DW      ?                       ;SEG cmd_line
                DW      OFFSET param1
c2      DW      ?                       ;SEG param1
                DW      OFFSET param2
```

Figure 7.15: *Program RUNH to load and execute WordStar.*

```
c3      DW      ?                   ;SEG param2
over_data:
;---------------------------------------------
; set up segments for parameter block
;---------------------------------------------
        MOV     [c1],DS             ;cmd line
        MOV     [c2],DS             ;FCB1
        MOV     [c3],DS             ;FCB2
;---------------------------------------------
; release memory to new program
;---------------------------------------------
        MOV     BX,(OFFSET pg_len-OFFSET code)/16+1
        MOV     AH,4Ah
        INT     21h
        JC      no_reduc
;---------------------------------------------
; save stack before executing program
;---------------------------------------------
        MOV     [stk_ptr],SP        ;save stack
        MOV     [stk_seg],SS
;---------------------------------------------
; load and execute program
;---------------------------------------------
        MOV     DX,OFFSET pgm_name
        MOV     BX,OFFSET par_blk
        MOV     AL,0
        MOV     AH,4Bh
        INT     21h
;---------------------------------------------
; restore stack after executing program
; use CS to be sure of location
;---------------------------------------------
        MOV     SP,CS:[stk_ptr]     ;restore stack
        MOV     SS,CS:[stk_seg]
        MOV     AH,4Ch
        INT     21h
;---------------------------------------------
; error messages
;---------------------------------------------
no_reduc:
        @write  ' Memory reduction failed'
        @go_dos
pg_len  LABEL   BYTE

code    ENDS
        END     strt
```

Figure 7.15: *(continued)*

```
0100 EB 10 20 52 55 4E 48 2C-20 30 31 2E 30 35 2E 38   .. RUNH, 01.05.8
0110 36 20 EB 35 00 00 00 00-58 52 44 51 4E 48 49 44   6 .5....XRDQNHID
0120 45 57 2E 43 4F 4D 00 00-00 00 00 00 00 00 00 00   EW.COM.........
```

Figure 7.16: *Beginning of the RUNH program*

After you rename WordStar to HIDEW and rename RUNH to WS, the scheme will be nearly invisible. The user who gives the regular command:

  WS FNAME

will see WordStar start up just as before. Thus it appears that WordStar is executed as usual. But if someone tries to copy WordStar to a floppy disk with the DOS command:

  COPY WS.COM A:

only a copy of our driver program will be obtained. You can make the deception even better by enlarging the driver program to about the size of WordStar. Load the program with the debugger, change the value in the CX register to a larger number, and save the new version with the W command.

SUMMARY

In this chapter we added four new macros to our library and we learned how to read a disk file. We wrote a program to display a WordStar file correctly on the video screen and another program to display the ASCII characters from an executable file. Then we wrote a program to change and display the read-only, hidden, and system attributes of disk files. Finally, we wrote two programs that can be used to execute hidden programs. In the next chapter we learn how to write disk files.

The beginning of your macro library should now look like this:

```
; Macros in this library
; @d_char       MACRO par?              ;display character
; @d_read       MACRO handle?,pointr?
```

```
; @dos_ver      MACRO                    ;get version
; @get_vec      MACRO  ?vec              ;interrupt vector
; @go_dos       MACRO                    ;return to DOS by 21h
; @head         MACRO  num?              ;header information
; @mak_buf      MACRO  name?, len?       ;make buffer
; @open         MACRO  pointr?           ;open disk file
; @read_bf      MACRO  loc               ;read input buffer
; @screen_mode  MACRO                    ;find screen type
; @set_vec      MACRO  ?vec              ;change interr vector
; @write        MACRO  text?             ;write text on screen
; @write_r      MACRO  addr?             ;display text at addr?
```

8

Writing
Disk Files

INTRODUCTION

In the previous chapter we learned how to write programs that read disk files. In this chapter we write the complementary type of programs, to write disk files. We also consider related operations such as renaming and deleting files. Then we will write a program to copy the video screen to disk, and we will consider filters—programs that copy a disk file but also change the contents in some way. We need to add three more macros to our library before we get to the programs.

MACRO @rename TO CHANGE A FILE NAME

We can, of course, change a file name with the DOS command REN. However, it is also possible for an executing program to change a file name. Let us see why we would want to do so.

We are going to write programs that create new disk files. If a file of the same name already exists, it will automatically be deleted when we create the new one. Therefore, when we create a new file, we should check to see whether a file of the same name already exists. If so, we can stop the program and alert the user. Alternatively, we can change the original name to something else. For example, we can change the extension to BAK.

Add macro @rename, shown in Figure 8.1, to your macro library. To rename a disk file, we place both the new name and the old name in memory and terminate them with zeros as usual. We point the DS:DX registers to the old name and the ES:DI registers to the new name. Our macro sets up the AH register for function 56 hex and executes interrupt 21 hex. The carry flag is set on return if an error occurred. We shall look for two types of error. The AL register has the value 3 if the old name

```
@rename MACRO
;; rename file or move across directories
;; enter macro with DS:DX=old name
;; and ES:DI=new name
        MOV     AH,56h
        INT     21h
        ENDM
```

Figure 8.1: *Macro @rename, to rename a disk file.*

and the new name refer to different disks. If the new name we have selected already exists, register AL has the error code 5.

If the name we choose for the new file is already in use, we must delete it before we can rename the other file. Therefore we need another macro.

MACRO @delete TO DELETE A DISK FILE

Just as we can delete disk files with the DOS command DEL, it is possible for our programs to delete disk files with function 41 hex of interrupt 21 hex. Enter macro *@delete*, given in Figure 8.2, into your macro library. We need to point the DS:DX registers to the file name we want to delete. Of course, the file name string ends with a zero. Our macro has one parameter, the pointer to the file name. The macro moves into the DX register the pointer to the file to be deleted, puts the value 41 hex into the AH register, and executes interrupt 21 hex. Our third new macro converts lowercase to uppercase.

CONVERTING LOWERCASE TO UPPERCASE

When we ran our Hello programs with DEBUG in Chapter 5, we saw that DOS places the command-line tail at location 82 hex at the beginning of our program. Lowercase letters are not converted to uppercase in this line, as they are in the 5D hex region. Sometimes, however, when we are interested in a particular letter of the alphabet, we do not care if it is present as uppercase or lowercase. For example, if we ask the user to respond with a Y or an N, we must expect to find one of four letters—Y,

```
@delete MACRO    pointr?
;; delete file at DS:DX
        PUSH     DX
        MOV      DX,pointr?
        MOV      AH,41h
        INT      21h
        POP      DX
        ENDM
```

Figure 8.2: *Macro @delete to delete a disk file.*

y, N, and *n.* We can simplify the analysis of the user's response by converting the answer to uppercase before checking the input. Then we only have to look for one of two characters—*Y* or *N.* Let us look at ASCII codes.

If we compare the ASCII codes for the letters *Y* and *y,* we can see that they differ by only one bit:

Y	0101 1001	(uppercase)
y	0111 1001	(lowercase)

The other letters are similar. Thus to change a lowercase letter to upper, we only have to turn off bit 5. We can do this by performing a logical AND with the value 5F hex:

	y	0111 1001	(lowercase)
AND	5F	0101 1111	
	Y	0101 1001	(uppercase)

If we perform this operation on an uppercase letter we get the same result:

	Y	0101 1001	(uppercase)
AND	5F	0101 1111	
	Y	0101 1001	(uppercase)

On the other hand, if we perform this operation on a number, like 9, we convert it to Ctrl-Y, which we don't want.

	9	0011 1001	(uppercase)
AND	5F	0101 1111	
		0001 1001	(Ctrl-Y)

Therefore, we must be careful to apply this method only to letters of the alphabet, not to numbers and special characters.

```
@ucase  MACRO
        LOCAL   notup?
;; Macro to change AL to upper case
;; Usage:  @ucase
        CMP     AL,'a'          ;;upper case?
        JB      notup?          ;;yes
        AND     AL,5Fh          ;;make upper
notup?:
        ENDM
```

Figure 8.3: *Macro @ucase to change lowercase letters to uppercase.*

Enter macro *@ucase,* shown in Figure 8.3, into your macro library. This macro operates on the byte in the AL register. First we make a check to ensure that the character is lowercase:

```
CMP     AL,'a'
JB      notup
```

We compare the character with a lowercase letter *a*. If the value is less than *a* (ASCII 97), we branch around the operation. Be sure to use the JB (jump if below) rather than the similar JL (jump if less) instruction. The JB instruction looks at the entire byte as the value, while the JL uses only the lower seven bits. It considers the highest bit to be a positive or negative sign.

We ignore the characters above the letter *z*—the braces, vertical bar, and tilde. You can include them if you think they will be important. Then you would add these lines:

```
CMP     AL,'z'
JA      notup
```

When we find a lowercase letter we perform the operation

```
AND     AL,5Fh
```

on the AL register, converting the letter to uppercase.

We also need another subroutine library before we begin our programs for this chapter.

SUBROUTINE LIBRARY TO PROCESS TWO FILE NAMES

In the previous chapter we created a subroutine library named GET_ONE-.LIB, which contained three procedures and an auxiliary input buffer. We accessed this library with an INCLUDE statement in our programs, so that we could process a file name entered by the user. Most of the programs in this chapter require the processing of two file names, and so we need to add another subroutine. The simplest technique is to copy the original library, using the name GET_TWO.LIB for the new copy. Then add procedure *gt_path2* and the macro establishing a second buffer, for the second file name, to the very beginning of the library. The new lines are given Figure 8.4. We will call this new procedure when we need to get a second file name. Let us look at a program that uses our new library.

MOVING A FILE FROM ONE DIRECTORY TO ANOTHER

In this section we write a program to move disk files from one directory to another on the same disk. This program is not very useful in itself,
but the macros and routines we develop here will be needed in other programs. Furthermore, this program is smaller and simpler than the others in
this chapter. Therefore, its operations will be easier to understand.

You can copy a disk file from one drive to another and from one directory to another by using the DOS COPY command. You can also change
the name of a disk file with the DOS command RENAME. However, the
RENAME command cannot change the directory name with which a file is

```
;*********************************************
; Get second parameter
;  DI points to beginning of name
;  If invalid, use auxiliary buffer
; Procdures required: get_name, scan_pa
; Output:        DI = points to first character
;*********************************************
gt_path2        PROC
;---------------------------------------------
; see if any characters are left
;---------------------------------------------
        OR      CX,CX           ;zero?
        JNZ     ck_par2         ;no
;---------------------------------------------
; get pathname from keyboard
;---------------------------------------------
no_par2m:
        @write  <cr,lf,'New path name: '>
        MOV     DI,OFFSET buff_ot ;pointer
        CALL    get_name
;---------------------------------------------
; check pathname referenced by DI
; carry flag set if invalid name
;---------------------------------------------
ck_par2:
        CALL    scan_pa
        JC      no_par2m
        RET
gt_path2        ENDP
;******** End of procedure gt_path2 ********
;---------------------------------------------
; auxiliary output buffer
;---------------------------------------------
hand2   DW      ?               ;dest handle
        @mak_buf buff_ot, 45
```

Figure 8.4: *New lines added to GET_ONE.LIB to make GET_TWO.LIB.*

associated. Of course, you can use the COPY command to move a file to another directory and then use the DOS DEL or ERASE command to delete the original version.

When you copy a program from one directory to another with the COPY command, the original file is duplicated, and so it appears in two places and takes twice as much disk space. By contrast, the program we are going to write does not duplicate a program, it merely changes the program name. Furthermore, we can change the associated directory name as well as the file name. Thus, it appears that we have moved the file from one directory to another.

Copy the TYPEW.ASM program from the previous chapter and give the new file the name *MOVE.ASM*. Change the program to look like Figure 8.5. Be sure to change the directive near the end of the program from GET_ONE.LIB to GET_TWO.LIB. The program begins as usual by calling procedure *get_path* to get the first parameter. As in our previous programs, the parameter is read from the default buffer at 80 hex if it was entered on the command line. Otherwise, we ask the user to enter the name, and we read the entry into the auxiliary input buffer. On returning to the main program, we open the file corresponding to the first parameter. We check the carry flag for an error and branch to label *error* if the flag is set. The only error we expect is the usual:

File not found

We can delete the next portion of the TYPEW previous program since our new program does not read text from the disk file. In its place, we put code to save the SI pointer to the first parameter by moving it to the DX register. The next section determines the second parameter, the new name of the file. We call our new subroutine named *gt_path2* for this purpose. This routine is similar to procedure *get_path*, except that we do not check for a parameter on the command line, and we display a slightly different prompt when a file name is needed:

New path name:

It is possible to combine subroutines *gt_path2* and *get_path* into a single routine; this is left as an exercise for the reader. We also need to establish two separate input buffers since both names must be in memory together during the renaming operation.

Procedure *gt_path2* begins by checking the CX register to see if there are any remaining characters in the buffer. If there are no more characters, we display the prompt and call procedure *get_name* to read the

```
GET_TWO.LIB

        PAGE    ,132
        TITLE   MOVE

COMMENT *
  January 12, 1985
  Rename file from one directory to another
  Usage:
        MOVE
        MOVE fname
        MOVE fname fname2
        MOVE fname prn
        MOVE \pathname\fname fname2
  Macros: @delete, @go_dos, @head, @mak buf, @open,
          @read_bf, @rename, @ucase, @write
  Librarys: mylib.equ, mylib.mac, get_two.lib
  *
        INCLUDE mylib.equ
        IF1
        INCLUDE mylib.mac
        ENDIF

code    SEGMENT
        ASSUME  CS:code, DS:code
        ORG     80h
buf_cnt DB      ?                       ;buffer length
buffer  LABEL   BYTE                    ;default buffer

        ORG     100h
strt:
        @head   ' MOVE, 01.12.86 '
;-----------------------------------------------
; get path name for old file
; SI points to beginning of name
;-----------------------------------------------
        CALL    get_path
        @open   SI
        JC      error   ;no file
        MOV     DX,SI
;-----------------------------------------------
; get path name for new file
; SI points to beginning of name
;-----------------------------------------------
        CALL    gt_path2
        MOV     DI,SI
try2:
        @rename
        JC      r_error         ;exists
        @go_dos                 ;to DOS
```

Figure 8.5: *Program MOVE to rename disk files.*

```
;-----------------------------------------
; error during opening of file
;-----------------------------------------
error:
        @write  'ERROR:'
        CMP     AX,2
        JNZ     e2
        @write  ' File not found'
e2:
        @go_dos
; error during renaming
r_error:
        @write  'ERROR:'
        CMP     AX,3
        JNZ     e3
        @write  ' Cannot change drive'
        @go_dos
e3:
        CMP     AL,5
        JNZ     e4
        @write  ' File exists. Delete it? (Y/N) '
        PUSH    DI                  ;save
        MOV     DI,OFFSET aux2  ;Y/N input buffer
        CALL    get_name            ;get char
        MOV     AL,[DI]
        POP     DI
        @ucase
        CMP     AL,'Y'
        JZ      e5
e4:
        @go_dos                     ;quit
e5:
        @delete DI
        JC      e6                  ;error
        JMP     try2                ;try again
e6:
        @write  ' ERROR: '
        CMP     AL,5
        JNZ     e7
        @write  'Write protected '
e7:
        @go_dos
; input buffer for Y/N response
        @mak_buf aux2,6
;-----------------------------------------
; gt_path2, get_path, ; get_name, scan_pa
; and auxiliary input buffer next
;-----------------------------------------
        INCLUDE get_two.lib

code    ENDS
        END     strt
```

Figure 8.5: *(continued)*

second parameter. Then, using procedure *scan_pa,* we check to see that the path name is valid.

On returning to the main program, we now have two path names. The DX register points to the first name and the DI and SI registers point to the second. Both are terminated by zero. Our *@rename* macro tries to change the first name to the second using function 56 hex of interrupt 21 hex. On returning from this routine, we check the carry flag for errors. We consider two possible errors: the two path names are on different drives, and the new name already exists. We cannot do anything about different drives except terminate the program with an error message, but we can delete the extra file.

If we find that the new name already exists (error 5), we ask the user for permission to delete it. We read the user's input with a third keyboard buffer. We save the original contents of the DI register on the stack and then point the DI register to the new buffer (*aux2*). Then we call procedure *get_name* to get the user's input. Although we only expect the user to enter the letter Y or N, we have provided for six characters, to allow for responses such as YES or NO. If more than six characters are typed, the computer beeps and does not accept any more. When the Return key is pressed, control returns to our program so that we can analyze the response.

We are only interested in the first character that was entered, the one register DI points to on return from the input routine. Therefore, we retrieve this character from the buffer using the DI register as a pointer. To avoid checking for both a lowercase and an uppercase letter, we convert the character to uppercase with our *@ucase* macro. We then check for the letter Y. If any other character has been entered, we terminate the program with our *@go_dos* macro. You might want to add two more lines of code at this point, to see if the letter N was entered. They would be someting like this:

```
CMP     AL,'N'
JNZ     (back to the error message)
```

If the letter Y was entered, we branch to our macro *@delete,* which is set up with parameter DI. The corresponding instructions move the pointer from the DI register to the DX register, as required by the delete function. We then execute function 41 hex of interrupt 21 hex to delete the target file name. On return from the delete function, we check the carry flag for error. The only error we expect is number 5, indicating that we are attempting to delete a read-only, hidden, or system file. You might want to add instructions at this point to reset the file attributes using function 43 hex. In that case, the program could delete the file. However, we simply terminate the program at this time.

If the deletion was successful, we branch to the label *try2* and execute the rename function again. We have been considering two possible errors, and the explicit error messages our program responds with. Another type of error, such as:

    MOVE   a:file1   b:

or

    MOVE   file1   \SUB\ *

gives the DOS error number 11, which is "invalid format." Our program responds with the generic message

    ERROR:

Create two working files to test our new program. Copy a small COM file, giving it the name DUM. Make second and third copies, named DUM2 and DUM3. Use the ATTR program from the previous chapter to write-protect DUM3. Assemble and run our new program; try out the various parts. Work on a RAM disk for fastest operation. Alternatively, use a floppy disk in case something goes wrong. (Of course, it is safe to use a hard disk if everything is correct.) Give the command

    MOVE   DUM   DUM4

Be sure to include two parameters that do not contain the * and ? symbols, or different drive names. Then give the command

    DIR   DUM *

Check to see that there are three files—DUM2, DUM3, and DUM4. Give the command again (pressing the F3 key and then Return) and see if you get the message

    ERROR: File not found

Give different drive names for the two parameters:

    MOVE   DUM4   A:DUM

and see if you get the error message

    Cannot change drive

Try to change the name to an existing file name:

    MOVE   DUM4   DUM2

When you are asked for permission to delete the target file, answer N. Then check the directory to see if the file is still there. Repeat the command answering Y, and see if the first parameter, *DUM4,* has disappeared. Finally, try to change the name to an existing file that is protected:

    MOVE   DUM2   DUM3

When you get the first error message, and the request to delete, enter a Y. The second error message should be

    ERROR: Write protected

We create a disk file next.

CREATING DISK FILES

In the previous chapter we wrote macro *@open* to access an existing disk file with function 3D hex. Then we wrote macro *@d_read* to read text from the opened file using function 3F hex. We are now going to write a similar pair of macros for creating new files. First we will write macro *@create* to make a new file, then we will write macro *@d_write* to write text to the new file.

In the previous chapter, when we deliberately tried to open a file that did not exist we received error number 2. Our program then displayed the corresponding meaning:

    ERROR: File not found

In this chapter we are going to write programs that create new disk files. Then we will use function 3C hex of interrupt 21 hex to create and open the new name, instead of our regular open function. However, there is a potential problem with this step.

Suppose we write a program to create a new file. The program reads the new name entered by the user, so that the new file can be created with function 3C hex. But when this function creates a new file, it automatically deletes any existing file with the same name. Thus, if the user accidentally types the name of an existing file, that file is deleted as the new file is created. As a precaution, then, we should check to see if a requested file already exists before using function 3C hex.

Previously, we used the @open macro:

    @open   SI, error

to open an existing file and check the carry flag for an error. If the carry flag was set, it meant that the file we wanted to open did not exist. Therefore, we branched to an error routine and displayed the message

    ERROR: File not found.

When we want to create a new file, we use the same macro, but we reverse the sense. We use the statement

    @open   SI, no_error

to ensure that the file name referenced by the SI pointer does *not* exist. If the carry flag is reset, it means that a file with the requested name already exists. We can display an error message such as

    ERROR: File already exists

and terminate the program.

There is another course of action when we find that a requested file already exists. We can change its extension to BAK, so that it can be saved as a backup file. (Of course, we might have to delete an existing BAK file of the same name, too.) Best of all would be to give the user a choice. For example, the message could be

    ERROR: Target file exists.
    Enter Q = quit, D = delete, B = backup:

Then the program terminates if the response is Q. But if the answer is D, we delete the original target file, and if the letter B is entered, we change the extension of the original file to BAK.

We will choose a third way in our next program. If we discover an existing file, we ask the user for permission to delete the file. If the answer is no, we terminate the program. If the answer is yes, we can proceed to the file creation. There is still one small problem, however.

DOS assigned a file handle when we executed the open function. If we now execute the create function, we will automatically delete the original file but not the corresponding file handle. The newly created file will be assigned a different file handle. Therefore, we should close the file we opened, to release the handle before we create the new file. We will consider the close function again after we learn how to write data to a disk file.

Of course, if the open operation returns with the carry flag set, indicating that the requested file does not exist, we are ready to create the new file. Let us write macros for creating, writing, and closing a disk file.

■ Creating a New Disk File With Macro @create

We have seen that a new disk file can be created with function 3C hex of interrupt 21 hex. We place the location of the file name into the DX register, set the CX register to the file attribute (normally zero), and the AH register to 3C hex, and issue interrupt 21 hex. Our next macro, *@create*, given in Figure 8.6, creates a new file for us. As in the *@open* macro, the parameter points to the location of the file name. Add this macro to your library.

```
@create MACRO    pointr?
;; macro to create a disk file for writing
;; pointr? is location of pathname
;; terminated with a zero
;; assigned handle or error code in BX
;; Usage:        @create  [DI]
;;               @create  <OFFSET buffer>
;;
        PUSH     DX
        PUSH     CX
        MOV      DX,pointr?
        XOR      CX,CX            ;;attribute zero
        MOV      AH,3Ch           ;;function
        INT      21h
        POP      CX
        POP      DX
        MOV      BX,AX            ;;handle
        ENDM
```

Figure 8.6: *Macro @create to create a new disk file.*

On return from the creation function, the carry flag is set if an error occurred. There are several possible errors: "no directory space"; "no file handles available"; and "existing name write-protected." However, these seem remote, and so we simply display the generic error message. If there is no error, the carry flag is cleared, and the assigned file handle appears in the AX register. Our macro moves the handle to the BX register. Now we have to write information to the new file.

■ Writing Information to a Disk File With Macro @d_write

Writing information to a disk file is similar to reading information from one. The data are placed in a memory buffer. The DX register points to the beginning of the buffer, the CX register has the number of bytes to write, and the BX register has the handle that was assigned by the create function. We put 40 hex in the AH register and issue interrupt 21 hex. The macro @d_write, given in Figure 8.7, creates the necessary code. Add it to your library.

This macro has two parameters. As in the corresponding @d_read macro, the first parameter is optional. It refers to the assigned handle that must be placed in the BX register. Since the @create macro placed the handle in this register, we can sometimes omit this parameter. The second parameter points to the data buffer in memory.

The carry flag is set on return from this operation if an error occurred. The important error is "disk full." If the carry flag is clear, the number of bytes that were written appears in the AX register. This should be the same as the value in the CX register.

```
@d_write MACRO  handle?,pointr?
;; Write to disk with assigned handle?
;; pointr? is location of pathname
;; CX has bytes to read, AX has bytes read
;; carry set if error
        PUSH    DX
        MOV     DX,pointr?
        IFNB    <handle?>
        MOV     BX,handle?
        ENDIF
        MOV     AH,40h          ;;function
        INT     21h
        POP     DX
        ENDM
```

Figure 8.7: Macro @d_write for writing data to disk.

If the number of bytes we need to write is larger than the buffer, we must issue the write function several times. On the other hand, we may read data from one disk file, process it, and then write the results to another disk file. In this way we alternately read and write data. In either case we have to close the file next. Let us write a macro for that.

CLOSING A DISK FILE WITH MACRO @close

When we have finished writing data to a new disk file, we must close the file, with function 3E hex. If we fail to close a new file, the disk directory will be incorrect and the file will be useless. Furthermore, the close function releases the assigned handle so that it can be reused for the next open or create operation. It is not necessary to close files that were opened only for reading, but doing so releases the handle for the next open or create operation.

Macro @close is given in Figure 8.8; copy it into your macro library. The optional parameter gives the assigned handle. Sometimes, the handle will already be in the BX register, and so we can omit the parameter from the macro implementation.

Let us write a program that writes a disk file.

SAVING AND RESTORING THE VIDEO SCREEN

As we have seen, the IBM PC can have one or two video screens that are memory mapped. Memory for the monochrome character screen

```
@close  MACRO   handle?
;; macro to close file with
;; handle?
;; carry set if error
        IFNB    <handle?>
        MOV     BX,handle?
        ENDIF
        MOV     AH,3Eh
        INT     21h
        ENDM
```

Figure 8.8: *Macro @close for closing a disk file.*

begins at segment B000 hex, while memory for the color/graphics screen starts at segment B800 hex. There are several ways to create a disk file of information transmitted to the screen. One way is to use the redirection symbol > on the command line. With this method, however, no information appears at all on the screen. Therefore, it is difficult to know what is happening and when a dump has been completed.

Our next program will create a disk file by directly saving the memory region corresponding to the appropriate display. This technique has several advantages, especially if both screens are available. We can save only the (ASCII) text, or we can save both the text and the attributes. We can incorporate the disk file directly into a report, or we can restore the screen by reading the disk file back into the video memory. We can execute our program from the monochrome screen to save the image of the color/graphics screen, and vice versa. If we only have one display, however, the command needed to run our program will appear at the bottom of the disk file (since it is needed to save the screen). Nevertheless, this may not be a problem if we only need to save a portion of the screen for a report.

Our next program will either read or write a file, but not both. Consequently, we only need to create one file name and so we use our *GET_ONE.LIB* library. Create a disk file named *SAVESCRN.ASM* and copy the program given in Figure 8.9. Let us go through the code.

Near the beginning we define the location of the monochrome and color/graphics screen memory segments (*m_mem* and *g_mem*). We define label *param2* at 6D hex so that we can look for a second parameter. This will be a single character selecting one of several options. We look for the first parameter at location 81 hex, the default input buffer. This will be the name of the file to read or write. We also use this area to store the pointer to the file name. Therefore, we define dual labels for location 80 hex—*pointr* is a word label and *buf_cnt* is a byte label.

Our usual *@head* macro encodes the progam name and date, and then we call subroutine *get_path* to get a file name. As before, this routine reads the file name at 81 hex if it was entered on the command line. Otherwise, the name is requested from the user. On return from the routine, we store the pointer to the file name at 80 hex since we no longer need this location for the file name. We check the first character for a question mark, a traditional way of asking for help. If a question mark is present, we branch to a routine that displays a help message. Otherwise, we move the character at 6D hex, corresponding to the second parameter, to the AL register. We again check for a question mark as a possible parameter.

If a question mark appears at location 6D hex, we also display the help message. Notice, however, that a question mark will appear at this

```
            PAGE    ,132
            TITLE   SAVESCRN

COMMENT *
  January 21, 1986
  Saves screen image as disk file
  Monochrome screen is default
  Parameter A saves data and attributes for entire screen
  Parameter C saves the entire screen
  Parameter R restores color screen from disk file
  Usage:
            SAVESCRN ?          display help message
            SAVESCRN fname      monochrome text
            SAVESCRN fname A    color attributes too
            SAVESCRN fname C    color text
            SAVESCRN fname M    monochrome text
            SAVESCRN fname R    restore color screen
  Macros: @create, @close, @d_read, @d_write,
          @go_dos, @head, @mak_buf, @open,
          @read_bf, @ucase, @write, @write_r
  *
            INCLUDE mylib.equ
            IF1
            INCLUDE mylib.mac
            ENDIF

m_mem     EQU     0B000h              ;monochrome memory
g_mem     EQU     0B800h              ;graphics memory

code      SEGMENT
          ASSUME  CS:code, DS:code

          ORG     6Dh
param2    LABEL   BYTE                ;second parameter
          ORG     80h
pointr    LABEL   WORD                ;file name pointer
buf_cnt   DB      ?                   ;buffer length
buffer    LABEL   BYTE                ;default buffer

          ORG     100h
strt:
          @head   ' SAVESCRN, 01.21.86 '
;--------------------------------------------
; get path name for disk file
; pointer returned in SI
;--------------------------------------------
          CALL    get_path
          MOV     [pointr],SI         ;save SI
; check for help request
          CMP     BYTE PTR [SI],'?'
          JZ      hlp
```

Figure 8.9: *Program SAVESCRN to save and restore the screen.*

```
; look for second parameter
        MOV     AL,[param2]
        CMP     AL,'?'
        JZ      hlp
        CMP     AL,'R'              ;restore screen
        JNZ     not_r
        JMP     restor
;---------------------------------------------
; display help message
;---------------------------------------------
hlp:
        @write_r <OFFSET help>
        @go_dos
not_r:
        MOV     BX,g_mem            ;set for color
        CMP     AL,'A'              ;save attrib
        JZ      save_at
        CMP     AL,'C'              ;color screen
        JZ      col
        CMP     AL,'M'
        JZ      mon
        CMP     AL,blank            ;default
        JNZ     hlp
mon:
        MOV     BX,m_mem            ;set monochrome
;---------------------------------------------
; move text from appropriate screen to buffer
;---------------------------------------------
col:
; use ES for source segment
        MOV     ES,BX
        XOR     SI,SI               ;screen pointer
        MOV     DI,OFFSET datbuff
        MOV     CX,25               ;lines
; move data for first 78 characters of each line
do_page:
        PUSH    CX
        MOV     CX,78               ;char/line
n_line:
        MOV     AL,ES:[SI]          ;get byte
        MOV     [DI],AL
        INC     SI
        INC     SI                  ;skip attribute
        INC     DI
        LOOP    n_line
        ADD     SI,4                ;move to next line
; end of line, add cr and lf to buffer
        MOV     BYTE PTR [DI],cr
        INC     DI
        MOV     BYTE PTR [DI],lf
        INC     DI
        POP     CX
```

Figure 8.9: *(continued)*

```
            LOOP    do_page
; reset ES to DS
            ASSUME  ES:code
            MOV     CX,DS
            MOV     ES,CX
            MOV     BYTE PTR [DI],eof ;mark end
            MOV     CX,2001          ;bytes to save
            JMP     SHORT m_eof
;------------------------------------------------
; move both data and attributes for color screen
;------------------------------------------------
save_at:
            MOV     DS,BX            ;set for color
            XOR     SI,SI           ;screen pointer
            MOV     DI,OFFSET datbuff
            MOV     CX,2000         ;words to move
            CLD                     ;move upward
            REP     MOVSW           ;do it
; reset DS to CS
            ASSUME  DS:code
            MOV     CX,CS
            MOV     DS,CX
            MOV     CX,4000         ;bytes to write
; get pointer to file name
m_eof:
            MOV     BP,CX           ;save count
;------------------------------------------------
; check that file does not exist
;------------------------------------------------
            MOV     DI,[pointr]     ;file pointer
            @open   DI,no_error
            @write  ' ERROR: File exists.'
            @write  ' Delete it? (Y/N) '
            PUSH    DI              ;save
            MOV     DI,OFFSET aux2  ;Y/N input buffer
            CALL    get_name        ;get char
            MOV     AL,[DI]
            POP     DI
            @ucase
            CMP     AL,'Y'
            JZ      e5              ;ok
            @go_dos                 ;quit
; input buffer for Y/N response
            @mak_buf aux2,4
e5:
            @close
;------------------------------------------------
; create new file
;------------------------------------------------
no_error:
            @create DI
            JC      error
```

Figure 8.9: *(continued)*

```
; write data to disk, CX has bytes to save
        MOV     CX,BP           ;restore count
        @d_write ,<OFFSET datbuff>
; check for error
        JC      error
        @close
        JC      error
        @go_dos
error:
        @write  'ERROR:'
        CMP     AX,2
        JNZ     e2
        @write  ' File not found'
e2:
        @go_dos
;-------------------------------------------------
; write disk file to color screen
;-------------------------------------------------
restor:
        @open   [pointr], error
        MOV     CX,4000         ;bytes to read
        @d_read ,<OFFSET datbuff>
        JC      error
        MOV     AX,g_mem        ;set for color
        MOV     ES,AX
        XOR     DI,DI           ;screen pointer
        MOV     SI,OFFSET datbuff
        MOV     CX,2000         ;words to move
        CLD                     ;move upward
        REP     MOVSW           ;do it
        @go_dos
;-------------------------------------------------
; procedures get_path, get_name, scan_pa
; and the auxiliary input buffer
;-------------------------------------------------
        INCLUDE get_one.lib
;-------------------------------------------------
; help message
;-------------------------------------------------
help    DB      ' Save or restore video screen with:',cr,lf
        DB      'SAVESCRN ?          display help message',cr,lf
        DB      'SAVESCRN fname      monochrome text',cr,lf
        DB      'SAVESCRN fname A    color attributes too',cr,lf
        DB      'SAVESCRN fname C    color text',cr,lf
        DB      'SAVESCRN fname M    monochrome text',cr,lf
        DB      'SAVESCRN fname R    restore color screen',cr,lf
        DB      '$'
datbuff LABEL   BYTE                    ;data buffer

code    ENDS
        END     strt
```

Figure 8.9: *(continued)*

location if the user entered an asterisk, since DOS converts an asterisk to a field of question marks. If no question mark appears, we check the second parameter for the letter R. This is a command to restore the color/ graphics screen, both text and attributes, by reading the file given as the first parameter. If we find an R, we branch to label *restor*.

We prepare to restore the color/graphics screen by opening the requested file and reading all 4000 bytes into a buffer at the end of the program. We use the *@open* and *@d_read* macros for this purpose. The CX register has the number of words to move (2000), the ES register points to the color/graphics memory segment, the DI register has the offset, initially zero, and SI points to the buffer at the end of the program. The string-move instruction then transfers the alternating characters and attributes to the color/graphics screen memory. We use the instruction

```
REP   MOVSW
```

(move string word) to move words, rather than bytes. Then we terminate the program with interrupt 20 hex.

Saving the Screen to a Disk File

Return to the label *not_r* near the beginning of the program. The remaining options create one of three disk files:

M   monochrome text (default)
C   color text
A   color text and attributes

We set the BX register to the color/graphics memory as the default. Then we check the second parameter for the letter A, to save all the color screen, both characters and attributes. This is the complement of the previous operation, where we restored the screen from a disk file.

Skip down to the label *save_at* to continue. We set the DS register to the segment of the color/graphics memory, the SI register to the offset (initially zero), the DI register to the buffer at the end of our program, and the CX register to the number of words (2000). Again we use the REP MOVSW string-move instructions, this time to copy data from the screen memory to our buffer. After moving the data, we reset the DS register to the code segment, using the CX register as an intermediate step. This is much faster than the traditional method:

```
PUSH   CS
POP    DS
```

We set the CX register to 4000, the number of bytes we want to write to disk. The new file is created with our *@create* macro, referenced by the pointer stored in memory at label *pointr*. We write all 4000 bytes with our *@d_write* macro, which executes function 40 hex of interrupt 21 hex. Finally, we close the new file with our *@close* macro. Notice that we omit the first parameter from macro *@d_write* and the parameter from *@close*, since the file handle is already located in the BX register.

■Saving Video Text to a Disk File

Return to the beginning of the program, label *not_r*. If the second parameter is the letter C, we save only the text characters of the color/ graphics screen, not the attributes of each displayed charater. As before, we move the information in the screen memory to the buffer at the end of the program. However, this step is more complicated now, since we cannot use the regular string-move command. We need to move every other byte of the screen memory to the buffer. But the characters will be adjacent in the new location. Therefore, the pointer to the screen memory must be incremented twice after each move, while the pointer to the buffer is incremented only once.

Another complication occurs because we want to be able to display the resulting disk file on the screen, using the DOS TYPE command. Each line of the screen contains 80 characters, but there are no carriage returns and line feeds in the screen memory. Therefore we will only transfer the first 78 characters of each line. Then we will add a carriage return and a line feed to the end of each line sent to the buffer.

We set the ES:SI registers to the color screen and the DI register to the buffer (DS already points to our program). The CX register is set to 25, the number of lines on the screen. This will control the outer loop. We push this value onto the stack and set CX to 78, the number of screen characters we read from each line. We move each byte from the ES:SI pointer to the AL register and then to the DS:DI pointer. The SI register, pointing to the video display memory, is incremented twice to skip over the video attribute. The DI register is incremented just once, so that the text in the buffer will be sequential. The LOOP command repeats these instructions 78 times, until CX = 0. We move the SI pointer to the beginning of the next line by adding the value 4. The carriage return and line feed are placed in the buffer to fill out the line to 80 characters. The outer loop count is restored to the CX register with the POP command. In this way we transfer one line of the screen for each execution of the outer loop. After transferring 2000 bytes to the buffer, we reset the ES register and place the end-of-file (EOF) marker in the buffer. The CX register is set to 2001 (including the EOF marker) and we branch to the label *m_eof* to write the disk file.

The fourth possibility for the second parameter is the letter M, to save the text from the monochrome screen. We also perform this operation if no second parameter is entered. The BX register is reset to the segment of the monochrome memory, and then the code continues as in the previous example. Assemble this program and try out the various features. If you have only one screen, save the text on that screen with the command:

SAVESCRN   TEXT M (or C)

Use the DIR command to see that the file has 2001 bytes. Clear the screen with the CLS command and then display the file with the command

TYPE TEXT

If you have both screens, change from one to the other (using the MODE command). Save the text of the monochrome screen from the color/graphics screen and vice versa. Fill the color/graphics screen with color and save the text and attributes:

SAVESCRN TEXTC A

Clear the screen and read back the file with the command:

SAVESCRN TEXTC R

In the next chapter we will write a program to switch screens and turn the color on or off.

Now let us consider filters.

FILTERS: CONVERTING ONE FILE INTO ANOTHER

A computer program that changes a disk file in some way is called a *filter*. For example, a filter program might replace each tab character with the corresponding number of blanks, remove all line feeds, or add a line feed after each carriage return. We created a filter of sorts in the previous chapter—the TYPEW program—and we are going to write two types of filter programs in this section. One will be easy to write but will run very slowly. The other will be harder to write but will run much faster. But first, let us look at the filter we have already written.

In the previous chapter we wrote the TYPEW program to convert a WordStar file to ASCII characters and display the result on the video screen. Then we tried a variation using the redirection symbol (>). Instead of sending the output to the video screen, we created a new disk file containing the ASCII output. The command was

```
TYPEW FILE.ASM > FILEOK.ASM
```

to convert the WordStar file named FILE.ASM to the ASCII file named FILEOK.ASM. However, this method is slow since the redirection feature handles characters singly rather than in blocks. Let us look at an easier— but even slower—method before looking at a harder but faster method.

Filtering Files with the DOS Redirection Feature

We previously created an output file by using the DOS redirection command. This program had the disadvantage of reading the name of the original file from user input. We had to include several operations, such as the open and disk-read commands. An alternative method is to use the redirection feature both to read the original file and then to create the new one. After that, our filter program is very simple, because there is no need for the open and disk-read commands. Of course, the disadvantage of this method is that the operation is very slow since we are both reading and writing single characters rather than blocks. Nevertheless, since DOS features such as tab expansion are available, this method may greatly simplify the programming. Furthermore, if we limit this method to filtering small files, it may not matter if the time increases from a few seconds to several minutes. We will write two different filters—one to raise lowercase letters to uppercase and another to convert the tab character to the equivalent number of spaces.

A Filter to Raise Lowercase Letters to Uppercase

The program shown in Figure 8.10 can convert the lowercase letters in a disk file to uppercase using the DOS redirection feature. Create a file named FILTERU.ASM and type up the program. It requires macros @go_dos, @head, and @ucase, but the subroutines GET_ONE and GET_TWO that we developed to handle disk files in the previous programs are not needed. Instead, we are going to use the standard input and output functions. Let us go through the code.

We begin our program in the usual way, except that we do not check the command line at 80 hex for a file name. Instead, we read one byte from the standard console input, using function 7:

```
MOV    AH,7
INT    21h
```

This function stops program operation until a character is available at the standard input device, which is normally the console keyboard. In this program, however, we are going to use redirection to read the input from a disk file. Furthermore, since we might want to change each character, we do not want to display it on the standard output at this time. Thus,

```
            PAGE    ,132
            TITLE   FILTERU

COMMENT *
  January 17, 1986
  program to convert WordStar files to ASCII
  Macros: @go_dos, @head
  *
            INCLUDE mylib.equ
            IF1
            INCLUDE mylib.mac
            ENDIF

code        SEGMENT
            ASSUME  CS:code,DS:code
            ORG     100h
start:
            @head   ' FILTERA,01.17.86'
nchar:
            MOV     AH,7            ;std input
            INT     21h             ;get character
            @ucase                  ;convert to upper
            MOV     DL,AL
            MOV     AH,6            ;direct i/o
            INT     21h             ;display it
            CMP     AL,eof          ;end of file?
            JNZ     nchar           ;done
            @go_dos                 ;return to DOS

code        ENDS
            END     start
```

Figure 8.10: *Filter to convert lowercase letters to uppercase.*

we use function 7, which, unlike regular console input, does not display the character on the screen.

Function 7 returns the character in the AL register. We convert it to uppercase if necessary by including our *@ucase* macro. Then, using function 6, we write the character to the standard output:

```
MOV    AH,6
INT    21h
```

This is normally the video screen. However, we will use redirection to send the character to the new disk file. Finally, we check the character for end-of-file. If that is what we find, we terminate with our *@go_dos* macro. Otherwise, we branch back to label *nchar* to read the next character.

Our program is extremely easy both to write and to change. For example, to convert the file *FILEL* to *FILEU,* give the command

```
FILTERU    <FILEL    >FILEU
```

Notice that we have used both redirection symbols: < and >. The first symbol indicates where the file is read from, the second where the results will go. Of course, if you omit the second parameter, the results appear on the video screen. If you omit both parameters, you can type lowercase characters at the keyboard and the equivalent uppercase characters will appear on the video screen. However, some of the control characters, such as the tab character and end-of-file, will appear as graphics characters on the screen. (This is a quick way to check out the program.)

We can easily change this program to perform other tasks. For example, to remove all line-feed characters, replace the *@ucase* macro with the lines

```
CMP    AL,lf
JE     nchar          ;skip
```

Then, when a line feed is encountered in the input, it is not sent to the output. Instead, we jump back the label *nchar* to get another character.

As another example, we can write the complementary program, to add a line feed after each carriage return. After the instructions

```
MOV    AL,6
INT    21h
```

add these statements:

```
CMP    AL,cr          ;carriage return?
JNZ    ceof           ;no
```

```
        MOV      AL,lf
        JMP      wchar
        ceof:
```

There is a potential problem with this technique. If the source and destination files are the same, as in this example:

```
FILTERU   <FILE   >FILE
```

the file named FILE will be lost. Because of the greatly increased time needed to filter a file, we will not generally use this method. We make an exception, however, when we want to expand the tab character.

We add another macro before starting the next program.

■ Macro @readch to Read One Keyboard Character and Display It

In the previous section we wrote a program to convert lowercase letters to uppercase using standard input and output. We used function 7 to get a character but not display it. Then, after inspecting the character and changing it if necessary, we wrote the character with function 6. The filtering actions we chose, changing lowercase to uppercase and removing or adding a line feed, were relatively simple. In our next example we write a filter to expand the tab character to the usual eight-character columns. This task can be complicated. Fortunately, function 1, which both reads and displays a keyboard character, also expands the tab character automatically.

Add macro *@readch,* shown in Figure 8.11, to your macro library.

■ Expanding the Tab Character with Redirection

Create a new file named TABS.ASM and type the program given in Figure 8.12. This version of our filter program uses function 1 both to read

```
@readch MACRO
;; read keyboard character into AL
;; and display on screen
        MOV      AH,1
        INT      21h
        ENDM
```

Figure 8.11: *Macro @readch to read a keyboard character and display it on the screen.*

and to write the character. The main feature of this function is that the tab character is automatically expanded. You may want to incorporate assembly-language programs into your technical articles, but the tab characters can cause trouble for word processors. You can convert the tab characters first using this program. Assemble this program and try it out. Give the command

TABS   <TABS.ASM   >TABS

Inspect the source and destination files with your editor and see that the tabs have been replaced by blanks. We write a fast filter program next.

FAST FILTERING OF FILES

In this section we are going to write programs that can filter disk files by reading both the source name and the target name from the user.

```
            PAGE    ,132
            TITLE   TABS

COMMENT *
   January 17, 1986
   expand tabs to eight columns
   Macros: @go_dos, @head, @readch
   *
            INCLUDE mylib.equ
            IF1
            INCLUDE mylib.mac
            ENDIF

code        SEGMENT
            ASSUME  CS:code,DS:code
            ORG     100h
start:
            @head   ' TABS,01.17.86 '
nchar:
            @readch                     ;get character
            CMP     AL,eof              ;end of file?
            JNZ     nchar               ;done
            @go_dos                     ;return to DOS

code        ENDS
            END     start
```

Figure 8.12: *Filter to expand tabs to eight columns.*

Alternatively, if only one file name is given, the new file will take the name of the original file.

We have written all the necessary routines that open, read, create, write, and close disk files. The new programs will be more complicated than the previous ones. However, they will draw heavily on our macros and subroutine libraries, thereby reducing the effort required to create them. Furthermore, the resulting programs will run very fast. This consideration is especially important for filtering large files, such as manuscripts for books and articles.

The MOVE program we wrote earlier in this chapter (Figure 8.5) read two file names from the user and used our library named GET_TWO.LIB. However, this program did not read or write disk files. On the other hand, our SAVESCREEN program (Figure 8.9) read only one file name from the user. However, it contains instructions for opening and reading an existing disk file and for creating, writing, and closing a new disk file. Since our next programs do all these activities, we will use the same routines in them. We begin with a variation of the program to convert lowercase letters to uppercase.

■ A Fast Program to Convert Lowercase Letters to Uppercase

Create a new file named UPPER.ASM and copy the program given in Figure 8.13. Many of the lines are the same as in the previous programs, so you can combine them to save some typing. Be sure to have the subroutine library named GET_ONE.LIB available. Let us go through the code.

We begin, as in the previous programs, by defining the block size to be 512×20 bytes. A block size this large will greatly increase the speed of our programs compared to filters that use redirection and byte-by-byte transfer, as in the previous section. We define the default console buffer at 80 hex and begin our code at 100 hex. We use the BP register as a flag to indicate whether the user enters one or two parameters. We set this register to zero at the beginning. We call routine *get_path* to get the first file name, the source file, and set the SI pointer to it. If the file name was not entered on the command line by the user, we ask the user to enter it now. We open the requested file and branch to our error routine if it cannot be found or opened. We reverse the sense of the branch, using an absolute branch, since the error routine is too far away for a conditional branch. If there is no error, we save the assigned handle in memory at location *hand1*.

```
                PAGE    ,132
                TITLE   UPPER, convert file to upper case

COMMENT *
  January 18, 1985
  Change file to upper case
  If only one file name given, the new file gets
  the original name and the original file is
  given the extension BAK
  Usage:
        UPPER
        UPPER fname
        UPPER fname fname2
        UPPER fname prn
        UPPER \pathname\fname fname2
  Macros: @create, @close, @d_read, @d_write,
          @delete, @go_dos, @head, @mak_buf,
          @open, @read_bf, @rename,
          @ucase, @write
  Libraries: mylib.equ, mylib.mac, get_one.lib
 *
        INCLUDE mylib.equ
        IF1
        INCLUDE mylib.mac
        ENDIF
blk_siz EQU     512*20

code    SEGMENT
        ASSUME  CS:code, DS:code
        ORG     80h
buf_cnt DB      ?                   ;buffer length
buffer  LABEL   BYTE                ;default buffer

        ORG     100h
strt:
        @head   ' UPPER, 01.18.86 '
        XOR     BP,BP               ;reset flag
;-------------------------------------------------
; get path name for first file
; SI points to beginning of name
; DI points to next path name
;-------------------------------------------------
        CALL    get_path
        @open   SI
        JNC     no_err
        JMP     error
no_err:
        MOV     [handl],BX          ;handle 1
;-------------------------------------------------
; check for second parameter
;-------------------------------------------------
```

Figure 8.13: *A fast filter to convert lowercase letters to uppercase.*

```
        OR      CX,CX           ;zero?
        JZ      no_par2         ;yes
;-------------------------------------------------
; get second parameter
;-------------------------------------------------
        CALL    scan_pa
        JC      no_par2         ;invalid parm
        INC     BP              ;set flag
        JMP     SHORT creat
no_par2:
        DEC     DI              ;name end
;-------------------------------------------------
; scan pathname for dot
;-------------------------------------------------
        MOV     CX,DI           ;name end+1
        SUB     CX,SI           ;count
        MOV     AL,period
        MOV     DI,SI
        REPNE   SCASB
        JNZ     no_dot
        DEC     DI              ;back to dot
;-------------------------------------------------
; DI points just beyond primary name
;-------------------------------------------------
no_dot:
        MOV     CX,DI
        SUB     CX,SI           ;name length
        PUSH    CX              ;save
        PUSH    SI              ;save
        MOV     [fpointr],SI    ;save
        MOV     DI,OFFSET temp
;-------------------------------------------------
; copy primary name to location temp
;-------------------------------------------------
        REP     MOVSB           ;copy name
        MOV     SI,OFFSET dollar ;.$$$0
        MOV     CX,5            ;characters
;-------------------------------------------------
; copy .$$$0 to end of temporary name
;-------------------------------------------------
        REP     MOVSB           ;copy extent
        POP     SI              ;original name
        POP     CX              ;count
        MOV     DI,OFFSET back
;-------------------------------------------------
; copy primary name to location back
;-------------------------------------------------
        REP     MOVSB           ;copy name
        MOV     SI,OFFSET bak   ;.BAK0
        MOV     CX,5            ;characters
```

Figure 8.13: *(continued)*

```
;------------------------------------------------
; copy .BAK0 to end of temporary name
;------------------------------------------------
        REP     MOVSB              ;copy extent
        MOV     SI,OFFSET temp     ;pointer
;------------------------------------------------
; create new file for temporary name
; SI points to beginning of name
;------------------------------------------------
creat:
        @create SI
        JC      error
        MOV     [hand2],BX         ;handle 2
;------------------------------------------------
; read source file
;------------------------------------------------
newbuff:
        MOV     CX,blk_siz         ;bytes to read
        @d_read [hand1],<OFFSET datbuff>
        JC      error
;------------------------------------------------
; AX has bytes read, done if zero
;------------------------------------------------
        OR      AX,AX              ;zero?
        JZ      exit               ;done
;------------------------------------------------
; save number of bytes
;------------------------------------------------
        PUSH    AX
        MOV     CX,AX              ;bytes
        MOV     SI,OFFSET datbuff  ;pointer
;------------------------------------------------
; filter each character
;------------------------------------------------
        CALL    do_char
        POP     CX                 ;bytes to write
;------------------------------------------------
; write CX bytes to new file
;------------------------------------------------
        @d_write [hand2],<OFFSET datbuff>
; check for error
        JC      error
        JMP     newbuff            ;next buffer
exit:
        @close  [hand2]
        JC      error
        OR      BP,BP              ;two names?
        JNZ     done               ;yes, quit
        MOV     DI,OFFSET back     ;new name
        @delete DI                 ;BAK file
```

Figure 8.13: *(continued)*

```
;-------------------------------------------------
; rename original file to BAK
;-------------------------------------------------
        MOV     DX,[fpointr]    ;old
        @rename
        JC      error
;-------------------------------------------------
; rename new file to original
;-------------------------------------------------
        MOV     DI,DX           ;new
        MOV     DX,OFFSET temp  ;old
        @rename
        JC      error
done:
        @go_dos                 ;to DOS
error:
        @write  'ERROR:'
        CMP     AX,2
        JNZ     e2
        @write  ' File not found'
e2:
        @go_dos
;-------------------------------------------------
; data area
;-------------------------------------------------
fpointr DW      ?               ;file pointer
hand2   DW      ?               ;second handle
bak     DB      '.BAK',0
dollar  DB      '.$$$',0
temp:   DB      40 DUP(?)
back:   DB      40 DUP(?)
;---------------------------------------------
; get_path, ; get_name, scan_pa
; and auxiliary input buffer next
;---------------------------------------------
        INCLUDE get_one.lib
;**********************************************
; Procedure to filter each byte of file
; Convert all lower-case characters to upper
; Terminate if end of file found
; Input:        SI = buffer pointer
;               CX = remaining characters
;**********************************************
do_char PROC
filter:
        MOV     AL,[SI]         ;next byte
        CMP     AL,eof          ;done?
        JZ      end_do          ;yes
        @ucase                  ;make upper
        MOV     [SI],AL
        INC     SI
        LOOP    filter
```

Figure 8.13: *(continued)*

```
end_do:
        RET
do_char ENDP
;******** End of procedure do_char ********
; buffer for disk data
datbuff LABEL    BYTE                ;data buffer

code    ENDS
        END      strt
```

Figure 8.13: *(continued)*

Using the instruction:

    OR   CX,CX

we check the CX register for zero to see if there are any characters left on the command line. If there are, we continue with the instructions. If only one parameter was entered, however, we assume that the user wants the new file to have the same name as the original. Therefore, we branch to the label *no_par2*. Our program distinguishes between two types of commands. In one case, the user enters the command

    UPPER FILE1 FILE2

and our program reads FILE1, filters the characters, and then writes the result to FILE2. But we frequently want to filter a file in a transparent manner, so that the new file will have the name of the old file. Then the command will be

    UPPER FILE1

with just one parameter. This time, our program will filter the file named FILE1 and place the results in the temporary file named FILE1.$$$. After successful completion of the filtering operation, the program will change the name of the original file to FILE1.BAK and then change the name of the temporary file to FILE1, so that we do not destroy the original file.

If the CX register indicates that a second parameter has been entered, we increment the BP flag, call procedure *scan_pa* to read the second file name, and branch to label *creat* to create the new file. But if only one parameter was entered, we branch to label *no_par2*. Our routine must now create two additional file names. Both will have the same primary name as the one entered by the user, but the extensions will be different. The new file will temporarily have the extension $$$. Then the extension of the original file is changed to BAK. Finally, the temporary extension of the new file is changed to the original name. For example, if the name FILE1.TXT was entered, we must create the names FILE1.$$$ and FILE1.BAK.

The first step is to decrement DI so that it points to the zero following the file name given by the user. We need to scan this name to find the location of the dot separating the first part of the name from the extension. The DI register points to the end of the name, and the SI pointer references the beginning. Therefore, the difference between them gives the number of characters in the name. We move the value in DI to the CX register and subtract the value in SI. We place in the AL register the dot we are scanning for, set the DI register to the beginning of the name, and execute the repeating string-scan instruction:

    REP   SCASB

On return from this instruction, the flag will be reset if no dot appears in the file name. This will be the case if the name has no extension. In that case, the DI register points just past the end of the name. We then branch to the label *no_dot*. Alternatively, if the zero flag is set, the dot has been found, and the DI register points to the first character past the dot. We therefore decrement DI so that it points to the dot. The SI register still points to the beginning of the name, and the DI register points to the end of the primary name. We place the difference between them, the length of the first name, into the CX register. The contents of CX and SI are saved on the stack for future use. We also save the contents of SI, in memory location *fpointr*. We are now ready to move the name to two other places.

We set the DI register to location *temp* and execute the string-move instruction:

    REP   MOVSB

This places a copy of the file name at label *temp*. We point the SI register to the label *dollar,* where we have stored the five characters—a period, three dollar signs, and a zero. We reset the CX register to 5 and execute the string-move instruction a second time. We have now constructed a file name such as

    FILE1.$$$0

We restore the SI and CX registers by popping the contents off the stack. Then we use the string-move routines two more times to generate the name:

FILE 1 .BAK

at location *bak*. We point the SI register to the beginning of the tempo-rary name at location *temp* and arrive at label *creat*. This is where we branched previously when a second parameter was entered. In that case, the SI register is pointing to the second name.

We create a new file with our *@create* macro, referencing either the second parameter if one was entered or our temporary parameter if only one parameter was entered. If there is no error, we save the assigned handle in location *hand2*. We now alternately read a block of data from the source file, filter the data, and then write it to the target file. We set the CX register to the block size and use our *@d_read* macro to read a block of data into the buffer at the end of our program. The AX register has the number of characters that were read. We check the value with the OR instruction to see if the value is zero. If so, we are done. Other-wise, we save the number on the stack with a PUSH statement, then move the number into the CX register, point the SI register to the buffer, and call the filter subroutine *do_char*. This routine is similar to the one we used in the previous chapter, except that we do not display the characters on the video screen. Furthermore, by changing only this filter routine, we can perform many different filtering operations. Let us move down to the filter routine *do_char*.

Our filter routine moves each character from the buffer referenced by the SI register into the AL register. We first check for the end-of-file char-acter and branch to the *end_do* label at the end of the routine if it is found. Otherwise, we perform the filtering operation—conversion to uppercase in this example—and return the character to the buffer. We loop according to the count in the CX register, incrementing the SI pointer to the buffer each time. When the CX register has been decre-mented to zero, all the characters in the buffer have been processed, and so we return to the main program. We pop the number of characters in the buffer into the CX register and write the characters to the new disk file using the code set up with our *@d_write* macro. The file handle is found at location *hand2*.

We alternatively read, filter, and write data until we reach the end of the file. Using the OR instruction, we check to see if the BP register is zero, indicating that only one file name was entered. If not, we terminate with a branch to the label *done*. On the other hand, if only one parameter was entered, the filtered file has the extension $$$. Therefore, we rename the extension of the original file, changing it to BAK (after deleting a possible previous file with this name). Then we rename the temporary $$$ file with the original name. This triple-naming technique ensures the integrity of the data. If for some reason we were unable to create the new file, the program will terminate with the original file intact.

This is a fairly long program, but by making only a few changes to our final *do_char* subroutine, we can create many different filters. Assemble our new program and run it. Make a working file from the assembly-language program. For example, give the command

```
COPY UPPER.ASM TEST.TXT
```

and then give the command

```
UPPER    TEST.TXT CON
```

The output should appear on the video screen (CON) in uppercase letters. Try the other possibilities, such as this:

```
UPPER    TEST.TXT TEST2
```

Then look at the new file with the TYPE command and see that the letters are uppercase. Finally, give only one parameter:

```
UPPER    TEST.TXT
```

Give the DIR command to see that two files exist—TEST.TXT and TEST-.BAK. Look at each with the TYPE command. The file TEST.TXT should have all the letters in uppercase. Let us create additional filters.

■ Converting a WordStar File to ASCII, Fast Version

In the previous chapter we wrote the program TYPEW to convert a WordStar file to ASCII and display the results on the video screen. We also used the redirection feature of DOS to place the result in a new disk file. But we learned that this is a slow process because the characters are handled one at time rather than in blocks. Our new version is very fast because we read up to 10,240 characters at a time. Furthermore, we only have to give a single file name to our program. For example, if we name our program TOASCII, we can recover an assembly-language or BASIC file named UPPER.ASM with the command

```
TOASCII   UPPER.ASM
```

Of course, the original file will be found under the name UPPER.BAK.

We can easily create our new filter program by making a few changes to the UPPER program. Copy UPPER.ASM and give the new program the name TOASCII.ASM. Change all occurrences of the name UPPER to TOASCII near the beginning and change the description near the beginning to describe the program. Replace the final procedure, *do_char,* with the version given in Figure 8.14. Assemble the program and try it out. Don't worry if you do not have a WordStar file. We will create one at the end of this section.

■ Converting an ASCII File to WordStar Format

As we saw previously, WordStar text files have "soft" carriage returns, carriage returns with the high bit set, at the end of each line within a paragraph. A regular carriage return (a "hard" return) appears at the end of the last line of a paragraph. However, if you create a document with another editor, there will be a a hard carriage return at the end of each line. If you want to use WordStar to edit a file created with another word processor, you must convert each hard carriage return within a paragraph to a soft return if you want to reform a paragraph. Furthermore, some spelling programs, such as SPELLIX, cannot work with a WordStar file. Therefore, if

```
;**********************************************
; Procedure to filter each byte of file
; Convert WordStar file to ASCII format
; Terminate if end of file found
; Input:        SI = buffer pointer
;               CX = remaining characters
;**********************************************
do_char PROC

filter:
        MOV     AL,[SI]             ;next byte
        CMP     AL,eof              ;file end?
        JZ      end_do
        AND     AL,7Fh              ;reset parity
        MOV     [SI],AL             ;change char
        INC     SI                  ;pointer
        LOOP    filter
end_do:
        RET
do_char ENDP
;******** End of procedure do_char ********
```

Figure 8.14: *Procedure do_char to convert WordStar files to ASCII.*

you want to check the spelling with such a program, you must convert the WordStar file to ASCII. Then, after checking the document, you must convert it back to WordStar format. The program we wrote in the previous section can create the ASCII file. We will now write the complementary program, to convert an ASCII file to WordStar format.

Make a copy of the previous program, giving the name TOWS.ASM (to WordStar) to the new file. Change the beginning comments to reflect the new program. Change the final procedure to match the listing shown in Figure 8.15. Most of the program is the same as TOASCII. However, procedure *do_char* is different. Therefore, let us look at it.

As in the previous programs, we use the SI register to move each character from the buffer into the AL register. However, we are also going to check two other characters—the previous one and the character two

```
;***********************************************
; Procedure to filter each byte of file
; Convert file to WordStar format
; Terminate if end of file found
; Input:        SI = buffer pointer
;               CX = remaining characters
;***********************************************
do_char PROC
        XOR     DX,DX           ;zero previous
filter:
        MOV     AL,[SI]         ;next byte
        CMP     AL,eof          ;file end?
        JE      end_do          ;yes, done
        CMP     AL,cr           ;carriage return
        JNZ     filt2           ;no change
        CMP     DL,lf           ;previous char
        JE      filt2           ;skip
        MOV     DH,[SI+2]       ;look ahead
        CMP     DH,blank        ;new paragraph?
        JE      filt2           ;yes, skip
        CMP     DH,cr           ;blank line?
        JE      filt2           ;yes, skip
        OR      AL,80h          ;set bit 7
        MOV     [SI],AL         ;change char
filt2:
        MOV     DL,AL           ;save char
        INC     SI              ;pointer
        LOOP    filter
end_do:
        RET
do_char ENDP
;******** End of procedure do_char ********
```

Figure 8.15: *Procedure do_char to convert ASCII files to WordStar format.*

ahead of the current one. We begin by setting the DX register to zero with the XOR command. After we get going, the DL register will contain the previous character and the DH register will contain the character two ahead of the present character.

We begin by comparing each character to the end-of-file marker and return to the calling routine if there is a match. Otherwise we check to see if the current character is a carriage return. If not, we skip on to the next character. When we find a carriage return, we check to see if the previous character (in the DL register) was a line-feed character. If so, we again skip on to the next character. Finally, we check to see if the next line is indented, indicating a new paragraph. If so, we also skip to the next character. On the other hand, if we find a carriage return within a paragraph, we convert it to a WordStar soft return by performing a logical OR with the value 80 hex. This operation sets the high-order bit. We conclude each pass by moving the current character from the AL register into the DL register.

Assemble the new program and try it out. If you do not use WordStar, make a test file from one of your regular ASCII text files that has definite paragraphs. Do not use an assembly-language file. Name the file TESTA-.TXT (test ASCII). If you use WordStar, make a small test file with the name TESTW.TXT (test WordStar). Convert it to ASCII with the previous program, giving the new version the name TESTA.TXT. Use this command:

```
TOASCII TESTW.TXT TESTA.TXT
```

Look at both files with the TYPE command. Convert the ASCII version to WordStar and display the results on the screen with the command

```
TOWS   TESTA.TXT CON
```

Then filter the file with a single parameter. Give the command

```
TOWS   TESTA.TXT
```

Look at both the new WordStar file, TESTA.TXT, and the previous version, TESTA.BAK, with the TYPE command. The WordStar version will be skewed over the screen with few carriage returns, while the ASCII version will look correct. We consider encryption next.

Encoding a File with XOR

By making a few changes to the previous program, we can turn it into a program for encoding, or encrypting, text. If your computer is used by others or is located in a public place, you may need to ensure the privacy of your disk files. Anyone can read your ASCII files by giving the TYPE command. If a file is coded, however, it cannot be read directly. It must first be decoded into its original form.

Make a copy of the previous program, using the name CRYPT.ASM for the new copy. As before, we need to change procedure *do_char* and the comments at the beginning of the program. But since we also need to make small changes throughout the program, the complete program is presented in Figure 8.16. Of course you still need the macro and equate libraries and the subroutine file GET_ONE.LIB.

Our new program is similar to the previous one. We are prepared to read one or two parameters that were entered on the command line. Furthermore, if no parameter is entered on the command line, we ask the user for one. However, if only one parameter is given, we do not ask for a second one. We make a backup file of the original and give the original name to the new file. We also ask the user to enter one character, a letter or a number, as a coding key. Finally, if only one file name was entered, we ask the user for permission to delete the original version after we have created the new file. We encrypt each character by performing an exclusive-OR operation with the key. The interesting feature of this technique is that an encoded file is returned to its normal form simply by running our coding program again using the same key. Let us see how that works.

Assemble the program so that you can try it out. Encrypt the assembly-language source program with the command

CRYPT   CRYPT.ASM CODED

Press the letter *a* when asked to enter the key character. Let us look at the result. If you try to read the coded file using the TYPE command, the screen will be filled with meaningless characters. However, we can study the coded version with DEBUG. Give the command

DEBUG CODED

and display the beginning of the file with the D command. The result will look like Figure 8.17. The ASCII representation on the right side does not show any information we can use. However, the uppercase letter A appears frequently, because the exclusive-OR operation between a letter and a blank changes the case of the letter. Therefore, it would be easy to guess the key letter by examining the coded file. If you try to decode this

```
            PAGE    ,132
            TITLE   CRYPT, convert file to upper case

COMMENT *
  January 18, 1985
  Crypt and decrypt a file with XOR
  Enter a single character as the key
  If only one file name given, the new file gets
  the original name and the original file is
  given the extension BAK
  Usage:
        CRYPT
        CRYPT fname
        CRYPT fname fname2
        CRYPT fname prn
        CRYPT \pathname\fname fname2
  Macros: @create, @close, @d_read, @d_write,
          @delete, @go_dos, @head, @mak_buf,
          @open, @read_bf, @readch,
          @rename, @ucase, @write
  Libraries: mylib.equ, mylib.mac, get_one.lib
 *
            INCLUDE mylib.equ
            IF1
            INCLUDE mylib.mac
            ENDIF
blk_siz EQU     512*20

code    SEGMENT
            ASSUME  CS:code, DS:code
            ORG     80h
buf_cnt DB      ?                   ;buffer length
buffer  LABEL   BYTE                ;default buffer

            ORG     100h
strt:
            @head   ' CRYPT, 01.18.86 '
            XOR     BP,BP           ;reset flag
;------------------------------------------------
; get path name for first file
; SI points to beginning of name
; DI points to next path name
;------------------------------------------------
            CALL    get_path
            @open   SI
            JNC     no_err
            JMP     error
no_err:
            MOV     [handl],BX      ;handle 1
;------------------------------------------------
; check for second parameter
;------------------------------------------------
```

Figure 8.16: *Program CRYPT.ASM to encrypt a disk file with the XOR operation.*

```
            OR          CX,CX              ;zero?
            JZ          no_par2            ;yes
;------------------------------------------------
; get second parameter
;------------------------------------------------
            CALL        scan_pa
            JC          no_par2            ;invalid parm
            INC         BP                 ;set flag
            JMP         SHORT creat
no_par2:
            DEC         DI                 ;name end
;------------------------------------------------
; scan pathname for dot
;------------------------------------------------
            MOV         CX,DI              ;name end+1
            SUB         CX,SI              ;count
            MOV         AL,period
            MOV         DI,SI
            REPNE       SCASB
            JNZ         no_dot
            DEC         DI                 ;back to dot
;------------------------------------------------
; DI points just beyond primary name
;------------------------------------------------
no_dot:
            MOV         CX,DI
            SUB         CX,SI              ;name length
            PUSH        CX                 ;save
            PUSH        SI                 ;save
            MOV         [fpointr],SI       ;save
            MOV         DI,OFFSET temp
;------------------------------------------------
; copy primary name to location temp
;------------------------------------------------
            REP         MOVSB              ;copy name
            MOV         SI,OFFSET dollar ;.$$$0
            MOV         CX,5               ;characters
;------------------------------------------------
; copy .$$$0 to end of temporary name
;------------------------------------------------
            REP         MOVSB              ;copy extent
            POP         SI                 ;original name
            POP         CX                 ;count
            MOV         DI,OFFSET back
;------------------------------------------------
; copy primary name to location back
;------------------------------------------------
            REP         MOVSB              ;copy name
            MOV         SI,OFFSET bak    ;.BAK0
            MOV         CX,5               ;characters
```

Figure 8.16: *(continued)*

```
;------------------------------------------------
; copy .BAK0 to end of temporary name
;------------------------------------------------
        REP     MOVSB           ;copy extent
        MOV     SI,OFFSET temp  ;pointer
;------------------------------------------------
; create new file for temporary name
; SI points to beginning of name
;------------------------------------------------
creat:
        @create SI
        JC      jerror
        MOV     [hand2],BX      ;handle 2
;------------------------------------------------
; read encrypting key
;------------------------------------------------
        @write  'Input one character for key: '
        @readch                 ;input key
        MOV     DL,AL           ;save in DL
;------------------------------------------------
; read source file
;------------------------------------------------
newbuff:
        MOV     CX,blk_siz      ;bytes to read
        @d_read [handl],<OFFSET datbuff>
        JNC     toor
jerror:
        JMP     error
;------------------------------------------------
; AX has bytes read, done if zero
;------------------------------------------------
toor:
        OR      AX,AX           ;zero?
        JZ      exit            ;done
;------------------------------------------------
; save number of bytes
;------------------------------------------------
        PUSH    AX
        MOV     CX,AX           ;bytes
        MOV     SI,OFFSET datbuff ;pointer
;------------------------------------------------
; filter each character
;------------------------------------------------
        CALL    do_char
        POP     CX              ;bytes to write
;------------------------------------------------
; write CX bytes to new file
;------------------------------------------------
        @d_write [hand2],<OFFSET datbuff>
; check for error
        JC      error
        JMP     newbuff         ;next buffer
```

Figure 8.16: *(continued)*

```
exit:
        @close  [hand2]
        JC      error
        OR      BP,BP           ;two names?
        JNZ     done            ;yes, quit
        MOV     DI,OFFSET back  ;new name
        @delete DI              ;BAK file
;-------------------------------------------------
; rename original file to BAK
;-------------------------------------------------
        MOV     DX,[fpointr]    ;old
        @rename
        JC      error
;-------------------------------------------------
; rename new file to original
;-------------------------------------------------
        MOV     DI,DX           ;new
        MOV     DX,OFFSET temp  ;old
        @rename
        JC      error
        @write  <cr,lf,'Delete Original? '>
        @readch
        @ucase
        CMP     AL,'Y'
        JNZ     done
        @delete <OFFSET back>
done:
        @go_dos                 ;to DOS
error:
        @write  'ERROR:'
        CMP     AX,2
        JNZ     e2
        @write  ' File not found'
e2:
        @go_dos
;-------------------------------------------------
; data area
;-------------------------------------------------
fpointr DW      ?               ;file pointer
hand2   DW      ?               ;second handle
bak     DB      '.BAK',0
dollar  DB      '.$$$',0
temp:   DB      40 DUP(?)
back:   DB      40 DUP(?)
;-------------------------------------------------
; get_path, ; get_name, scan_pa
; and auxiliary input buffer next
;-------------------------------------------------
        INCLUDE get_one.lib
```

Figure 8.16: *(continued)*

```
;***********************************************
; Procedure to filter each byte of file
; Encrypt file with XOR
; Terminate if end of file found
; Input:         SI = buffer pointer
;                CX = remaining characters
;***********************************************
do_char PROC
filter:
        MOV     AL,[SI]             ;next byte
        CMP     AL,eof              ;done?
        JZ      end_do              ;yes
        XOR     AL,DL               ;key
        MOV     [SI],AL
        INC     SI
        LOOP    filter
end_do:
        RET
do_char ENDP
;********* End of procedure do_char *********
; buffer for disk data
datbuff LABEL   BYTE                ;data buffer

code    ENDS
        END     strt
```

Figure 8.16: *(continued)*

file using the uppercase letter A as the key, most of the information will be readable.

Return the encoded file to its original form by running CRYPT exactly the same way as before, using the same key. The DEBUG display should look like Figure 8.18. Run the program a third time and press the 2 key above the letter W for the encryption key. Now the DEBUG display should look like Figure 8.19. This time, the number 8 appears frequently, because the exclusive-OR between the line feed and the ASCII 2 gives ASCII 8. However, if you try to decode the file with the key of 8, it will still be meaningless. Let us go through the code.

The instructions are the same as the previous programs up to the label *newbuff*. Change the statement just before this label from

    JC   error

to

    JC   jerror

The new instructions we add place the error routine out of reach for a conditional jump. Therefore, we branch to a stepping-stone label. The following new code asks for the key character from the user. The response is read using DOS function I and stored in the DL register. We saw previously that this function displays the character on the video screen after it has been entered at the keyboard. You might want to use function 8 instead, so that the key character does not show on the video screen. But then the user will have to take care to press the desired key.

We add a comment and four new lines of code just before *newbuff*. The

```
0100 68 31 20 26 24 68 4D 50-52 53 6C 6B 68 35 28 35    hl &$hMPRSlkh5(5
0110 2D 24 68 22 33 38 31 35-4D 41 02 0E 0F 17 04 13    -$h"3815MA......
0120 15 41 07 08 0D 04 41 15-0E 41 14 11 11 04 13 41    .A...A..A.....A
0130 02 00 12 04 6C 6B 6C 6B-22 2E 2C 2C 24 2F 35 41    ....lklk".,,$/5A
0140 4B 6C 6B 41 41 2B 00 0F-14 00 13 18 41 50 59 4D    KlkAA+......APYM
0150 41 50 58 59 54 6C 6B 41-41 22 13 18 11 15 41 00    APXYTlkAA"....A.
0160 0F 05 41 05 04 02 13 18-11 15 41 00 41 07 08 0D    ..A........A.A...
0170 04 41 16 08 15 09 41 39-2E 33 6C 6B 41 41 24 0F    .A....A9.31kAA$.
```

Figure 8.17: *Display of file encoded with the letter a.*

```
0100 09 50 41 47 45 09 2C 31-33 32 0D 0A 09 54 49 54    .PAGE.,132...TIT
0110 4C 45 09 43 52 59 50 54-2C 20 63 6F 6E 76 65 72    LE.CRYPT, conver
0120 74 20 66 69 6C 65 20 74-6F 20 75 70 70 65 72 20    t file to upper
0130 63 61 73 65 0D 0A 0D 0A-43 4F 4D 4D 45 4E 54 20    case....COMMENT
0140 2A 0D 0A 20 20 4A 61 6E-75 61 72 79 20 31 38 2C    *.. January 18,
0150 20 31 39 38 35 0D 0A 20-20 43 72 79 70 74 20 61    1985.. Crypt a
0160 6E 64 20 64 65 63 72 79-70 74 20 61 20 66 69 6C    nd decrypt a fil
0170 65 20 77 69 74 68 20 58-4F 52 0D 0A 20 20 45 6E    e with XOR..  En
```

Figure 8.18: *Display of decoded file.*

```
0100 3B 62 73 75 77 3B 1E 03-01 00 3F 38 3B 66 7B 66    ;bsuw;....?8;f{f
0110 7E 77 3B 71 60 6B 62 66-1E 12 51 5D 5C 44 57 40    ~w;q`kbf..Q]\DW@
0120 46 12 54 5B 5E 57 12 46-5D 12 47 42 42 57 40 12    F.T[^W.F].GBBW@.
0130 51 53 41 57 3F 38 3F 38-71 7D 7F 7F 77 7C 66 12    QSAW?8?8q}..w|f.
0140 18 3F 38 12 12 78 53 5C-47 53 40 4B 12 03 0A 1E    .?8..xS\GS@K....
0150 12 03 0B 0A 07 3F 38 12-12 71 40 4B 42 46 12 53    .....?8..q@KBF.S
0160 5C 56 12 56 57 51 40 4B-42 46 12 53 12 54 5B 5E    \V.VWQ@KBF.S.T[^
0170 57 12 45 5B 46 5A 12 6A-7D 60 3F 38 12 12 77 5C    W.E[FZ.j}`?8..w\
```

Figure 8.19: *Display of file encoded with the character 2.*

next occurrence of:

```
JC   error
```

is also changed to this:

```
        JNC toor
jerror:
        JMP error
toor:
```

Move down to label *done* and insert more new lines. This new section asks the user for permission to delete the original file if only one file name was entered. You might want to add this feature to the previous programs.

Finally, we change procedure *do_char*. Each character is copied from the buffer referenced by the SI register to the AL register. We first check for end-of-file, then we perform an exclusive-OR operation with the current character and the key in register DL. The converted character is returned to the buffer, and the SI pointer is incremented.

The coding technique is not very sophisticated, but it will prevent casual access to your files. Furthermore, the coding program is easy to use. The same operation is used for encoding and for decoding, and the program will readily delete the original file for you. Let us consider a different type of filter.

Removing or Deleting Characters

The filter programs in the previous examples changed the characters in our file, but they did not alter the size of the file. Sometimes, however, we may need to delete or insert characters as we filter the file. Let us consider two cases.

Removing the Line-Feed Character

ASCII and WordStar text files written on the IBM PC have both a carriage return and a line feed at the end of each line, and so it is possible to inspect such files with the DOS TYPE command. When transmitting a file over the telephone to a large computer, however, we must remove all line feeds. The large computer automatically adds a line feed after each carriage return. If you send a line-feed character after each carriage return, there will be two line feeds at the end of each line. This will cause your text to be displayed with double spacing. Therefore, you should remove the line-feed characters from a file before sending it over the telephone. Earlier in this chapter we wrote such a filter using the DOS redirection feature. Converting our present program to perform this task is more complicated, but the new version will run faster.

We can keep the file the same size if we replace each line feed with another character, say a blank. But it would be better simply to reduce the size of the file. One method is to establish two buffers and two pointers. The original file is read into the source buffer using the SI pointer. Then, after filtering each character, we move it to the destination buffer using the DI pointer. Similarly, we can write a complementary filter to add a line-feed character after each carriage return. You will need such a program if you inadvertently remove the line feeds from the wrong program. Also, if you receive a program over the phone line that has been processed to remove line feeds, you will have to restore them. The conversion of our filter program to the new form is left as an exercise for the reader.

SUMMARY

In this chapter we learned how to rename disk files, create new disk files, and delete disk files. We wrote several new programs: one moves a disk file from one directory to another; a second creates a disk file from the information displayed on either the monochrome or the graphics screen. Then we developed filters to expand the tab character, to raise lowercase letters to uppercase, and to convert WordStar files to ASCII and back again. Finally, we wrote a program to encrypt our files so that they cannot easily be read by others.

In the next chapter we consider programs for special applications.

The beginning of your macro library should now look like this:

```
; Macros in this library
; @close          MACRO   handle?
; @create         MACRO   pointr?            ;disk file
; @d_char         MACRO   par?              ;display character
; @d_read         MACRO   handle?,pointr?
; @d_write        MACRO   handle?,pointr?
; @delete         MACRO   pointr?
```

```
; @dos_ver       MACRO                          ;get version
; @get_vec       MACRO  ?vec                    ;interrupt vector
; @go_dos        MACRO                          ;return to DOS by 21h
; @head          MACRO  num?                    ;header information
; @mak_buf       MACRO  name?, len?
; @open          MACRO  pointr?                 ;open disk file
; @read_bf       MACRO  loc?                    ;read input buffer
; @readch        MACRO                          ;read/display character
; @rename        MACRO                          ;DX to DI
; @screen_mode   MACRO                          ;find screen type
; @set_vec       MACRO  ?vec                    ;change interr vector
; @ucase         MACRO                          ;change AL to uppercase
; @write         MACRO  text?                   ;write text on screen
; @write_r       MACRO  addr?                   ;display text at addr?
```

9

Miscellaneous Programs

INTRODUCTION

In the previous chapters we developed a set of macros, and we wrote several useful programs that made the IBM PCs easier to use. We will write two more macros and six additional programs in this final chapter. One program installs graphics characters for an Epson printer, a second program interchanges keyboard keys, and a third program switches video screens and turns color on or off. The fourth program changes the printer mode, the fifth program displays hexadecimal addresses in a readable fashion, and the final program increases the usable memory size to 704K bytes. We begin with a new macro.

MACRO @lprint TO SEND CHARACTERS TO THE PRINTER

We previously wrote macro *@write* to send a string of characters to the video screen with function 9 of interrupt 21 hex. Since there is no equivalent function for the printer, our macro must send characters one at time, using function 5. Add macro *@lprint,* given in Figure 9.1, to your macro library. When we use this macro, we add the string we want to print as a parameter. The macro begins by saving four working registers on the stack. The code then branches over the string of characters to be printed. The DI register points to the first character, the CX register has the number of characters in the string, and the AH register is loaded with function number 5. In a small loop, each character referenced by the DI register is moved from memory to the DL register and interrupt 21 hex is executed. As in the *@print* macro, the parameter may contain literal text surrounded by apostrophes, constants, and symbols. When elements of the parameter are separated by commas, we must surround the parameter with a pair of angle brackets. This macro is more suitable for long strings than short ones. For our next example, in which we only need to send three characters to the printer, it would be shorter to load each character in turn into DL and execute interrupt 21 hex. Nevertheless, the macro

        @lprint <esc,'m',4>

clearly shows the three characters that are sent to the printer.
    Now we write our graphics program.

CHANGING IBM GRAPHICS TO EPSON GRAPHICS

We have seen that the standard ASCII character set contains 128 characters and is implemented with seven of the eight bits of each byte. IBM PC defines the other 128 characters as Greek letters, mathematical symbols, and graphics characters needed to draw boxes. If you attach an IBM PC graphics printer to an IBM PC, graphics characters that are displayed on the video screen will appear at the printer when the Shift-PrtSc combination is pressed.

Epson printers can be connected to an IBM PC and they render the first 128 ASCII characters correctly. Unfortunately, because Epson uses a different "extended" character set, boxes on the video screen are printed as italic letters rather than as graphics symbols. While the Epson printer can print boxes and other graphics symbols, these symbols are accessed through different codes than on the IBM. Therefore, there must first be a translation from the codes for the IBM graphics symbols to the corresponding Epson codes. Our next program performs this translation.

```
@lprint MACRO    text?
        LOCAL    around,mesg,next
;; Macro to send text to printer
;; Usage:        @lprint  <esc,'m',3>

        PUSH     AX
        PUSH     CX
        PUSH     DX
        PUSH     DI
        JMP      SHORT around

mesg    DB       text?
around:                            ;;write
        MOV      DI,OFFSET mesg
        MOV      CX,around-mesg    ;;length
        MOV      AH,5              ;;printer
next:
        MOV      DL,[DI]           ;;get byte
        INT      21h
        INC      DI
        LOOP     next
        POP      DI
        POP      DX
        POP      CX
        POP      AX
        ENDM
```

Figure 9.1: *Macro @lprint to send a string of characters to the printer.*

Characters are sent to the printer through interrupt 17 hex. Therefore, if we intercept this interrupt vector, we can inspect all characters that are sent to the printer. Then, whenever we find an IBM box character, we can change it to the corresponding Epson character. Unfortunately, the conversion is not exact. The IBM character set can create both single-line and double-line boxes, while the Epson set only has single-line characters. Nevertheless, boxes on the video screen can now be printed as boxes.

The program shown in Figure 9.2 consists of two parts, an installation program and a memory-resident interrupt handler. The installation program establishes the interrupt handler in memory, saves the original vector for interrupt 17, changes interrupt 17 so that it branches into our program, turns on the Epson graphics character set, and then directs DOS to raise the starting address for future programs, so that the handler will remain resident and not be overwritten.

The new routine intercepts, via interrupt 17 hex, characters sent to the printer by any means—Shift-PrtSc, Ctrl-PrtSc, or output to PRN. If an IBM box character is found, the routine substitutes the corresponding Epson character and passes it along to the BIOS routine. Otherwise, the original character is transmitted. Thus, this program acts as a filter. The handler branches to the original interrupt vector after analyzing each character, and so our interrupt handler remains resident in memory until the computer is turned off or reset. We wrote a resident program called FILL in Chapter 6. However, that program did not change the interrupt vectors; it simply reduced the memory size.

Because more than one resident program may need to intercept a particular interrupt vector, we should be careful how we change an interrupt vector. For example, suppose the original vector points to ROM BIOS location F000:E987 hex and a resident handler intercepts the vector and redirects control to its own routine at 6000:102. When the resident program has completed its task, it will branch to the original ROM BIOS address at F000:E987 hex. If a second resident handler is installed at another address, say 7000:102 hex, it must patch the interrupt vector to point to itself also. That is, the new routine is inserted into the chain of events. When control leaves the second handler, however, a branch must be made to the previous interrupt address, at 6000:102, not to the original vector at F000:E987 hex. If the second resident program does not save the previous value of the interrupt vector, but simply branches to the original ROM BIOS interrupt address, the first resident program will no longer operate. Its interrupt address is bypassed, and thus is never called. Unfortunately, many commercial programs incorrectly change the interrupt vectors in this way.

When there is printer output, our PRINTGR program checks the characters. It looks for character codes that produce both single-lined and

```
              PAGE    ,132
              TITLE   PRINTGR, install graphics

COMMENT *
  January 21, 1986
  Program to print graphics on non-IBM printers
  using patch to INT 17h
  Use lookup table
  Macros: @get_vec, @lprint, @set_vec, @write
  INT 27h
 *
              INCLUDE mylib.equ        ;equates
              IF1
              INCLUDE mylib.mac        ;macro library
              ENDIF

; box characters (single lines)
bulc    EQU     218                    ;upper left corner
burc    EQU     191                    ;upper right corner
bllc    EQU     192                    ;lower left corner
blrc    EQU     217                    ;lower right corner
bmt     EQU     194                    ;middle top
bmb     EQU     193                    ;middle bottom
bml     EQU     195                    ;middle left
bmr     EQU     180                    ;middle right
vert    EQU     179                    ;vertical
horiz   EQU     196                    ;horizontal
cross   EQU     197                    ;cross
; box characters (double lines)
dulc    EQU     201                    ;upper left corner
durc    EQU     187                    ;upper right corner
dllc    EQU     200                    ;lower left corner
dlrc    EQU     188                    ;lower right corner
dmt     EQU     203                    ;middle top
dmb     EQU     202                    ;middle bottom
dml     EQU     204                    ;middle left
dmr     EQU     185                    ;middle right
dvert   EQU     186                    ;vertical
dhoriz  EQU     205                    ;horizontal
dcross  EQU     206                    ;cross
; Epson characters
eulc    EQU     87h                    ;upper left corner
eurc    EQU     88h                    ;upper right corner
ellc    EQU     89h                    ;lower left corner
elrc    EQU     8Ah                    ;lower right corner
emt     EQU     82h                    ;middle top
emb     EQU     81h                    ;middle bottom
eml     EQU     84h                    ;middle left
emr     EQU     83h                    ;middle right
evert   EQU     86h                    ;vertical
ehoriz  EQU     85h                    ;Epson horizontal
```

Figure 9.2: *Program to change IBM box characters to the corresponding Epson characters.*

```
;------------------------------------------------
; begin resident code and installation routine
;------------------------------------------------
code    SEGMENT
        ASSUME  CS:code, DS:code, ES:code
        ORG     100h

;------------------------------------------------
; resident code begins here
;------------------------------------------------
strt:   JMP     SHORT over_data
        DB      ' PRINTGR,I2.22.85 '
o_vec   LABEL   WORD
org_vec DD      0

; Table of original scan codes
tabl    DB      bulc,burc,bllc,blrc
        DB      bmt,bmb,bml,bmr
        DB      vert,horiz,cross
; double lines
        DB      dulc,durc,dllc,dlrc
        DB      dmt,dmb,dml,dmr
        DB      dvert,dhoriz,dcross
tabl    EQU     $-tabl          ;table length

; Table of new (Epson) scan codes
tab2    DB      eulc,eurc,ellc,elrc
        DB      emt,emb,eml,emr
        DB      evert,ehoriz,'+'
        DB      eulc,eurc,ellc,elrc
        DB      emt,emb,eml,emr
        DB      evert,ehoriz,'+'
;------------------------------------------------
; begin patch code
;------------------------------------------------
        ASSUME  DS:NOTHING      ;use CS not DS
new:
; check for printer output (AH = 0)
        OR      AH,AH           ;print?
        JNZ     cont2           ;no
; check for non-ASCII character
        CMP     AL,80h
        JB      cont2           ;no
; save register contents
        STI                     ;turn on interr
        PUSH    ES
        PUSH    DI
        PUSH    CX
; check for a box character
        MOV     CX,CS
        MOV     ES,CX           ;establish ES
        MOV     DI,OFFSET tabl  ;original
```

Figure 9.2: *(continued)*

```
            MOV     CX,tabl         ;table length
            REPNE   SCASB           ;search tabl
            JNE     cont            ;no match
            ADD     DI,tabl-1       ;point to tab2
            MOV     AL,CS:[DI]      ;new scan code
cont:
            POP     CX
            POP     DI
            POP     ES
cont2:
            JMP     [org_vec]       ;continue
;------------------------------------------------------------
; end of resident code
;------------------------------------------------------------
; installation code begins here
;------------------------------------------------------------
            ASSUME  DS:code         ;use DS again
over_data:
            @write  <cr,lf,'Installing graphic printer set.'>
;------------------------------------------------------------
; get original printer vector at 17h
;------------------------------------------------------------
            @get_vec 17h
;------------------------------------------------------------
; save original vector
;------------------------------------------------------------
            MOV     o_vec,BX
            MOV     o_vec+2,ES
;------------------------------------------------------------
; point interrupt vector 17h to this program
;------------------------------------------------------------
            MOV     DX,OFFSET new   ;starting point
            @set_vec 17h            ;change vector
;------------------------------------------------------------
; turn on Epson graphics set
;------------------------------------------------------------
            @lprint <esc,'m',4>
;------------------------------------------------------------
; quit and stay resident
;------------------------------------------------------------
            MOV     DX,OFFSET over_data ;code length
            INT     27h                 ;done
code        ENDS
            END     strt
```

Figure 9.2: (continued)

double-lined boxes in the IBM graphics set. There are 11 different symbols for each type of box. The symbols correspond to the four corners, the vertical and horizontal lines, midline tees for dividing a box into several smaller boxes, and a cross for the interior. When a code for one of these IBM graphics characters is found, it is changed to the corresponding Epson character code before being sent to the printer.

Create a new file, named PRINTGR.ASM, and add the program given in Figure 9.2. Let us go through the code. We begin by defining the two types of IBM box characters. Symbols such as *bulc* stand for "box, upper-left corner." The symbols for double-line characters begin with the letter *d,* and those for the corresponding Epson characters begin with the letter *e.* The Epson characters are given for a model LX-80 printer. If you have a different model, check the manual to see if the symbols are the same. One character, the cross, is missing from the Epson portion of our table. We will use a regular plus symbol in its place.

After defining the code segment, we set the instruction pointer to 100 hex. The first instruction of the installation program branches over the resident portion of the program to the label *over_data*. We will return to the resident code shortly, but for now continue with the label *over_data* at the end of the resident code.

We begin by displaying a message on the video screen, to inform the user that the graphics printer set is being installed. Then we retrieve the original vector at interrupt 17 hex, using our *@get_vec* macro. The segment value is returned in the ES register, and the offset is in the BX register. We store the original vector at location *o_vec* near the beginning of the resident section of our program. Of course, this is the address to which our resident program will branch when it has finished its task.

In the next step, we change interrupt vector 17 hex to point to our resident program at label *new*. The change is made with instructions in our macro *@set_vec*. Then we turn on the Epson graphics set with the *@lprint* macro. The three characters Esc, m, and 4 are required. You may need to change these to a different set for your printer. We terminate the installation program by setting the resident-program length to the label *over_data*. Then we terminate with interrupt 27 hex. Let us now look at the resident code.

The resident instructions begin at label *strt* and include the branch needed by the installation program. This is followed by the program heading, the storage location for the original interrupt vector, and the table of box characters beginning at label *tab1*. The resident code follows. The installation program changed interrupt 17 hex so that it branches to the label *new* in our resident program.

Our program analyzes all characters that are sent to the printer. However, we must be careful not to change any registers unless we first save the original contents on the stack. Furthermore, we will not know the value of the DS register. Therefore, we must use the CS register-override instruction for the resident program. We inform the assembler that we will not be using the DS register by including the directive

ASSUME DS:NOTHING

Our resident code begins by checking the AH register for the value zero, with the OR instruction. This operation, of course, does not change the value in AH. If AH is zero, there is output for the printer. But if AH is not zero, we branch to the address of the original interrupt vector, now stored at location *org_vec*. Otherwise, we check the character in AL to see if a regular ASCII character is present. If so, we skip further checking and continue with the original interrupt address. If we find a potential graphics character, we enable interrupts with the STI instruction. We also save the contents of the three registers ES, DI, and CX on the stack since we use them in our interrupt handler. We compare the character in the AL register to the 22 IBM box characters stored at location *tab1*. We use the scan-string instruction, SCASB, for this test. If we find a match, we substitute the corresponding Epson character from table *tab2*. We restore the original contents of the saved registers and branch to the original interrupt vector.

The interrupt handler we wrote in this section contains all the essential parts, and so you can alter it to intercept other interrupt vectors. Let us look at a more complicated resident program.

INTERCHANGING KEYS THROUGH THE ROM BIOS

In this section we write a resident interrupt handler to change some of the keyboard keys. Some of the IBM PC keys seem to be in inconvenient places. For example, the backslash key is to the left of the Z key, and the left Shift key is to the left of the backslash key. By contrast, most keyboards, including the PC AT, have the Shift key immediately to the left of the Z key. Another problem is the Return key on the right side; the tilde key appears to be where the Return key should be. If the original placement of these keys seems awkward, you can change their meaning to something else.

It is easy to change the regular ASCII keys with the DOS program called ANSI.SYS, but it is not possible to change the Shift and Return keys with this method. Another possible technique is a commercial program, such as Superkey or Prokey. However, these programs are so large that they take up valuable memory space. We will use a third method, a resident interrupt handler that intercepts ROM BIOS interrupt 9. As we learned in Chapter 1, this is a hardware interrupt that is activated each time a key is pressed. At such times, the CPU stops its current task and reads the scan code sent by the keyboard processor. The scan code is simply a serial number assigned to each key; it is not related to the ASCII character set transmitted by a regular video terminal.

The interrupt handler we write in this section is more complicated and more likely to cause trouble than the one used in PRINTGR. We cannot be as polite as we were before. Here, we do not save the original value of the interrupt vector, but simply branch to the ROM BIOS when we are through. If another program has previously changed this interrupt, it will no longer operate.

Our resident program intercepts the interrupt as before. However, at this point the interrupt indicates only that a key has been pressed. There is no character available yet. The ROM BIOS normally reads the character when it gains control through interrupt 9. Therefore, our resident driver must read the character to see if it is one we want to change. It does this by duplicating the first part of the ROM BIOS keyboard routine.

After reading the character, our routine compares it with a list of the keys we want to change. This task is complicated by the fact that the keyboard sends one character when a key is pressed and another when the key is released. Therefore, if we want to interchange two keys, we must look for four different characters.

Our program changes four keys, and so we must look for eight characters. We set up a table of the original characters, starting at label *tab1*. The new values are placed in the next table, starting at label *tab2*. The "release" code immediately follows each corresponding "press" code. Notice that we get the value of the release code by adding 80 hex to the press code.

Besides interchanging the left Shift and backslash keys, we assign the tilde key to the minus sign next to the PgUp key. Then we change the tilde key into an extra Return key.

After our resident program reads the scan code into the AL register, we use the SCASB instruction to scan the first table for a match. If a match is found, we move the corresponding new character from the second table into the AL register and branch into the ROM BIOS routine.

Since we have duplicated the first part of the ROM BIOS keyboard code, we must not branch to the beginning of that routine as we did in the previous program; we must branch past the code we have already executed. Unfortunately, there are several different versions of the ROM BIOS in use. Therefore, the installation program must determine where to jump.

As we have seen, the IBM PC and XT computers use one of four different ROM BIOS versions. The earlier versions use a slightly different arrangement than the later versions, and so we must branch to a different place, depending on the ROM BIOS version. As you might expect, the PC AT uses yet another version, and, of course, the IBM copies use still other versions.

We want to change keys only on the IBM PCs, not the PC AT or PC copies. Therefore our installation program moves the ROM date and the computer type into the installation program and displays the ROM date on the video screen (as we did in Chapter 4). If the computer is found to be an AT or a PC copy, the appropriate message is displayed and the program terminates without installing the interrupt code. But if the computer is a regular IBM PC, we check to see if this keyboard program has already been installed. We read interrupt vector 9 with our @get_vec macro and see if it has been changed. If so, we display the message

> **KEYSWAP already installed.**
> **Do you want to remove it? (Y/N)**

We read the user's response with our *@readch* macro and convert it to uppercase with our *@ucase* macro. If the answer is Y, we restore interrupt 9 to its original value, bypassing our routine. We set the DS:DX registers to the vector and execute our macro *@set_vec*. Now the keyboard is restored to its original form and we display the appropriate message on the screen. Of course, we cannot recover the small amount of memory space occupied by our resident program until the computer is reset.

If our program has not already been run, we check the two middle digits of the ROM date to see which version is present. The resident code is originally programmed for the later version of ROM; if we find an earlier version, we must increment the branch point twice. Then we display a message on the screen describing the keys that are changed. We patch interrupt vector 9 so that it points to our resident program and terminate the installation program with interrupt 27 hex.

Create a file named KEYSWAP.ASM by copying the program named ROM-DATE, which we wrote in Chapter 4. Change the file to look like Figure 9.3. If you have an IBM PC, run the program and see that the four keys left Shift, backslash, tilde, and far minus have been changed. Run the program a second time to see that the keys are returned to their normal forms.

We need to add another macro for our next program.

CHANGING THE SCREEN TYPE WITH MACRO @screen_set

Earlier, we wrote macro *@screen_mode* to determine the current video mode. That macro creates instructions to execute function F hex of ROM BIOS interrupt 10 hex. This function returns the current mode in the AL register. We learned that modes 0–6 describe the color graphics screen,

```
                PAGE     ,132
                TITLE    KEYSWAP, swap shift and backslash

        COMMENT *
          January 21, 1986
          Program to swap shift and backslash keys
          using patch to INT 9 or
          return INT 9 to original value
                  Scan code  To
                     41       28    tilde to return
                     74       41    minus to tilde
                     42       43    shift to backslash
                     43       42    backslash to shift

          Checks for ROM dates:
                     04/24/81      PC-0              FF
                     10/19/81      PC-1              FF
                     10/27/82      PC-2              FF
                     11/08/82      PC-XT, portable   FE
                     01/10/84      PC-AT             FC
                     06/10/85      PC-AT, 30 MB      FC

          Code is setup for PC-2 and XT
          Early PCs omitted PUSH AX and POP AX
          Don't change PC-AT
          Macros: @get_vec, @go_dos, @readch,
                  @set_vec, @ucase, @write, @write_r
            INT 27h
         *
        ; scan codes
        c_ret  EQU     28                    ;carriage return
        tilde  EQU     41                    ;tilde
        l_shift EQU    42                    ;shift scan code
        b_slash EQU    43                    ;backslash code
        minus  EQU     74                    ;lone minus key

                INCLUDE mylib.equ            ;equates
                IF1
                INCLUDE mylib.mac            ;macro library
                ENDIF


        ;------------------------------------------
        ; ROM BIOS routines
        ;------------------------------------------
        rombios SEGMENT AT 0F000h
                ORG     0E987h
        kb_int  LABEL   FAR                  ;keyboard interr
                ORG     0E9A4h
        cont_kb LABEL   FAR                  ;continue interr
                ORG     0FFF5h
        date    LABEL   FAR                  ;ROM date
        rombios ENDS
```

Figure 9.3: *Program to interchange keys by changing interrupt 9.*

```
;-----------------------------------------------
; begin resident code and installation routine
;-----------------------------------------------
code    SEGMENT
        ASSUME  CS:code, DS:code, ES:code
        ORG     100h

strt:   JMP     SHORT over_data
;-----------------------------------------------
; resident code begins here
;-----------------------------------------------
        DB              ' KEYSWAP,A.R.Miller,01.21.86 '
; Table of original scan codes
tabl    DB              l_shift,l_shift+80h ;left shift
        DB              b_slash,b_slash+80h ;backslash
        DB              tilde,tilde+80h
        DB              minus,minus+80h
tabl    EQU     $-tabl

; Table of new scan codes
tab2    DB              b_slash,b_slash+80h ;backslash
        DB              l_shift,l_shift+80h ;left shift
        DB              c_ret,c_ret+80h
        DB              tilde,tilde+80h
new:
;-----------------------------------------------
; copy of ROM BIOS for interrupt 9
;-----------------------------------------------
        STI
        PUSH    AX
        PUSH    BX
        PUSH    CX
        PUSH    DX
        PUSH    SI
        PUSH    DI
        PUSH    DS
        PUSH    ES
        CLD
; next four ROM bytes are in a subroutine
        PUSH    AX
        MOV     AX,40h
        MOV     DS,AX
        POP     AX
        IN      AL,60h
        PUSH    AX
        IN      AL,61h
        MOV     AH,AL
        OR      AL,80h
        OUT     61h,AL
        XCHG    AH,AL
        OUT     61h,AL
        POP     AX
```

Figure 9.3: *(continued)*

```
;-----------------------------------------------
; end of original ROM BIOS code
; check scan codes for keys to switch
;-----------------------------------------------
        MOV     DI,CS
        MOV     ES,DI           ;establish ES
        MOV     DI,OFFSET tab1  ;original
        MOV     CX,tab1         ;table length
        REPNE   SCASB           ;search tab1
        JNE     to_rom          ;no match
        ADD     DI,tab1-1       ;point to tab2
        MOV     AL,CS:[DI]      ;new scan code
to_rom:                         ;far JMP
        JMP     cont_kb         ;continue ROM
;-----------------------------------------------
; end of resident code
;-----------------------------------------------
; installation code begins here
;-----------------------------------------------
over_data:
        MOV     AX,rombios      ;0F000h
        ASSUME  DS:rombios
        MOV     DS,AX
        MOV     SI,OFFSET date  ;source
        MOV     DI,OFFSET r_date ;destination
        MOV     CX,10           ;date and type
;-----------------------------------------------
; copy ROM date
;-----------------------------------------------
        REP     MOVSB
        ASSUME  DS:code
        MOV     AX,CS
        MOV     DS,AX           ;reset DS
; terminate string with dollar sign
        MOV     BYTE PTR [doll],'$'
;-----------------------------------------------
; check for slash in date
;-----------------------------------------------
        CMP     BYTE PTR [r_slash],'/'
        JZ      sl              ;ok
        JMP     not_it          ;not IBM
;-----------------------------------------------
; display ROM date
;-----------------------------------------------
sl:
        @write_r <OFFSET p_ver>
;-----------------------------------------------
; check for PC-AT
;-----------------------------------------------
```

Figure 9.3: *(continued)*

```
        MOV     AL,[c_type]
        CMP     AL,0FCh
        JNZ     not_pc
        JMP     pc_at
;-----------------------------------------------------------
; check if already installed
;-----------------------------------------------------------
not_pc:
        @get_vec 9                  ;get INT 9
        MOV     AX,ES
        CMP     AH,0f0h             ;original?
        JNZ     got_it              ;already installed
;-----------------------------------------------------------
; check ROM version
;-----------------------------------------------------------
        MOV     AX,[rd2q]           ;ROM day
        CMP     AX,'72'             ;PC-2 (27)
        JZ      swap                ;ok
        CMP     AX,'80'             ;XT (08)
        JZ      swap                ;ok
        CMP     AX,'42'             ;PC-0 (24)
        JZ      rom2                ;ok
        CMP     AX,'91'             ;PC-1 (19)
        JZ      rom2                ;ok
        JMP     not_it              ;not a PC
;-----------------------------------------------------------
; increase ROM address by two for PC-0 and 1
;-----------------------------------------------------------
rom2:
        MOV     DI,OFFSET to_rom+1
        INC     BYTE PTR [DI]
        INC     BYTE PTR [DI]
;-----------------------------------------------------------
; change interrupt vector at 9
;-----------------------------------------------------------
swap:
        @write_r <OFFSET sw_mes>
        MOV     DX,OFFSET new    ;starting point
        @set_vec 9
;-----------------------------------------------------------
; quit and stay resident
;-----------------------------------------------------------
        MOV     DX,OFFSET over_data ;code length
        INT     27h                 ;done
;-----------------------------------------------------------
; keyswap already installed, terminate
;-----------------------------------------------------------
got_it:
        @write  <cr,lf,'KEYSWAP already installed'>
        @write  <cr,lf,'Do you want to remove it? (Y/N)'
        @readch
        @ucase
```

Figure 9.3: *(continued)*

```
                CMP       AL,'Y'
                JNE       done
;------------------------------------------------------------
; return interrupt vector 9 to original value
;------------------------------------------------------------
                ASSUME    DS:rombios
                MOV       AX,rombios
                MOV       DS,AX
                MOV       DX,OFFSET kb_int ;0E987h
                @set_vec  9                ;set INT 9
                MOV       AX,CS
                MOV       DS,AX            ;reset DS
;------------------------------------------------------------
; display message
;------------------------------------------------------------
                @write    <cr,lf,'Keyboard returned to normal'>
done:
                @go_dos                    ;quit
;------------------------------------------------------------
; IBM PC AT
;------------------------------------------------------------
pc_at:
                @write    <cr,lf,'A PC AT'>
                @go_dos                    ;quit
;------------------------------------------------------------
; not an IBM PC or PC-XT
;------------------------------------------------------------
not_it:
                @write    <cr,lf,'Not an IBM PC'>
                @go_dos                    ;quit
;------------------------------------------------------------
; Data area
;------------------------------------------------------------
p_ver    DB       'ROM Version:'
r_date   DB       'xx'
r_slash  DB       '/'
rd2q     LABEL    WORD
         DB       'xx/82'
doll     DB       '?'
c_type   DB       '?'       ;computer type

sw_mes   DB       cr,lf
         DB       'Left shift and backslash interchanged'
         DB       cr,lf,'Tilde becomes return key'
         DB       cr,lf,'Far minus becomes tilde key$'

code     ENDS
         END      strt
```

Figure 9.3: *(continued)*

while mode 7 is the monochrome screen. In the next program we are going to change the screen mode according to the value in the AL register. Add macro @screen_set, shown in Figure 9.4, to your macro library. This macro generates code to execute function 0 of interrupt 10 hex, which sets the video mode according to the value specified in the AL register.

Now let us see how to change the video screen.

CHANGING THE VIDEO SCREEN

Our next program changes the appearance of the video screen. It can reverse the foreground and background colors so that you see dark letters on a light background. And if you have a color/graphics screen, you can change from 80 to 40 characters per line and back. You can also turn the color on or off. If you have both a monochrome and a color/graphics screen, this program can switch from one screen to the other. (The DOS program MODE can also change screens and the number of characters per line.) After you switch from one screen to the other, you can turn off the inactive screen. If you have only a black-and-white graphics monitor, you can use our program to turn off the color mode to produce a sharper image.

The @screen_set macro we wrote in the last section can change the characteristics of a video screen. For example, to change to a color/graphics screen with 40 characters per line, we set the AL register to mode 1. Our macro sets the AH register to zero and executes interrupt 10 hex. Unfortunately, we cannot use this method to change from one screen to the other. Thus, if the monochrome screen is current and we use @screen_set to change to the graphics screen, DOS will ignore the request. That is, function 0 of interrupt 10 hex cannot change from one type of screen to the other. Our program, however, will accomplish this feat by trickery.

```
@screen_set      MACRO
;; Macro to change screen mode
;; Number in AL is mode:
;;
         PUSH    AX       ;;save
         XOR     AH,AH    ;;zero
         INT     10h
         POP     AX
         ENDM
```

Figure 9.4: *Macro @screen_set to change the screen mode.*

We learned in Chapter 5 that the BIOS maintains a data area at the low end of memory, just above the interrupt vectors. The byte at location 410 hex (0:410 or 40:10) contains a list of the hardware currently attached to the computer, as shown in Table 9.1. This includes the printers, disk drives, serial ports, memory, and the current video screen characteristics. The value stored at this location generally reflects the switch settings on the system board. One switch setting determines whether the monochrome screen or the graphics screen will be selected when you start your computer. However, once the computer is running, you can change this equipment byte.

If the system switch is set for the monochrome screen and you want to change to the graphics screen, simply change the video mode bits, 4 and 5, of the byte at 410 hex to indicate a graphics screen. Then use our *@screen_set* macro with AL set to 3 (80-column color) and execute Function 0 of interrupt 10 hex to bring up the color text screen.

The screen program is given in Figure 9.5. Create a file named SCREEN.ASM and enter the program. The beginning comments show how to use the program, describe the equipment byte at 410 hex, and explain the flags used by the program to determine which video screens are present. Let us go through the code.

Bit	Meaning
F, F	Number of parallel ports
D	(Not used)
C	Game adapter
B, A, 9	Number of serial ports
8	(Not used)
7, 6	Number of floppy disks
5, 4	Initial video mode where:
	11 = monochrome
	10 = 80 × 25 graphics
	01 = 40 × 25 graphics
3, 2	System-board RAM
1	(Not used)
0	Boot from floppy disk

Table 9.1: *The 16-bit equipment list at 410 hex.*

```
            PAGE     ,132
            TITLE    SCREEN - Determine type and change

COMMENT *
   January 23, 1986
   Determines screen type with INT 10h, AH=0Fh
   Changes screen type with INT 10h, AH=0
   Yellow on blue for color modes
   Reverse video R parameter
   Usage:
      SCREEN                display type
      SCREEN ?              display help
      SCREEN B              b/w graphics
      SCREEN C              color graphics
      SCREEN M              monochrome screen
      SCREEN O              turn off graphics screen
      SCREEN R              reversed current screen
      SCREEN 40             set 40 characters/line
      SCREEN 80             set 80 characters/line

   Value in AL is mode:
         0   40x25 B/W
         1   40x25 color
         2   80x25 B/W
         3   80x25 color
         7   80x25 monochrome

   Equipment flags at 40:10 show:
         bit 4 = 1 if monochrome
                 0 if graphics

   Location s_type has:
         1h if color/graphics only
         70h if monochrome only
         71h if both adapters
   Macros: @go_dos, @head, @screen_mode,
         @screen_set, @write, @write_r
   INT 10h
      *
         INCLUDE mylib.equ
         IF1
         INCLUDE mylib.mac
         ENDIF

m_mem   EQU      0B000h   ;monochrome memory
g_mem   EQU      0B800h   ;graphics memory
yell    EQU      1Eh      ;yellow on blue

stor    SEGMENT AT 40h
        ORG      10h                    ;equipment flag
equip_f LABEL    FAR
stor    ENDS
```

Figure 9.5: *Program to change video screens.*

```
CODE      SEGMENT
          ASSUME   CS:code,DS:code
          ORG      5Dh
param     LABEL    BYTE                    ;first parameter

          ORG      100h
strt:
          @head    'SCREEN, 01.23.86 '
;------------------------------------------------
; see if monochrome memory exists
;------------------------------------------------
          MOV      AX,m_mem
          MOV      ES,AX
          CALL     det_sc
          JNE      ch_grap          ;no monochrome
          MOV      BYTE PTR [s_type],70h ;set for mono
;------------------------------------------------
; see if graphics memory exists
;------------------------------------------------
ch_grap:
          MOV      AX,g_mem
          MOV      ES,AX
          CALL     det_sc
          JNE      ch2              ;no graphics
          INC      BYTE PTR [s_type] ;set for graphics
ch2:
          ASSUME   ES:stor
          MOV      AX,stor
          MOV      ES,AX
;------------------------------------------------
; determine current screen mode, and save in BL
;------------------------------------------------
          @screen_mode             ;read mode
          MOV      BL,AL            ;save state
;------------------------------------------------
; check for parameter at 5Dh
;------------------------------------------------
          MOV      CL,[param]
          CMP      CL,blank         ;parameter?
          JNE      not_bl           ;yes
          JMP      nopar            ;no
;------------------------------------------------
; check for help request
;------------------------------------------------
not_bl:
          CMP      CL,'?'           ;help?
          JNE      not_h            ;no
;------------------------------------------------
; display help message
;------------------------------------------------
hlp:
          @write_r <OFFSET help>
          @go_dos                  ;quit
not_h:
          CMP      CL,'R'           ;reverse?
```

Figure 9.5: *(continued)*

```
            JNE      not_rv            ;no
;------------------------------------------------
; reverse current screen
;------------------------------------------------
            MOV      DX,m_mem          ;screen memory
            MOV      AL,70h            ;reverse video
            CMP      BL,7              ;monochrome?
            JZ       rev               ;yes
            MOV      DX,g_mem
            TEST     BL,1              ;color?
            JZ       rev               ;no
            INC      AL                ;make 71 hex
rev:
            CALL     ch_att
            @go_dos                    ;done
not_rv:
            CMP      CL,'M'            ;monochrome?
            JNE      notm              ;no
;------------------------------------------------
; see if monochrome screen present
;------------------------------------------------
            TEST     BYTE PTR [s_type],11110000b
            JZ       mon3
;------------------------------------------------
; Change from graphics screen to monochrome
; by setting bit 4 of equipment flag at 40:10
;------------------------------------------------
            OR       BYTE PTR ES:[equip_f],00010000b
            MOV      AL,7              ;monochrome
            @screen_set                ;make change
            @go_dos                    ;done
mon3:
            @write   <cr,lf,'No monochrome adapter'>
            @go_dos                    ;done
notm:
            MOV      AH,7              ;attribute
            MOV      DX,g_mem          ;screen memory
            CMP      CL,'O'            ;turn off
            JNZ      not_off
;------------------------------------------------
; turn off inactive screen
;------------------------------------------------
            CMP      BL,7
            JE       turn_o
            MOV      DX,m_mem          ;screen memory
turn_o:
            CALL     cl_scr
            @go_dos
;------------------------------------------------
; change graphics screen according to parameter
;------------------------------------------------
not_off:
            AND      BL,0011b          ;make text mode
            CMP      CL,'8'            ;80 char?
            JNE      n80               ;no
```

Figure 9.5: *(continued)*

```
; set 80 character width
        OR      BL,10b          ;set bit 1
        JMP     SHORT setc
n80:
        CMP     CL,'4'          ;40 char?
        JNE     n40             ;no
; set 40 character width
        AND     BL,001b         ;reset bit 1
        JMP     SHORT setc
n40:
        CMP     CL,'B'          ;b/w?
        JNE     nbw             ;no
; set b/w mode
        AND     BL,010b         ;reset bit 0
        JMP     SHORT setc
; set color mode
nbw:
        CMP     CL,'C'
        JE      s_col
        JMP     hlp             ;give help
s_col:
        OR      BL,1            ;set bit 0
;-----------------------------------------------
; see if graphics screen present
;-----------------------------------------------
setc:
        TEST    BYTE PTR [s_type],00001111b
        JNZ     gra3
        @write  <cr,lf,'No graphics adapter'>
        @go_dos                 ;done
;-----------------------------------------------
; change from monochrome to graphics screen by
; resetting bit 4 of equipment flag at 40:10
;-----------------------------------------------
gra3:
        AND     BYTE PTR ES:[equip_f],11101111b
        MOV     AL,BL           ;screen type
        @screen_set             ;make change
        TEST    BL,1            ;color?
        JZ      nocol           ;no
        MOV     AH,yell         ;yellow/blue
nocol:
        CALL    cl_scr          ;set attr
        @go_dos                 ;done
;-----------------------------------------------
; display current screen mode
;-----------------------------------------------
nopar:
        MOV     AL,BL
        CMP     AL,7            ;monochrome?
        JNE     not_mon         ;no
        @write  ' Monochrome Screen'
        @go_dos                 ;done
not_mon:
```

Figure 9.5: *(continued)*

```
                AND     AL,1                ;even or odd?
                JZ      even
                @write  'COLOR'
                JMP     SHORT odd
        even:
                @write  ' B/W '
        odd:
                @write  ' Graphics Screen'
                @go_dos
        s_type  DB      0                   ;screens avail
        ;*****************************************************
        ; Determine if monochrome or graphics adapter      *
        ; is present                                        *
        ;                                                   *
        ; On input:  ES has segment                         *
        ; On exit:   Zero flag set if memory present        *
        ;*****************************************************
        det_sc  PROC    NEAR
                MOV     CX,55AAh            ;pattern
                MOV     DI,0FA0h            ;off screen
                MOV     ES:[DI],CH          ;01010101 pattern
                MOV     AL,ES:[DI]
                CMP     AL,CH
                JNE     no_mem              ;no memory
                MOV     ES:[DI],CL          ;10101010 pattern
                MOV     AL,ES:[DI]
                CMP     AL,CL
        no_mem:
                RET
        det_sc  ENDP
        ;*********** End of procedure det_sc ***********
        ;*****************************************************
        ; clear screen and select foreground and background
        ; INPUT:
        ;       AH = video attribute
        ;       DX = screen segment
        ;*****************************************************
        cl_scr  PROC    NEAR
                MOV     ES,DX               ;screen segment
                XOR     DI,DI               ;screen beginning
                MOV     AL,blank            ;blank char
                MOV     CX,2000             ;words
                REP     STOSW               ;fill screen
                RET
        cl_scr  ENDP
        ;*********** End of procedure cl_scr ************
        ;*****************************************************
        ; change video attribute for current screen
        ; INPUT:
        ;       AL = video attribute
        ;       DX = video segment
        ;*****************************************************
```

Figure 9.5: *(continued)*

```
ch_att    PROC
          MOV       ES,DX            ;screen segment
          XOR       DI,DI            ;screen beginning
          MOV       CX,2000          ;bytes
n_att:
          INC       DI               ;attribute
          STOSB
          LOOP      n_att
          RET
ch_att    ENDP
;*********** End of procedure ch_att *************
;------------------------------------------------
; help message
;------------------------------------------------
help      DB        'Commands are:',cr,lf
          DB        'SCREEN         show current mode',cr,lf
          DB        'SCREEN ?       display this message',cr,lf
          DB        'SCREEN B       set b/w graphics',cr,lf
          DB        'SCREEN C       set color graphics',cr,lf
          DB        'SCREEN M       set monochrome screen',cr,lf
          DB        'SCREEN O       turn off graphics screen',cr,lf
          DB        'SCREEN R       reverse screen',cr,lf
          DB        'SCREEN 4       set 40 characters/line',cr,lf
          DB        'SCREEN 8       set 80 characters/line',cr,lf
          DB        '$'

code      ENDS
          END       strt
```

Figure 9.5: *(continued)*

We define two constants, representing the memory segments for the monochrome screen (B000 hex) and the color/graphics screen (B800 hex). We also define the attribute for yellow lettering on a blue background (1E hex) for use with color mode. If you want a different set of colors, change this definition. We define a separate segment at 40 hex to locate the address of the equipment flag. As before, we are careful not to define data at this location, so that we can convert the EXE file to a COM file.

Our code segment begins by defining the parameter at 5D. This program expects only single-character parameters. Therefore, it is easier to read them at this location than at the usual buffer at 80 hex.

The code begins at 100 hex with the program header. Our first instructions determine which video screen adapter cards (which drive video monitors) are present. We set the ES register to the segment of the monochrome memory and then call procedure *det_sc*. The subroutine first writes the byte 55 hex (an alternating pattern of zeros and ones) to a nondisplayed portion of the screen memory. Then the pattern is read back to see if it is the same. If so, we write the pattern AA hex (an alternating pattern of ones and zeros). Again the pattern is read back. If the correct pattern is read back both times, we conclude that there is valid memory at this location. Otherwise, we note that there is no monochrome screen adapter. The zero flag is set if memory is present.

We have seen that the video screens display 25 lines of 80 columns of 16-bit words, and so the first 4000 bytes appear on the screen. But the video boards contain 4096 bytes. Therefore, we choose offset FA0 hex, the 4001st byte, to write our pattern, because this location does not show on the screen.

On returning to the main program, we set our program flag, *s_type,* to the value 70 hex if a monochrome adapter is present. We next check for a color/graphics adapter. We set the ES register to the segment of the color/graphics memory and call procedure *det_sc* again. We write the same two patterns as before, and we set the zero flag if memory is present. On returning to the main program, we increment the program flag if a color/graphics memory ("adapter") is present.

Now that we have determined which video "screens" are available, we set the ES register to the segment of the BIOS data area at 40 hex. Using our *@screen_mode* macro, we determine the current video screen mode and save the state in the BL register. We check for a parameter at 5D hex. If there is no parameter, we display the current screen type. If a question mark was entered as a parameter, we display a help message, showing how to use the program.

We next check the parameter for the letter *R,* which requests a reversal of the current video screen. We make the change by writing directly to the current screen memory (which amounts to writing directly to the screen). We set the DX register to the segment of the video screen and select a video attribute of 70 hex. This produces reverse video for both the monochrome screen and the (black-and-white) graphics screen with color off. If color is turned on, however, we increment this value to 71 hex to produce blue letters on a gray background. We call procedure *ch_att* to change the video attributes directly. Let us look at this routine.

Procedure *ch_att* changes the screen attribute by writing the attribute character to alternate positions of the video screen. The transfer is performed with the store-string instruction, STOSB. We enter this routine with the DX register pointing to the appropriate screen memory. The AL register contains the attribute. We set the DI pointer to zero and the CX register to 2000, the number of characters on the screen. We first increment the DI pointer so that it references the attribute byte. Then the STOSB instruction moves the byte from the AL register to the memory location referenced by the ES:DI registers. After the byte is transferred, the DI register is automatically incremented. However, we must increment it again so that it points to the next attribute. The LOOP command performs the operation 2000 times.

We next check for a parameter of M, a request to switch to the monochrome screen. If we find this parameter, we first check the program flag to see if the monochrome screen is present. If not, we display an error message and terminate the program. Otherwise, we call subroutine *mk_mono* to change to the monochrome screen. This routine sets bit 4 of the equipment flag. Then we set the AL register to 7 for monochrome mode and execute interrupt 10 hex.

The parameter O is next; this is a request to turn off the inactive screen. If you have both a monochrome and a graphics screen you can switch from one to the other. At such times you may want to turn off the inactive screen, that is, make it black. We call procedure *cl_scr* for this purpose. This routine is similar to procedure *ch_att*, except that we write into every location on the screen memory rather than just the attribute locations. We call this routine with the segment of the inactive screen in the DX register and the video attribute in the AH register. The routine sets the CX register to 2000, the number of words on the screen. Then it loads a blank into the AL register and repeatedly executes the store-string instruction, STOSW, on the AX register. We blank the screen by choosing attribute 7.

The remaining parameters, B, 40, 80, and C, change the graphics screen. However, we only expect one of the four text modes, 0–3. Therefore we turn off the bits that designate the graphics modes, 4–6, by performing a logical AND with the screen mode and the number 3. The second bit of the mode determines the screen width. When this bit is set there are 80 characters per line, and when it is reset there are 40 characters per line. If the parameter 8 (or 80) was given, then, we perform a logical OR with the binary value 10 to turn on this bit. By contrast, if the parameter 4 (or 40) was entered, we reset the bit by performing a logical AND with the value 1. These changes do not alter the color.

We turn color on or off in a similar way. The least-significant bit is set for a color display and reset for black-and-white. Therefore, if the parameter B (for black-and-white) was entered, we perform a logical AND with the value 2. If the parameter C (for color) was given, we perform a logical OR with the value 1. The value in the BL register now reflects the desired video mode. We check the program byte to see if a color/graphics screen is present. If not, the program is terminated with an error message. Otherwise, we set bit 4 of the BIOS equipment flag at 410 hex. Then, using our *@screen_set* macro, we make the change with interrupt 10 hex. Finally, if color is wanted, we set up the attribute for yellow lettering on a blue background and call procedure *cl_scr* to make the change.

CHANGING THE PRINTER MODE

Earlier in this chapter we wrote a resident interrupt handler to change IBM graphics characters to Epson printer-graphics characters. Our next program changes the printer mode. Dot-matrix printers can be set to any of several different modes, such as italics, compressed letters, wide (expanded) letters, boldface, letter-quality, and tiny type. Additional options include vertical line height (six or eight lines per inch) and disabling the paper-out sensor (so you can print on single sheets). These features are selected by sending the appropriate characters to the printer. Let us consider several ways to select printer features.

If you want a printout of your assembly listings, you will probably need to set your printer to compressed type, to accomodate the width of the listing. The usual symbol for this mode is the byte 0F hex, or Ctrl-O.

We learned in Chapter 5 that we can change the printer typeface by creating a short program to send the appropriate characters to the printer. Let us look at a better way.

Our next program can efficiently change eight printer options: bold, compressed, italic, letter-quality, tiny, or wide type; vertical spacing of either six or eight lines per inch; and disabling the paper-out sensor or not. The entire program is less than 1000 bytes long. Furthermore, it can be executed with parameters from a batch file. If parameters are not given, a menu appears on the screen. The user moves the cursor through the menu and then makes the selection with the Return key.

The program given in Figure 9.6 is designed for an Epson LX-80 printer, but it will also work on many other dot-matrix printers. Just to be sure, check the definitions given in the data area near the beginning of the program against the values given in your owner's manual. Create a file named PRINTER.ASM and type up the program. Let us go through the code.

The definitions begin by setting the top line of the menu to the fourth line of the screen. Then the segments for both the monochrome and color/graphics memory are defined. We also define attributes for normal monochrome (light letters on a dark background), yellow letters on a blue background (for a color screen), and blinking reversed video. The keys for up and down cursor movement are also defined. You can save some typing by copying the characters for the box from the PRINTGR program given earlier in this chapter.

We begin the code segment by defining the first parameter at location 5D hex and the second parameter at 6D hex. As in the previous program, we only expect parameters that are a single letter, and so it is easier to read the parameters at these locations than at 80 hex. The instructions start at 100 hex with a branch over the data area. We write in our usual header without using our *@head* macro. Then we establish a storage location for the normal video attribute, 7 for a monochrome or black-and-white screen. The program will change it to yellow-on-blue for a color/graphics screen. The next section defines the character strings that activate or disable each of the printer's features. A table of labels referencing the desired features comes next. The first eight entries activate a feature, while the second eight entries disable the corresponding feature. Notice that entries are arranged in alphabetical order, as they will appear in the menu on the screen.

The instructions start next, at the label *over*. We determine the current screen mode using our *@screen_mode* macro. We set the ES register to the segment of the current screen. In addition, if the color/graphics screen is current, we set location *norml* to attribute yellow.

We check the second parameter to see if the letter O was entered, to disable a feature (turn it off). If so, we branch to the label *off*. Otherwise, we check the first parameter. If no parameter was entered, we branch to label *help* and display the menu on the screen. The user is presented with a list of options surrounded by a double-lined box (Figure 9.7). Initially, the top item is shown in blinking, reverse-video type. The highlighted item can be moved up or down by pressing the up- or down-arrow keys. When the desired item is highlighted, it is selected by pressing the Return key. Alternatively, pressing the Esc or End key terminates the program without making a change. Let us look at the cursor routine.

After the menu is written on the screen with our *@write_r* macro, we make the first menu item blink in reverse video. We call procedure *ch_att* with the blinking attribute, F0 hex, in the AL register. This subroutine is similar to the one in the previous program. Instead of changing the entire screen, however, we only change 16 characters. We use the SI register as a pointer to the menu item (0–7), and the BP register marks the screen position. We read the keyboard using function 8 of interrupt 21 hex. This function waits for the user to type something and returns immediately with a character; it does not wait for a Return key to be pressed. Furthermore, it does not display the character on the screen. If a regular ASCII key is pressed, the value is available in the AL register. We therefore check this register for the Esc key and terminate the program if we find it. We then check for the Return key. If this character is found we process the corresponding menu item that is highlighted. If neither Esc nor

```
              PAGE    ,132
              TITLE   PRINTER

COMMENT *
   January 25, 1986
   Program to change characteristics of
   dot matrix printer
   USAGE:
           PRINTER B          (bold, comp and wide)
           PRINTER C          (compressed)
           PRINTER I          (italics)
           PRINTER L          (letter quality)
           PRINTER P          (paper-out sensor)
           PRINTER T          (tiny)
           PRINTER W          (wide)
           PRINTER 8          (lines/inch)
   turn off with O
           PRINTER B  O       (bold off)
           PRINTER C  O       (compressed off)
           PRINTER T  O       (tiny off)
           PRINTER W  O       (wide off)
           PRINTER 8  O       (8 lines off)
   Macros: @go_dos, @screen_mode, @write_r
   INT 21h functions 5, 8
   *
           INCLUDE mylib.equ
           IF1
           INCLUDE mylib.mac
           ENDIF

first_l EQU    4                   ;first line select
m_mem   EQU    0B000h              ;monochrome memory
g_mem   EQU    0B800h              ;graphics memory
normb   EQU    07                  ;B/W normal attribute
yellow  EQU    1Eh                 ;color normal attribute
blink   EQU    0F0h                ;blinking, reverse
up_arr  EQU    72                  ;up cursor
down_ar EQU    80                  ;down cursor
;-------------------------------------------------
; box characters (double lines)
;-------------------------------------------------
bulc    EQU    0C9h                ;upper left corner
burc    EQU    0BBh                ;upper right corner
bllc    EQU    0C8h                ;lower left corner
blrc    EQU    0BCh                ;lower right corner
bver    EQU    0BAh                ;vertical
bhor    EQU    0CDh                ;horizontal

code    SEGMENT
        ASSUME  CS:code, DS:code
        ORG     5Dh
param1  LABEL   BYTE                ;first parameter
```

Figure 9.6: *Program to change the printer mode.*

```
          ORG       6Dh
param2    LABEL     BYTE                    ;second parameter

          ORG       100h
strt:
          JMP       SHORT over
;------------------------------------------------
; Data area
;------------------------------------------------
          DB        ' PRINTER, 01.25.86 '
norml     DB        normb                  ;default to B/W
; bold, both compressed and wide
bolc      DB        0Fh,esc,57h,'1'
bolcl     EQU       $-bolc
bolco     DB        12h,esc,57h,'0'
bolcol    EQU       $-bolco
; compressed type
comc      DB        0Fh
comcl     EQU       $-comc
comco     DB        12h
comcol    EQU       $-comco
; tiny type
tinc      DB        esc, '3', 16h, 0Fh, esc, 53h, '1'
tincl     EQU       $-tinc
tinco     DB        12h,esc,54h,1Bh,32h
tincol    EQU       $-tinco
; wide type
widc      DB        esc,57h,'1'
widcl     EQU       $-widc
widco     DB        esc,57h,'0'
widcol    EQU       $-widco
; letter quality
letc      DB        esc,'x',1
letcl     EQU       $-letc
letco     DB        esc,'x',0
letcol    EQU       $-letco
; eight lines per inch
eigc      DB        esc,'0'
eigcl     EQU       $-eigc
eigco     DB        esc,'2'
eigcol    EQU       $-eigco
; paper-out sensor
papc      DB        esc,'9'
papcl     EQU       $-papc
papco     DB        esc,'8'
papcol    EQU       $-papco
; italics type
itac      DB        esc,'4'
itacl     EQU       $-itac
itaco     DB        esc,'5'
itacol    EQU       $-itaco
```

Figure 9.6: *(continued)*

```
;----------------------------------------------
; index to messages
;----------------------------------------------
table   LABEL   WORD
        DW      OFFSET bol
        DW      OFFSET com
        DW      OFFSET ita
        DW      OFFSET let
        DW      OFFSET tin
        DW      OFFSET wid
        DW      OFFSET eig
        DW      OFFSET pap

        DW      OFFSET bol_off
        DW      OFFSET com_off
        DW      OFFSET ita_off
        DW      OFFSET let_off
        DW      OFFSET tin_off
        DW      OFFSET wid_off
        DW      OFFSET eig_off
        DW      OFFSET pap_off

tablel  EQU     $-table             ;length
n_com   EQU     tablel/2
n_coml  EQU     n_com-1
last_l  EQU     first_l+n_coml      ;last line number
top_l   EQU     first_l*2*80+2      ;first line position
bot_l   EQU     last_l*2*80+2       ;last line position

over:
        XOR     BP,BP               ;zero
; determine screen type
        @screen_mode
;set ES for screen memory
        MOV     BX,m_mem            ;mono mode
        CMP     AL,7                ;mono?
        JZ      mono                ;yes
        MOV     BX,g_mem            ;graphics mode
        TEST    AL,1                ;color?
        JZ      mono                ;b/w mode
; graphics screen in color mode
        MOV     BYTE PTR [norml],yellow ;set color
mono:
        MOV     ES,BX
;----------------------------------------------
; check for second parameter
;----------------------------------------------
        MOV     AL,[param2]
        CMP     AL,'O'
        JZ      off
```

Figure 9.6: *(continued)*

```
;-------------------------------------------------
; check for first parameter
;-------------------------------------------------
        MOV     AL,[paraml]
        CMP     AL,blank
        JNZ     n_hlp
        JMP     help                    ;no parameter
n_hlp:
        CMP     AL,'B'
        JZ      bol                     ;bold
        CMP     AL,'C'
        JZ      com                     ;compressed
        CMP     AL,'L'
        JZ      let                     ;letter quality
        CMP     AL,'8'
        JZ      eig                     ;8 lines/inch
        CMP     AL,'P'
        JZ      pap                     ;paper-out sensor
        CMP     AL,'I'
        JZ      ita                     ;italics
        CMP     AL,'T'
        JZ      tin                     ;tiny
        CMP     AL,'W'
        JZ      wid
        JMP     help
;-----------------------------------------------
; repeat macro for sending string to printer
; compress, tiny, wide, letter, 8/inch
;-----------------------------------------------
        IRP     ?X,<bol,wid,let,eig,tin,com,pap,ita>
?X:
        MOV     DI,OFFSET ?X&c
        MOV     CX,?X&l
        JMP     SHORT send
        ENDM
;---------------------------------------
; send string to printer
;---------------------------------------
send:
        MOV     AH,5
next:
        MOV     DL,[DI]         ;pointer
        INT     21h
        INC     DI
        LOOP    next
        JMP     done
;---------------------------------------
; turn off feature
;---------------------------------------
off:
; check first parameter
```

Figure 9.6: *(continued)*

```
        MOV     AL,[param1]
        CMP     AL,'B'          ;bold?
        JZ      bol_off         ;yes
        CMP     AL,'T'          ;tiny?
        JZ      tin_off         ;yes
        CMP     AL,'C'          ;compressed?
        JZ      com_off         ;yes
        CMP     AL,'L'          ;letter quality?
        JZ      let_off         ;yes
        CMP     AL,'8'          ;8 lines/inch?
        JZ      eig_off         ;yes
        CMP     AL,'P'          ;paper-out?
        JZ      pap_off         ;yes
        CMP     AL,'I'          ;italics?
        JZ      ita_off         ;yes
        CMP     AL,'W'          ;wide?
        JZ      wid_off         ;yes
        JMP     SHORT help      ;no
;-----------------------------------------------
; repeat macro for sending string to printer
; turn off compress, tiny, wide, letter, 8/inch
;-----------------------------------------------
        IRP     ?X,<bol,wid,let,eig,tin,com,pap,ita>
?X&_off:
        MOV     DI,OFFSET ?X&co
        MOV     CX,?X&col
        JMP     SHORT send
        ENDM
;----------------------------------------
; correlate help menu to task
; SI is index into table
;----------------------------------------
selct:
        ADD     SI,SI           ;double value
        JMP     WORD PTR [SI+OFFSET table]
;----------------------------------------
; no parameter, show options
;----------------------------------------
help:
;---------------------------------------------------
; display help message
;---------------------------------------------------
        @write_r <OFFSET h_msg>
        XOR     SI,SI           ;zero
        MOV     BP,top_l        ;save value
        MOV     DI,BP           ;first line
        MOV     AL,blink        ;reverse blinking
        CALL    ch_att          ;make change
;---------------------------------------------------
; keyboard input without echo
;---------------------------------------------------
key_in:
```

Figure 9.6: *(continued)*

```
              MOV      AH,8
              INT      21h
              CMP      AL,esc         ;quit?
              JZ       done           ;yes
              CMP      AL,cr          ;select
              JZ       selct
              OR       AL,AL          ;zero?
              JNZ      key_in         ;no, wait for cursor
; first character is zero, get extended code
              MOV      AH,8           ;get auxiliary byte
              INT      21h
              CMP      AL,down_ar
              JNZ      not_dn
; move reversed block down one line
              MOV      DI,BP          ;restore
              MOV      AL,[norml]
              CALL     ch_att         ;make normal
              CMP      SI,n_coml
              JZ       too_low
              INC      SI             ;line counter
              ADD      BP,2*80        ;next line
              JMP      SHORT rever
; cursor at bottom, move to top
too_low:
              XOR      SI,SI          ;reset
              MOV      BP,top_l       ;save value
              JMP      SHORT rever
not_dn:
              CMP      AL,up_arr
              JNZ      not_up
; move reversed block up one line
              MOV      DI,BP
              MOV      AL,[norml]
              CALL     ch_att         ;make normal
              OR       SI,SI          ;already top?
              JZ       too_high
              DEC      SI             ;line count
              SUB      BP,2*80        ;next line
rever:
              MOV      DI,BP
              MOV      AL,blink       ;reverse blinking
              CALL     ch_att         ;make change
              JMP      key_in
; cursor at top, move to bottom
too_high:
              MOV      SI,n_coml
              MOV      BP,bot_l
              JMP      rever
not_up:
              CMP      AL,79          ;end key
              JNZ      key_in         ;try again
done:
```

Figure 9.6: *(continued)*

```
        OR      BP,BP
        JZ      done2
        MOV     DI,BP
        MOV     AL,[norml]          ;stop blinking
        CALL    ch_att              ;make normal
done2:
        @go_dos
;**********************************************************
; Routine to change video attribute for 16 characters
; On entry:     ES = video screen segment
;               DI = offset into screen memory
;               AL = video attribute
;**********************************************************
ch_att  PROC
        MOV     CX,16               ;block length
nexta:
        INC     DI                  ;skip char
        STOSB                       ;store
        LOOP    nexta
        RET
ch_att  ENDP
;*************** End procedure ch_att  **************
h_msg   DB      '  PRINTER Version 4.1',cr,lf
        DB      'The dot-matrix printer can be set to'
        DB      ' following modes:',cr,lf
        DB      bulc,16 DUP(bhor),burc,cr,lf
        DB      bver,'Bold type       ',bver,cr,lf
        DB      bver,'Compressed type ',bver,cr,lf
        DB      bver,'Italics type    ',bver,cr,lf
        DB      bver,'Letter quality  ',bver,cr,lf
        DB      bver,'Tiny type       ',bver,cr,lf
        DB      bver,'Wide type       ',bver,cr,lf
        DB      bver,'Eight lines/inch',bver,cr,lf
        DB      bver,'Paper-out sensor',bver,cr,lf

        DB      bver,'Bold OFF        ',bver,cr,lf
        DB      bver,'Compressed OFF  ',bver,cr,lf
        DB      bver,'Italics OFF     ',bver,cr,lf
        DB      bver,'Letter OFF      ',bver,cr,lf
        DB      bver,'Tiny OFF        ',bver,cr,lf
        DB      bver,'Wide OFF        ',bver,cr,lf
        DB      bver,'Six lines/inch  ',bver,cr,lf
        DB      bver,'Paper-out OFF   ',bver,cr,lf
        DB      bllc,16 DUP(bhor),blrc,cr,lf
        DB      'Move cursor to the desired selection'
        DB      ' and press the Return key.',cr,lf
        DB      'Press <Esc> to cancel.'
        DB      ' For direct execution enter:',cr,lf
        DB      ' PRINTER  X   where X is B, C,'
        DB      ' I, L, T, W, P, or 8.',cr,lf
        DB      'Turn off feature with:  PRINTER  X  O$'
code    ENDS
        END     strt
```

Figure 9.6: *(continued)*

Return is found, we check for zero in the AH register, meaning that a special, nonalphanumeric key was pressed.

If zero is not found we loop back to label *key_in* and read another character. If we find a zero, however, it means that a character corresponding to an extended code was entered. (The extended codes are given in Appendix B.) The extended codes include the cursor keys, function keys, and certain keys pressed in combination with the Alt key or Ctrl key. We execute function 8 a second time to get the extended code for the key that was pressed. We are looking for the up or down arrow, corresponding to the value 72 or 80. If we find one of these two characters, we move the highlighted block in the corresponding direction. If we find the End key, we terminate the program.

The cursor is moved in two steps. First we change the attribute of the current position back to normal, then we change the attribute of the new position to blinking. We retrieve the current position from the BP register and place it in the DI register. We also set the attribute to the value at location *norml*. This will be light-on-dark for a monochrome or black-and-white screen and yellow-on-blue for a color screen. Then we call procedure

```
C:\ASM>prtest
  PRINTER Version 4.1
The dot-matrix printer can be set to following modes:

┌─────────────────┐
│Bold type        │
│Compressed type  │
│Italics type     │
│Letter quality   │
│Tiny type        │
│Wide type        │
│Eight lines/inch │
│Paper-out sensor │
│Bold OFF         │
│Compressed OFF   │
│Italics OFF      │
│Letter OFF       │
│Tiny OFF         │
│Wide OFF         │
│Six lines/inch   │
│Paper-out OFF    │
└─────────────────┘

Move cursor to the desired selection and press the Return key.
Press <Esc> to cancel. For direct execution enter:
  PRINTER  X  where X is B, C, I, L, T, W, P, or 8.
Turn off feature with:  PRINTER  X  0▪
```

Figure 9.7: *Menu for printer program.*

ch_att to make the change. Before we select the new position, we must see if we are at one extreme or the other of the menu. For example, if the cursor is at the top and the down arrow is pressed we move the cursor down one line, but if the up arrow is pressed we move the cursor to the bottom line, wrapping the cursor around.

Selecting a Menu Item

When the Return key is pressed, the SI register is pointing to the selected menu item. We branch to label *selct* to find the corresponding code. The SI register serves as a pointer or index to the menu items displayed on the screen. It is also an index into the "jump" table that references the corresponding instructions. We double the value in SI by adding SI to itself. Then we branch to the label referenced by SI in our jump table near the beginning of the code. For example, if SI has a value of 1, it means that the second item in the menu was selected. After we double the value in SI and add it to the table offset, we direct a branch to the label *com* by performing a JMP [*label*] instruction, setting compressed type. The corresponding code points the DI register to the appropriate string (*comc*) and the CX register to the number of items in the string (*comcl*). The instructions in this region are created by the IRP in-line macro we considered in Chapter 7. We branch to label *send* to transmit the string to the printer. Finally, we branch to label *done,* where we return the blinking cursor to normal and terminate the program.

If a parameter was entered on the command line, we process the request directly; we do not display the menu. This method is ideal for batch operation. We first check for a second parameter of O, a request to turn off a feature. Then we process the first parameter, branching to the appropriate label. For example, the parameter C causes a branch to label *com,* as in the previous example. Now, however, after sending the appropriate string to the printer, we branch to label *done.* We check the BP register for zero to see if a parameter was entered. If so, we skip over the code to restore the screen and terminate the program.

We unscramble addresses with our next program.

DISPLAYING BYTES ARABIC-STYLE

Hexadecimal displays, such as those generated by the D command of the debugger, are typically written from left to right. Two hexadecimal characters written together constitute each byte. However, there is an inconsistency in this type of display. The two characters (nibbles) that represent the byte are displayed with the larger (higher-valued) character on the left and the smaller value on the right. When a 16-bit address is represented in this way, the bytes appear to be reversed. Thus the instruction

JMP done

from the previous program is shown as

E9 02DC JMP done

in the assembly listing. This indicates that the label *done* is located at address 2DC hex. However, if we examine the bytes in a memory display, the three bytes would appear as

E9 DC 02

That is, the DC is located between the E9 and 02 bytes. The comforting rule is that the higher (most-significant) half of the address (2 in this case) is higher in memory (that is, at a numerically larger address) than the lower half (DC).

If we use the D command of the debugger to look at the BIOS interrupt area at the beginning of memory, we see something like this:

```
0000 72 30 E3 00 47 01 70 00–C3 E2 00 F0 47 01 70 00
0010 47 01 70 00 54 FF 00 F0–47 FF 00 F0 47 FF 00 F0
0020 DF 01 D7 5C 2F 01 B2 63–DD E6 00 F0 DD E6 00 F0
```

Each four bytes, eight characters, represents one interrupt vector. Consider, for example, interrupt 5, the PrtSc command located at address 14 hex. The interrupt address is

F000:FF54

However, it appears in the listing as 54 FF 00 F0. Notice what happens if we reverse the order of the bytes in the middle line:

```
F0 00 FF 47 F0 00 FF 47–F0 00 FF 54 00 70 01 47 0010
```

Now the vector for interrupt 5 appears in a natural order. Let us consider another example.

A further complexity arises when we display the file-allocation table (FAT). The FAT is a set of numbers describing where each file is located on the disk. Floppy disks and small hard disks use a 12-bit FAT, while larger disks use a 16-bit FAT. You can inspect the first two sectors of the FAT for drive B by giving this DEBUG command:

    LDS:100 1 1 2

The first parameter is the load address, the next designates drive B, the third selects the first sector number, and the last parameter is the number of sectors to be read. If you then give the command

    D170 L10

you might see something like this:

    6884:0170 C0 04 4D E0 04 4F 00 05–51 20 05 53 40 05 55 60

Although it is not readily apparent, the FAT numbers on this line are

    4C 4D 4E 4F 50 51 52 53 54 55

We can see this relationship by displaying the line backward:

    60 55 05 40 53 05 20 51–05 00 4F 04 E0 4D 04 C0 6884:0170

Then we can split the nibbles:

    60 55 0 54 0 53 0 52 0 51–0 50 0 4F 0 4E 0 4D 0 4C 0

and read the line from right to left.

Several authors have criticized the backward design of the FAT, but in fact, the design is correct. The problem lies in the mixing of Arabic and Roman notation. Arabic is written from right to left, and so the system of Arabic numerals also increases from right to left. The tens are to the left of the units, the hundreds are to the left of the tens, and so on. We have accepted this backward notation without question. The problem is that we insist on displaying successive bytes in Roman fashion, from left to right. Thus, when we represent a 32-bit interrupt vector as four bytes, we arrange the two nibbles in each byte in Arabic fashion from right to left. But then we arrange successive bytes in Roman fashion from left to right. In this way we scramble 12-bit, 16-bit, and 32-bit numbers in our displays.

Microsoft compromises by reversing the 16-bit addresses but then runs the bytes together to indicate that they are reversed. Thus, in the listing that we considered above:

E9 02DC JMP done

the DC byte is located between the E9 and 02 bytes in memory. Now consider the appearance when displayed in Arabic style:

02 DC E9 JMP done

or perhaps:

JMP done 02 DC E9

The program listed in Figure 9.8 is designed to make your displays easier to read. Create a file named ADUMP.ASM and type up the program. Assemble it and try it out. Execute it without a parameter and the result will look like Figure 9.9. Look at the second line, starting at address 10 hex (on the right). Move left to interrupt 5, address 14 hex. Compare the vector there to the value we found from DEBUG:

F000:FF54

Notice how much easier it is to read. You can display the next line by pressing the down-arrow key and the next page by pressing the PgDn key. You can also go backward, but the entire screen is refreshed for each line, which greatly slows down the display.

Terminate the program with the Esc key. Run ADUMP again, but give two parameters:

ADUMP 40 0

specifying segment 40, the BIOS data area at offset 0. The first line contains the parallel and serial port addresses. The next line has the equipment list at 40:10. Let us go through the program.

We begin by defining the four cursor keys—the up and down arrows, PgUp and PgDn. We also define the two parameters at locations 5D and 6D hex. We expect only hexadecimal numbers at these locations. After coding the heading, we identify the program name on the screen and give directions for use. We set the SI and ES registers to zero as the default. Then we point the DI register to the first parameter area and check for

```
          PAGE     ,132
          TITLE    ADUMP

COMMENT *
  January 25, 1096
  Display a portion of memory in hex and ASCII
  Successive hex bytes are reversed in Arabic fashion
  Usage:
          ADUMP
          ADUMP   400        ;offset
          ADUMP   5300 0     ;segment, offet
    Macros: @d_char, @go_dos, @head, @ucase,
          @write, @write_r
  INT 21h function 8
  *
          INCLUDE mylib.equ
          IF1
          INCLUDE mylib.mac
          ENDIF

up_arr  EQU      72                  ;up cursor
down_ar EQU      80                  ;down cursor
pg_up   EQU      73                  ;previous screen
pg_dn   EQU      81                  ;next screen

code    SEGMENT
        ASSUME   CS:code, DS:code
        ORG      5Dh
param1  DB       ?                   ;parameter 1
        ORG      6Dh
param2  DB       ?                   ;parameter 2

        ORG      100h
strt:
        @head    ' ADUMP, 01.25.86 '
        @write_r <OFFSET mesl>
; set segment and offset to zero
        XOR      SI,SI               ;zero offset
        MOV      ES,SI               ;segment
; check if parameter was entered
        MOV      DI,OFFSET param1
        CMP      BYTE PTR [DI],blank ;anything?
        JZ       t_lines
; convert parameter from ASCII hex to binary in SI
        CALL     get_hex
        MOV      SI,DX
; check if second parameter was entered
        MOV      DI,OFFSET param2
        CMP      BYTE PTR [DI],blank ;anything?
        JZ       t_lines
        MOV      ES,SI
; convert parameter from ASCII hex to binary in SI
```

Figure 9.8: Program ADUMP for Arabic display of hexadecimal numbers.

```
        CALL    get_hex
        MOV     SI,DX
;------------------------------------------------
; start display of 16 lines
; ES has segment, SI has offset
;------------------------------------------------
t_lines:
        @write_r <OFFSET mes2>
        MOV     CX,21               ;lines
n_line:
        @write  <cr,lf>             ;new line
; display address and 16 hex bytes
        CALL    do_hex
; display ASCII
        CALL    do_ascii
        ADD     SI,16               ;next line
        LOOP    n_line
; wait for keyboard input
        CALL    get_in
        CMP     AL,esc              ;quit?
        JZ      done                ;yes
        CMP     AL,cr               ;next page?
        JNZ     not_cr              ;no
        JMP     t_lines
not_cr:
        CMP     AL,pg_dn
        JNZ     not_pd
        JMP     t_lines             ;next page
not_pd:
        CMP     AL,up_arr
        JNZ     not_ua              ;prev line
; back up pointer one line and redisplay
        SUB     SI,22*16
        JMP     t_lines
not_ua:
        CMP     AL,pg_up
        JNZ     not_tl              ;prev page
; back up pointer one page and redisplay
        SUB     SI,42*16
        JMP     t_lines
not_tl:
        MOV     CX,1
        CMP     AL,blank
        JZ      n_line              ;next line
        CMP     AL,down_ar
        JZ      n_line              ;next line
done:
        @go_dos
; translation table binary to ASCII hex
hex_tab DB      '0123456789ABCDEF'
```

Figure 9.8: *(continued)*

```
;*****************************************
; Convert binary number in AL to hex and
;   and display on screen
; Input:          AL = byte
;*****************************************
outhex  PROC
        PUSH    DX
        MOV     DL,AL                   ;save
        REPT    4                       ;times 16
        SHR     AL,1
        ENDM
        CALL    outhx                   ;high half
        MOV     AL,DL                   ;get back
        CALL    outhx                   ;low half
        MOV     AL,DL                   ;restore
        POP     DX
        RET
outhex  ENDP
;********  End outhex  *******************
;*****************************************
; convert four bits in AL to hex and
; display on screen
;*****************************************
outhx   PROC
        AND     AL,0Fh                  ;low 4 bits
        PUSH    BX
        MOV     BX,OFFSET hex_tab
        XLAT    hex_tab
        @d_char AL                      ;display
        POP     BX
        RET
outhx   ENDP
;********  End outhx  *******************
;*****************************************
; Convert ASCII hex to binary
; Input:          DI points to string
; Output:         DX = binary value
;*****************************************
get_hex PROC
        PUSH    AX
        XOR     AX,AX                   ;zero
        MOV     DX,AX                   ;DX too
g_hex2:
        MOV     AL,[DI]
        SUB     AL,'0'                  ;make binary
        JL      g_hex_b                 ;too low
        CMP     AL,10
        JL      g_hex_g                 ;ok
        @ucase                          ;make upper
        SUB     AL,'A'-'9'-1            ;adjust for A-F
        JL      g_hex_b                 ;too low
```

Figure 9.8: (continued)

```
                CMP       AL,15
                JG        g_hex_b         ;too large
        ; add new character to sum
        g_hex_g:
                REPT      4
                SHL       DX,1
                ENDM
                ADD       DX,AX
                INC       DI
                JMP       g_hex2          ;next char
        ; end of string
        g_hex_b:
                POP       AX
                RET

        get_hex ENDP
        ;************* End of get_hex *********
        ;******************************************
        ; display address and 16 hex bytes
        ; Input:        SI = pointer
        ; Output:       SI is 16 larger
        ;******************************************
        do_hex  PROC
                MOV       DI,SI
                ADD       DI,16
                PUSH      CX
                MOV       CX,16           ;one line
        next_ch:
                DEC       DI              ;next
                MOV       AL,ES:[DI]
                CALL      outhex
                PUSH      BX
                MOV       BL,blank
        ; put a minus sign at quarter points
                MOV       AX,DI
                AND       AL,0fh
                JZ        not_min         ;line end
                AND       AL,3
                JNZ       not_min
                MOV       BL,'-'          ;minus
        not_min:
                @d_char BL
                POP       BX
                LOOP      next_ch
                POP       CX
                @d_char blank
        ; display address at right side
                PUSH      BX
        ; display segment address
                MOV       BX,ES
                MOV       AL,BH
                CALL      outhex          ;high half
```

Figure 9.8: *(continued)*

```
                MOV     AL,BL
                CALL    outhex          ;low half
                @d_char ':'             ;colon
; display offset address
                MOV     BX,SI           ;offset
                MOV     AL,BH
                CALL    outhex          ;high half
                MOV     AL,BL
                POP     BX
                CALL    outhex          ;low half
                RET
do_hex   ENDP
;************* End of do_hex  ***********
;*******************************************
; display 16 ASCII bytes
; control characters shown as period
; extended character translated to ASCII
;
; Input:         SI = pointer
;*******************************************
do_ascii PROC
                @write  <blank,blank>
                MOV     DI,SI
                PUSH    CX
                MOV     CX,16           ;one line
next_as:
                MOV     AL,ES:[DI]
                AND     AL,7Fh          ;make ASCII
                CMP     AL,7Fh          ;DEL?
                JZ      d_per           ;yes
                CMP     AL,blank        ;too small?
                JNB     nbl
d_per:
; change to period
                MOV     AL,period
nbl:
                @d_char AL
                INC     DI              ;next
                LOOP    next_as
                POP     CX
                RET
do_ascii ENDP
;************* End of do_ascii  *********
;*******************************************
; wait for character from keyboard
; don't echo on screen
; if extended code, two calls are made
;
; Output:        AL = character
;*******************************************
```

Figure 9.8: *(continued)*

```
get_in   PROC
         MOV     AH,8
         INT     21h
         OR      AL,AL           ;zero?
         JNZ     get_2           ;no
; get extended code
         INT     21h
get_2:
         RET
get_in   ENDP
;*************   End of get_in   **********
mes1     DB      '     Arabic display--Hex goes'
         DB      ' from right to left',cr,lf
         DB      ' Active keys are: down and up'
         DB      ' arrows, PgDn, PgUp, and Esc$'
mes2     DB      cr,lf,lf,' F  E  D  C  B  A  9  8'
         DB      ' 7  6  5  4  3  2  1  0  SEGM'
         DB      ' ADDR  0123456789ABCDEF$'

code     ENDS
         END     strt
```

Figure 9.8: *(continued)*

an entry. If there is one, we call procedure *get_hex* to convert the ASCII hex characters to binary. Let us consider that routine.

Routine *get_hex* begins by setting the AX and DX registers to zero. The AX register will hold each of the characters in turn. The DX register will contain the complete binary number. We move the first ASCII character into AX and subtract an ASCII zero to convert the number to binary. If the character is a letter from A to F, we must additionally subtract 7. If the character is valid, we shift the previous result left four bits and add the new value. We do this to each character until there are no more. Then we return to the main program and move the value into the SI register.

We then check the second parameter. If there is only one parameter, it becomes the offset in the SI register. But if two parameters are present, we shift the first parameter into the ES register and call routine *get_hex* a second time. On return from this routine, we move the new value into the SI register. Of course, if no parameter was entered, we begin the display at address zero. Now that the starting segment and offset are set, we can begin the display.

We write a header over the table, reminding the user that the hexadecimal display goes from right to left. We call procedure *do_hex* to display the hex bytes in reverse order. We add 16 to the address and work backwards to the starting address. We add a minus sign every four bytes to set off the 32-bit groups. The binary-to-ASCII hexadecimal conversion is performed by procedure *outhex*. It produces two characters from each byte by calling procedure *outhx* twice. This procedure converts binary numbers to ASCII by using the XLAT instruction. We set up a table:

hex_tab DB '0123456789ABCDEF'

giving the sequence of ASCII hex numbers. The original binary number is the index into the table. With the binary number in the AL register and the offset of the table in the BX register, we simply give the command

XLAT hex_tab

and the conversion is performed. We then display the character on the screen with our *@d_char* macro and call procedure *do_ascii* to display the ASCII equivalent of each character or a decimal point if the character is not printable.

After displaying 21 lines of data, we stop and wait for input. We call procedure *get_in* to monitor the keyboard. The input is obtained from function 8, as in the previous program. A value of zero is found if a special key has been pressed. Then we execute the function a second time to get the extended code. We look for five keys. If the Esc key is pressed, we terminate the program. If the down arrow is pressed, we display one more line, and if the PgDn key is pressed we display another 21 lines. In the same way, the up arrow moves the display back one line and the PgUp key moves it back 21 lines. Unfortunately, the last two operations refresh the screen. As a result, the program is rather time-consuming. It would be faster to write the information directly to the video screen. Then the screen would be updated instantly. This improvement is left as an exercise for the reader.

```
     Arabic display--Hex goes from right to left
     Active keys are: down and up arrows, PgDn, PgUp, and Esc
      F  E  D  C  B  A  9  8  7  6  5  4  3  2  1  0   SEGM ADDR
     00 70 01 47-F0 00 E2 C3-00 70 01 47-00 E3 30 72   0000:0000
     F0 00 FF 47-F0 00 FF 47-F0 00 FF 54-00 70 01 47   0000:0010
     F0 00 E6 DD-F0 00 E6 DD-63 B2 01 2F-5C D7 01 DF   0000:0020
     00 70 01 47-F0 00 EF 57-F0 00 E6 DD-F0 00 E6 DD   0000:0030
     06 61 01 7E-F0 00 F8 41-F0 00 F8 4D-F0 00 F0 65   0000:0040
     63 CF 01 50-F0 00 E8 2E-F0 00 F8 59-F0 00 E7 39   0000:0050
     00 70 01 40-F0 00 FE 6E-F0 00 E6 F2-F6 00 00 00   0000:0060
     F0 00 00 00-00 00 05 22-F0 00 F0 A4-F0 00 FF 53   0000:0070
     05 90 02 99-05 90 02 8C-63 ED 03 5C-00 E3 0B 07   0000:0080
```

Figure 9.9: *Arabic display of BIOS interrupt vectors.*

We enlarge the available RAM memory in the next and last program.

INCREASING THE MEMORY TO 704K BYTES

We have seen that the maximum amount of memory DOS can normally use is 640K bytes, ending with segment 9000 hex. We also saw that the video-screen memory begins at segment B000 hex. Therefore, there is an unused 64K-byte block of memory at segment A000 hex. The program presented in this section allows you to expand DOS into this segment so that 704K bytes of memory are available for your programs. Of course, you cannot use this program unless you have memory in segment A000 hex. Therefore, you will need to add another memory board. Some memory boards, such as the AST SixPak, cannot be addressed to this region, while others, such as the IBM 64/256 board, can. After adding the new memory and addressing it to the A000 hex segment, run the program given in Figure 9.10. This resets the maximum RAM memory to 704K bytes.

Our program performs several services. The maximum memory size, stored in the BIOS data area at 40:13 hex, must be increased and the new memory set to zero to avoid parity errors. After making these changes, we reset the computer so that it will reload DOS. Finally, we must ensure that our program does not perform these services a second time. Create a file named MEM704.ASM. Type up the program given in Figure 9.10 and assemble it. Let us go through the source listing.

We begin by establishing the segment in the BIOS data area at 40 hex. Then we define the location within this segment where the maximum memory size is stored (location 13 hex). We begin the code segment next, as usual, starting with the program name and date and a branch over this information. We then check the word at 40:13 (label *mem_siz*) to see if the value stored there is already 704K (2C0 hex). If so, we terminate the program. However, if this is the first time the program has been run, we first check that there is 704K bytes of memory installed in the computer. We write two patterns, 55 hex and AA hex, as we did with the SCREEN program earlier in this chapter. If there is no memory in the A000 hex segment, we display an error message and terminate the program.

If 704K bytes of memory is present, we change the BIOS word at 40:13 hex to 2C0 hex, set the new memory to zero, write a message on the screen to inform the user, and then reboot the system with interrupt 19 hex.

Let us consider the code that sets the memory to zero. The IBM PC uses parity-checked memory. Each eight-bit byte has an associated ninth bit

```
            PAGE    ,132
            TITLE   704K - set memory to 704K bytes
COMMENT *
    Increase memory to 704K bytes by changing
    BIOS data word at 40:13 hex
    Set new memory to zero
    February 22, 1986
  *
            INCLUDE mylib.equ
            IF1
            INCLUDE mylib.mac
            ENDIF

old_siz EQU     640             ;old mem size
new_siz EQU     704             ;new mem size
new_seg EQU     0A000h          ;704K segment


; BIOS data area
bios_d  SEGMENT AT 40h
        ORG     13h
mem_siz LABEL   WORD            ;memory size
bios_d  ENDS


code    SEGMENT
        ASSUME  CS:code,DS:code, ES:bios_d
        ORG     100h
strt:
        @head   ' MEM704,02.22.86 '
; point to memory size in BIOS data area
        MOV     AX,bios_d       ;zero
        MOV     ES,AX
        MOV     SI,OFFSET mem_siz
; check if already run
        CMP     WORD PTR ES:[SI],new_siz
        JNE     ok
        @go_dos                 ;quit
; check for memory at A000 hex
ok:
        MOV     BX,ES           ;save ES
        MOV     AX,new_seg
        MOV     ES,AX           ;ES=A000
        XOR     DI,DI           ;offset
        MOV     AX,55AAh        ;01010101
        MOV     ES:[DI],AH      ;55 hex
        CMP     AH,ES:[DI]      ;ok?
        JNZ     no_mem          ;no
        MOV     ES:[DI],AL      ;AA hex
        CMP     AL,ES:[DI]      ;ok?
        JNZ     no_mem          ;no
; set memory size for 704K bytes
        MOV     CX,ES           ;save ES
        MOV     ES,BX           ;ES=40
```

Figure 9.10: *Program MEM704 to increase memory size to 704K bytes.*

```
              MOV      WORD PTR ES:[SI],new_siz
              MOV      ES,CX            ;ES=A000
; fill new memory with zeros
              XOR      AX,AX            ;zero word
              MOV      DI,AX            ;zero location
              MOV      CX,8000h         ;32K words
              REP      STOSW            ;do it
              @write   <' Memory now 704K bytes',cr,lf>
              INT      19h              ;reboot system
; no memory at A000 hex, terminate without change
no_mem:
              @write   'No memory at A000 hex, aborting'
              @go_dos

code          ENDS
              END      strt
```

Figure 9.10: *(continued)*

that is used for a parity check. The sum of the nine bits must have zero parity. When any byte is read, the parity bit is checked to see that there is no error. However, this scheme can only work properly if the parity bits are correctly set on startup. This can be accomplished by writing a zero in each memory location. The system sets the memory to zero only up through 640K bytes. Therefore, the new memory in the A000 segment will not be set to zero. If you try to read from the new memory, you will get a parity error and the computer will lock up. If you first fill the new memory with zeros, however, everything will be all right.

Our program sets the new 64K bytes of memory to zero with the store-string (STOSW) instruction. We point the ES:DI registers to the beginning of the memory at segment A000 hex, set the AX register to the zero we want to write, set the CX register to 64K bytes (8000 hex words), and combine the REP instruction with the STOSW instruction. From now on, your programs can use as much as 704K bytes of memory. You might want to establish a 360K-byte RAM disk with the VDISK program. Then you will still have 344K bytes of usable memory.

If you run the CHKDSK program after establishing a 360K-byte RAM disk, you will see something like this:

720896 bytes total memory
281472 bytes free

Since 1K bytes of memory is 2^{10} or 1024, not 1000, 704K bytes means

720,896. We can also think of this as 11 segments (0 through A) times 64K (65,536).

While this technique works properly with both the monochrome and the graphics adapter, there is a potential problem. The IBM Enhanced Graphics Adapter (EGA) uses part of the A000 hex segment, and so you cannot use this technique when an EGA is installed in your computer.

SUMMARY

In this chapter we added two new macros and wrote several new programs. Some of them were rather long, but useful. Furthermore, techniques such as resident interrupt drivers and binary-to-hex translation with the XLAT operation will be useful in other programs you write. You now have a kit of useful routines in addition to the many programs we have written, and you have 64K bytes more memory to help you. You should be able to write many new and interesting programs. Have fun.

The beginning of your macro library should now look like this:

```
; Macros in this library
;   @close          MACRO   handle?
;   @create         MACRO   pointr?              ;disk file
;   @d_char         MACRO   par?                 ;display character
;   @d_read         MACRO   handle?,pointr?
;   @d_write        MACRO   handle?,pointr?
;   @delete         MACRO   pointr?
;   @dos_ver        MACRO                        ;get version
;   @get_vec        MACRO   ?vec                 ;interrupt vector
;   @go_dos         MACRO                        ;return to DOS by 21h
;   @head           MACRO   num?                 ;header information
;   @lprint         MACRO   text?                ;text to printer
;   @mak_buf        MACRO   name?, len?
;   @open           MACRO   pointr?              ;open disk file
;   @read_bf        MACRO   loc?                 ;read input buffer
;   @readch         MACRO                        ;read/display character
;   @rename         MACRO                        ;DX to DI
;   @screen_mode    MACRO                        ;find screen type
;   @screen_set     MACRO                        ;change screen type
;   @set_vec        MACRO   ?vec                 ;change interr vector
;   @ucase          MACRO                        ;change AL to upper case
;   @write          MACRO   text?                ;write text on screen
;   @write_r        MACRO   addr?                ;display text at addr?
```

A The ASCII Character Set

Character Set (00-7F) Quick Reference

DECIMAL VALUE ➡		0	16	32	48	64	80	96	112
⬇	HEXA DECIMAL VALUE	0	1	2	3	4	5	6	7
0	0	BLANK (NULL)	►	BLANK (SPACE)	0	@	P	`	p
1	1	☺	◄	!	1	A	Q	a	q
2	2	☻	↕	"	2	B	R	b	r
3	3	♥	‼	#	3	C	S	c	s
4	4	♦	¶	$	4	D	T	d	t
5	5	♣	§	%	5	E	U	e	u
6	6	♠	▬	&	6	F	V	f	v
7	7	•	↨	'	7	G	W	g	w
8	8	◘	↑	(	8	H	X	h	x
9	9	○	↓	)	9	I	Y	i	y
10	A	◙	→	*	:	J	Z	j	z
11	B	♂	←	+	;	K	[	k	{
12	C	♀	∟	,	<	L	\	l	¦
13	D	♪	↔	—	=	M	]	m	}
14	E	♫	▲	.	>	N	∧	n	~
15	F	☼	▼	/	?	O	_	o	△

Character Set (88-FF) Quick Reference

DECIMAL VALUE ➡		128	144	160	176	192	208	224	240
⬇	HEXA DECIMAL VALUE	8	9	A	B	C	D	E	F
0	0	Ç	É	á	▓	└	╨	∝	≡
1	1	ü	æ	í	▒	┴	╤	β	±
2	2	é	Æ	ó	▓	┬	╥	Γ	≥
3	3	â	ô	ú	│	├	╙	π	≤
4	4	ä	ö	ñ	┤	─	╘	Σ	∫
5	5	à	ò	Ñ	╡	┼	╒	σ	∫
6	6	å	û	ª	╢	╞	╓	µ	÷
7	7	ç	ù	º	╖	╟	╫	τ	≈
8	8	ê	ÿ	¿	╕	╚	╪	₫	°
9	9	ë	Ö	⌐	╣	╔	┘	θ	•
10	A	è	Ü	¬	║	╩	┌	Ω	·
11	B	ï	¢	½	╗	╦	█	δ	√
12	C	î	£	¼	╝	╠	█	∞	n
13	D	ì	¥	¡	╜	═	█	φ	2
14	E	Ä	₧	«	╛	╬	█	∈	■
15	F	Å	ƒ	»	┐	╧	█	∩	BLANK 'FF'

Technical Reference Manual, pp.7-12–7-13, © 1984 International Business Machines Corporation

B The Extended Keyboard Codes

The keys on the IBM PC keyboard are assigned numbers, called scan codes, that range from 1 to 83. They are identified in Appendix H. When a key is pressed, the keyboard computer transmits the corresponding scan code to the computer in the system unit. The main computer converts these codes to ASCII if possible and sends the result to the keyboard buffer. However, certain keys and key combinations cannot be represented in ASCII. For those keys, two bytes are sent to the input buffer. The first byte is a zero; the second byte is the extended code given in the following table. If the extended code is between 15 and 83, it corresponds to the scan code. For example, pressing the F1 key gives the two bytes 0, 59 since the scan code for the F1 key is 59.

However, there are additional codes with numbers above 83. These correspond to the shifted function, arrow, and number keys. They are also identified in the table. Finally, it is not possible to send the ASCII null code of zero, since a zero indicates an extended code. Therefore, the value of 3 is to be used for this character. It is generated with Ctrl-2.

Hexadecimal	Decimal	Keystrokes
3	3	Ctrl-2 (Null)
F	15	Shift-tab
10	16	Alt-Q
11	17	Alt-W
12	18	Alt-E
13	19	Alt-R
14	20	Alt-T
15	21	Alt-Y
16	22	Alt-U
17	23	Alt-I
18	24	Alt-O
19	25	Alt-P
1E	30	Alt-A
1F	31	Alt-S
20	32	Alt-D
21	33	Alt-F
22	34	Alt-G
23	35	Alt-H
24	36	Alt-J
25	37	Alt-K
26	38	Alt-L

Hexadecimal	Decimal	Keystrokes
2C	44	Alt-Z
2D	45	Alt-X
2E	46	Alt-C
2F	47	Alt-V
30	48	Alt-B
31	49	Alt-N
32	50	Alt-M
3B	59	F1
3C	60	F2
3D	61	F3
3E	62	F4
3F	63	F5
40	64	F6
41	65	F7
42	66	F8
42	67	F9
44	68	F10
46	70	Ctrl-Break
47	71	Home
48	72	Up arrow
49	73	PgUp
4B	75	Left arrow
4D	77	Right arrow
4F	79	End
50	80	Down arrow
51	81	PgDn
52	82	Ins
53	83	Del
54–5D	84–93	Shift-F1 through F10
5E–67	94–103	Ctrl-F1 through F10
6B–71	104-113	Alt-F1 through F10
72	114	Ctrl-PrtSc
73	115	Ctrl-Left arrow
74	116	Ctrl-Right arrow
75	117	Ctrl-End

Hexadecimal	Decimal	Keystrokes
76	118	Ctrl-PgDn
77	119	Ctrl-Home
78–83	120–131	Alt-1–9, 0, –, =
84	132	Ctrl-PgUp

C The 8088 Instruction Set

ADD	**ADD** destination,source Addition			**Flags** O D I T S Z A P C X X X X X X
Operands	Clocks	Transfers*	Bytes	Coding Example
register, register	3	—	2	ADD CX, DX
register, memory	9 + EA	1	2-4	ADD DI, [BX].ALPHA
memory, register	16 + EA	2	2-4	ADD TEMP, CL
register, immediate	4	—	3-4	ADD CL, 2
memory, immediate	17 + EA	2	3-6	ADD ALPHA, 2
accumulator, immediate	4	—	2-3	ADD AX, 200

AND	**AND** destination,source Logical and			**Flags** O D I T S Z A P C 0 X X U X 0
Operands	Clocks	Transfers*	Bytes	Coding Example
register, register	3	—	2	AND AL,BL
register, memory	9 + EA	1	2-4	AND CX,FLAG__WORD
memory, register	16 + EA	2	2-4	AND ASCII [DI],AL
register, immediate	4	—	3-4	AND CX,0F0H
memory, immediate	17 + EA	2	3-6	AND BETA, 01H
accumulator, immediate	4	—	2-3	AND AX, 01010000B

CALL	**CALL** target Call a procedure			**Flags** O D I T S Z A P C
Operands	Clocks	Transfers*	Bytes	Coding Examples
near-proc	19	1	3	CALL NEAR__PROC
far-proc	28	2	5	CALL FAR__PROC
memptr 16	21 + EA	2	2-4	CALL PROC__TABLE [SI]
regptr 16	16	1	2	CALL AX
memptr 32	37 + EA	4	2-4	CALL [BX].TASK [SI]

CBW	**CBW** (no operands) Convert byte to word			**Flags** O D I T S Z A P C
Operands	Clocks	Transfers*	Bytes	Coding Example
(no operands)	2	—	1	CBW

CLC	**CLC** (no operands) Clear carry flag			**Flags** O D I T S Z A P C 0
Operands	Clocks	Transfers*	Bytes	Coding Example
(no operands)	2	—	1	CLC

CLD	**CLD** (no operands) Clear direction flag			**Flags** O D I T S Z A P C 0
Operands	Clocks	Transfers*	Bytes	Coding Example
(no operands)	2	—	1	CLD

---

* For the 8086, add four clocks for each 16-bit word transfer with an odd address. For the 8088, add four clocks for each 16-bit word transfer. Mnemonics © Intel, 1978.

CLI	CLI (no operands) Clear interrupt flag			Flags	O D I T S Z A P C 0
Operands	**Clocks**	**Transfers***	**Bytes**		**Coding Example**
(no operands)	2	—	1		CLI

CMC	CMC (no operands) Complement carry flag			Flags	O D I T S Z A P C X
Operands	**Clocks**	**Transfers***	**Bytes**		**Coding Example**
(no operands)	2	—	1		CMC

CMP	CMP destination,source Compare destination to source			Flags	O D I T S Z A P C X X X X X X
Operands	**Clocks**	**Transfers***	**Bytes**		**Coding Example**
register, register	3	—	2		CMP BX, CX
register, memory	9 + EA	1	2-4		CMP DH, ALPHA
memory, register	9 + EA	1	2-4		CMP [BP + 2], SI
register, immediate	4	—	3-4		CMP BL, 02H
memory, immediate	10 + EA	1	3-6		CMP [BX].RADAR [DI], 3420H
accumulator, immediate	4	—	2-3		CMP AL, 00010000B

CMPS	CMPS dest-string,source-string Compare string			Flags	O D I T S Z A P C X X X X X X
Operands	**Clocks**	**Transfers***	**Bytes**		**Coding Example**
dest-string, source-string	22	2	1		CMPS BUFF1, BUFF2
(repeat) dest-string, source-string	9 + 22/rep	2/rep	1		REPE CMPS ID, KEY

CWD	CWD (no operands) Convert word to doubleword			Flags	O D I T S Z A P C
Operands	**Clocks**	**Transfers***	**Bytes**		**Coding Example**
(no operands)	5	—	1		CWD

DAA	DAA (no operands) Decimal adjust for addition			Flags	O D I T S Z A P C X X X X X X
Operands	**Clocks**	**Transfers***	**Bytes**		**Coding Example**
(no operands)	4	—	1		DAA

DAS	DAS (no operands) Decimal adjust for subtraction			Flags	O D I T S Z A P C U X X X X X
Operands	**Clocks**	**Transfers***	**Bytes**		**Coding Example**
(no operands)	4	—	1		DAS

* For the 8086, add four clocks for each 16-bit word transfer with an odd address. For the 8088, add four clocks for each 16-bit word transfer. Mnemonics © Intel, 1978.

DEC	DEC destination Decrement by 1				Flags	O D I T S Z A P C X X X X X
Operands		Clocks	Transfers*	Bytes	Coding Example	
reg16		2	—	1	DEC AX	
reg8		3	—	2	DEC AL	
memory		15 + EA	2	2-4	DEC ARRAY [SI]	

DIV	DIV source Division, unsigned				Flags	O D I T S Z A P C U U U U U
Operands		Clocks	Transfers*	Bytes	Coding Example	
reg8		80-90	—	2	DIV CL	
reg16		144-162	—	2	DIV BX	
mem8		(86-96) + EA	1	2-4	DIV ALPHA	
mem16		(150-168) + EA	1	2-4	DIV TABLE [SI]	

ESC	ESC external-opcode,source Escape				Flags	O D I T S Z A P C
Operands		Clocks	Transfers*	Bytes	Coding Example	
immediate, memory		8 + EA	1	2-4	ESC 6,ARRAY [SI]	
immediate, register		2	—	2	ESC 20,AL	

HLT	HLT (no operands) Halt				Flags	O D I T S Z A P C
Operands		Clocks	Transfers*	Bytes	Coding Example	
(no operands)		2	—	1	HLT	

IDIV	IDIV source Integer division				Flags	O D I T S Z A P C U U U U U
Operands		Clocks	Transfers*	Bytes	Coding Example	
reg8		101-112	—	2	IDIV BL	
reg16		165-184	—	2	IDIV CX	
mem8		(107-118) + EA	1	2-4	IDIV DIVISOR_BYTE [SI]	
mem16		(171-190) + EA	1	2-4	IDIV [BX].DIVISOR_WORD	

---

* For the 8086, add four clocks for each 16-bit word transfer with an odd address. For the 8088, add four clocks for each 16-bit word transfer. Mnemonics © Intel, 1978.

IMUL		IMUL source Integer multiplication			Flags	O D I T S Z A P C X U U U U X
Operands		Clocks	Transfers*	Bytes	Coding Example	
reg8		80-98	—	2	IMUL CL	
reg16		128-154	—	2	IMUL BX	
mem8		(86-104) + EA	1	2-4	IMUL RATE BYTE	
mem16		(134-160) + EA	1	2-4	IMUL RATE WORD [BP] [DI]	

IN		IN accumulator,port Input byte or word			Flags	O D I T S Z A P C
Operands		Clocks	Transfers*	Bytes	Coding Example	
accumulator, immed8		10	1	2	IN AL, 0FFEAH	
accumulator, DX		8	1	1	IN AX, DX	

INC		INC destination Increment by 1			Flags	O D I T S Z A P C X X X X X
Operands		Clocks	Transfers*	Bytes	Coding Example	
reg16		2	—	1	INC CX	
reg8		3	—	2	INC BL	
memory		15 + EA	2	2-4	INC ALPHA [DI] [BX]	

INT		INT interrupt-type Interrupt			Flags	O D I T S Z A P C 0 0
Operands		Clocks	Transfers*	Bytes	Coding Example	
immed8 (type = 3)		52	5	1	INT 3	
immed8 (type ≠ 3)		51	5	2	INT 67	

INTR †		INTR (external maskable interrupt) Interrupt if INTR and IF=1			Flags	O D I T S Z A P C 0 0
Operands		Clocks	Transfers*	Bytes	Coding Example	
(no operands)		61	7	N/A	N/A	

INTO		INTO (no operands) Interrupt if overflow			Flags	O D I T S Z A P C 0 0
Operands		Clocks	Transfers*	Bytes	Coding Example	
(no operands)		53 or 4	5	1	INTO	

---

* For the 8086, add four clocks for each 16-bit word transfer with an odd address. For the 8088, add four clocks for each 16-bit word transfer.

† NTR is not an instruction; it is included only for timing information.

Mnemonics © Intel, 1978.

IRET	IRET (no operands) Interrupt Return			Flags	O D I T S Z A P C R R R R R R R R
Operands	Clocks	Transfers*	Bytes	Coding Example	
(no operands)	24	3	1	IRET	

JA/JNBE	JA/JNBE short-label Jump if above/Jump if not below nor equal			Flags	O D I T S Z A P C
Operands	Clocks	Transfers*	Bytes	Coding Example	
short-label	16 or 4	—	2	JA ABOVE	

JAE/JNB	JAE/JNB short-label Jump if above or equal/Jump if not below			Flags	O D I T S Z A P C
Operands	Clocks	Transfers*	Bytes	Coding Example	
short-label	16 or 4	—	2	JAE ABOVE EQUAL	

JB/JNAE	JB/JNAE short-label Jump if below/Jump if not above nor equal			Flags	O D I T S Z A P C
Operands	Clocks	Transfers*	Bytes	Coding Example	
short-label	16 or 4	—	2	JB BELOW	

JBE/JNA	JBE/JNA short-label Jump if below or equal/Jump if not above			Flags	O D I T S Z A P C
Operands	Clocks	Transfers*	Bytes	Coding Example	
short-label	16 or 4	—	2	JNA NOT ABOVE	

JC	JC short-label Jump if carry			Flags	O D I T S Z A P C
Operands	Clocks	Transfers*	Bytes	Coding Example	
short-label	16 or 4	—	2	JC CARRY SET	

JCXZ	JCXZ short-label Jump if CX is zero			Flags	O D I T S Z A P C
Operands	Clocks	Transfers*	Bytes	Coding Example	
short-label	18 or 6	—	2	JCXZ COUNT DONE	

JE/JZ	JE/JZ short-label Jump if equal/Jump if zero			Flags	O D I T S Z A P C
Operands	Clocks	Transfers*	Bytes	Coding Example	
short-label	16 or 4	—	2	JZ ZERO	

* For the 8086, add four clocks for each 16-bit word transfer with an odd address. For the 8088, add four clocks for each 16-bit word transfer. Mnemonics © Intel, 1978.

JG/JNLE	JG/JNLE short-label Jump if greater/Jump if not less nor equal			Flags	O D I T S Z A P C
Operands	**Clocks**	**Transfers***	**Bytes**	**Coding Example**	
short-label	16 or 4	—	2	JG GREATER	

JGE/JNL	JGE/JNL short-label Jump if greater or equal/Jump if not less			Flags	O D I T S Z A P C
Operands	**Clocks**	**Transfers***	**Bytes**	**Coding Example**	
short-label	16 or 4	—	2	JGE GREATER_EQUAL	

JL/JNGE	JL/JNGE short-label Jump if less/Jump if not greater nor equal			Flags	O D I T S Z A P C
Operands	**Clocks**	**Transfers***	**Bytes**	**Coding Example**	
short-label	16 or 4	—	2	JL LESS	

JLE/JNG	JLE/JNG short-label Jump if less or equal/Jump if not greater			Flags	O D I T S Z A P C
Operands	**Clocks**	**Transfers***	**Bytes**	**Coding Example**	
short-label	16 or 4	—	2	JNG NOT_GREATER	

JMP	JMP target Jump			Flags	O D I T S Z A P C
Operands	**Clocks**	**Transfers***	**Bytes**	**Coding Example**	
short-label	15	—	2	JMP SHORT	
near-label	15	—	3	JMP WITHIN_SEGMENT	
far-label	15	—	5	JMP FAR_LABEL	
memptr16	18 + EA	1	2-4	JMP [BX].TARGET	
regptr16	11	—	2	JMP CX	
memptr32	24 + EA	2	2-4	JMP OTHER.SEG [SI]	

JNC	JNC short-label Jump if not carry			Flags	O D I T S Z A P C
Operands	**Clocks**	**Transfers***	**Bytes**	**Coding Example**	
short-label	16 or 4	—	2	JNC NOT_CARRY	

JNE/JNZ	JNE/JNZ short-label Jump if not equal/Jump if not zero			Flags	O D I T S Z A P C
Operands	**Clocks**	**Transfers***	**Bytes**	**Coding Example**	
short-label	16 or 4	—	2	JNE NOT_EQUAL	

---

* For the 8086, add four clocks for each 16-bit word transfer with an odd address. For the 8088, add four clocks for each 16-bit word transfer. Mnemonics © Intel, 1978.

JNO	**JNO** short-label Jump if not overflow			Flags	O D I T S Z A P C
Operands		Clocks	Transfers*	Bytes	Coding Example
short-label		16 or 4	—	2	JNO NO_OVERFLOW

JNP/JPO	**JNP/JPO** short-label Jump if not parity / Jump if parity odd			Flags	O D I T S Z A P C
Operands		Clocks	Transfers*	Bytes	Coding Example
short-label		16 or 4	—	2	JPO ODD_PARITY

JNS	**JNS** short-label Jump if not sign			Flags	O D I T S Z A P C
Operands		Clocks	Transfers*	Bytes	Coding Example
short-label		16 or 4	—	2	JNS POSITIVE

JO	**JO** short-label Jump if overflow			Flags	O D I T S Z A P C
Operands		Clocks	Transfers*	Bytes	Coding Example
short-label		16 or 4	—	2	JO SIGNED_OVRFLW

JP/JPE	**JP/JPE** short-label Jump if parity / Jump if parity even			Flags	O D I T S Z A P C
Operands		Clocks	Transfers*	Bytes	Coding Example
short-label		16 or 4	—	2	JPE EVEN_PARITY

JS	**JS** short-label Jump if sign			Flags	O D I T S Z A P C
Operands		Clocks	Transfers*	Bytes	Coding Example
short-label		16 or 4	—	2	JS NEGATIVE

LAHF	**LAHF** (no operands) Load AH from flags			Flags	O D I T S Z A P C
Operands		Clocks	Transfers*	Bytes	Coding Example
(no operands)		4	—	1	LAHF

LDS	**LDS** destination,source Load pointer using DS			Flags	O D I T S Z A P C
Operands		Clocks	Transfers	Bytes	Coding Example
reg16, mem32		16 + EA	2	2-4	LDS SI,DATA.SEG [DI]

* For the 8086, add four clocks for each 16-bit word transfer with an odd address. For the 8088, add four clocks for each 16-bit word transfer. Mnemonics © Intel, 1978.

LEA	**LEA** destination,source			Flags	O D I T S Z A P C
Operands	Clocks	Transfers*	Bytes		Coding Example
reg16, mem16	2 + EA	—	2-4		LEA BX, [BP] [DI]

LES	**LES** destination,source			Flags	O D I T S Z A P C
Operands	Clocks	Transfers*	Bytes		Coding Example
reg16, mem32	16 + EA	2	2-4		LES DI, [BX].TEXT__BUFF

LOCK	**LOCK** (no operands)			Flags	O D I T S Z A P C
Operands	Clocks	Transfers*	Bytes		Coding Example
(no operands)	2	—	1		LOCK XCHG FLAG,AL

LODS	**LODS** source-string			Flags	O D I T S Z A P C
Operands	Clocks	Transfers*	Bytes		Coding Example
source-string	12	1	1		LODS CUSTOMER__NAME
(repeat) source-string	9 + 13/rep	1/rep	1		REP LODS NAME

LOOP	**LOOP** short-label			Flags	O D I T S Z A P C
Operands	Clocks	Transfers*	Bytes		Coding Example
short-label	17/5	—	2		LOOP AGAIN

LOOPE/LOOPZ	**LOOPE/LOOPZ** short-label			Flags	O D I T S Z A P C
Operands	Clocks	Transfers*	Bytes		Coding Example
short-label	18 or 6	—	2		LOOPE AGAIN

LOOPNE/LOOPNZ	**LOOPNE/LOOPNZ** short-label			Flags	O D I T S Z A P C
Operands	Clocks	Transfers*	Bytes		Coding Example
short-label	19 or 5	—	2		LOOPNE AGAIN

NMI†	**NMI** (external nonmaskable interrupt)			Flags	O S I T S Z A P C
	Interrupt if NMI = 1				0 0
Operands	Clocks	Transfers*	Bytes		Coding Example
(no operands)	50˙	5	N/A		N/A

---

* For the 8086, add four clocks for each 16-bit word transfer with an odd address. For the 8088, add four clocks for each 16-bit word transfer.

† NTR is not an instruction; it is included only for timing information.

Mnemonics © Intel, 1978.

MOV				MOV destination, source Move		Flags	O D I T S Z A P C
Operands	**Clocks**	**Transfers***	**Bytes**	**Coding Example**			
memory, accumulator	10	1	3	MOV ARRAY [SI], AL			
accumulator, memory	10	1	3	MOV AX, TEMP__RESULT			
register, register	2	—	2	MOV AX,CX			
register, memory	8 + EA	1	2-4	MOV BP, STACK__TOP			
memory, register	9 + EA	1	2-4	MOV COUNT [DI], CX			
register, immediate	4	—	2-3	MOV CL, 2			
memory, immediate	10 + EA	1	3-6	MOV MASK [BX] [SI], 2CH			
seg-reg, reg16	2	—	2	MOV ES, CX			
seg-reg, mem16	8 + EA	1	2-4	MOV DS, SEGMENT__BASE			
reg16, seg-reg	2	—	2	MOV BP, SS			
memory, seg-reg	9 + EA	1	2-4	MOV [BX].SEG__SAVE, CS			

MOVS				MOVS dest-string, source-string Move string		Flags	O D I T S Z A P C
Operands	**Clocks**	**Transfers***	**Bytes**	**Coding Example**			
dest-string, source-string	18	2	1	MOVS LINE EDIT__DATA			
(repeat) dest-string, source-string	9 + 17/rep	2/rep	1	REP MOVS SCREEN, BUFFER			

MOVSB/MOVSW				MOVSB/MOVSW (no operands) Move string (byte/word)		Flags	O D I T S Z A P C
Operands	**Clocks**	**Transfers***	**Bytes**	**Coding Example**			
(no operands)	18	2	1	MOVSB			
(repeat) (no operands)	9 + 17/rep	2/rep	1	REP MOVSW			

MUL				MUL source Multiplication, unsigned		Flags	O D I T S Z A P C X U U U U X
Operands	**Clocks**	**Transfers***	**Bytes**	**Coding Example**			
reg8	70-77	—	2	MUL BL			
reg16	118-133	—	2	MUL CX			
mem8	(76-83) + EA	1	2-4	MUL MONTH [SI]			
mem16	(124-139) + EA	1	2-4	MUL BAUD__RATE			

NEG				NEG destination Negate		Flags	O D I T S Z A P C X X X X X 1*
Operands	**Clocks**	**Transfers***	**Bytes**	**Coding Example**			
register	3	—	2	NEG AL			
memory	16 + EA	2	2-4	NEG MULTIPLIER			

*0 if destination = 0

---

* For the 8086, add four clocks for each 16-bit word transfer with an odd address. For the 8088, add four clocks for each 16-bit word transfer. Mnemonics © Intel, 1978.

NOP	NOP (no operands) No Operation			Flags	O D I T S Z A P C
Operands	**Clocks**	**Transfers***	**Bytes**	**Coding Example**	
(no operands)	3	—	1	NOP	

NOT	NOT destination Logical not			Flags	O D I T S Z A P C
Operands	**Clocks**	**Transfers***	**Bytes**	**Coding Example**	
register	3	—	2	NOT AX	
memory	16 + EA	2	2-4	NOT CHARACTER	

OR	OR destination,source Logical inclusive or			Flags	O D I T S Z A P C 0 X X U X 0
Operands	**Clocks**	**Transfers***	**Bytes**	**Coding Example**	
register, register	3	—	2	OR AL, BL	
register, memory	9 + EA	1	2-4	OR DX, PORT ID [DI]	
memory, register	16 + EA	2	2-4	OR FLAG BYTE, CL	
accumulator, immediate	4	—	2-3	OR AL, 01101100B	
register, immediate	4	—	3-4	OR CX, 01H	
memory, immediate	17 + EA	2	3-6	OR [BX].CMD WORD, 0CFH	

OUT	OUT port,accumulator Output byte or word			Flags	O D I T S Z A P C
Operands	**Clocks**	**Transfers***	**Bytes**	**Coding Example**	
immed8, accumulator	10	1	2	OUT 44, AX	
DX, accumulator	8	1	1	OUT DX, AL	

POP	POP destination Pop word off stack			Flags	O D I T S Z A P C
Operands	**Clocks**	**Transfers***	**Bytes**	**Coding Example**	
register	8	1	1	POP DX	
seg-reg (CS illegal)	8	1	1	POP DS	
memory	17 + EA	2	2-4	POP PARAMETER	

POPF	POPF (no operands) Pop flags off stack			Flags	O D I T S Z A P C R R R R R R R R R
Operands	**Clocks**	**Transfers***	**Bytes**	**Coding Example**	
(no operands)	8	1	1	POPF	

* For the 8086, add four clocks for each 16-bit word transfer with an odd address. For the 8088, add four clocks for each 16-bit word transfer. Mnemonics © Intel, 1978.

PUSH	**PUSH** source Push word onto stack				Flags	O D I T S Z A P C
Operands		**Clocks**	**Transfers***	**Bytes**	**Coding Example**	
register		11	1	1	PUSH SI	
seg-reg (CS legal)		10	1	1	PUSH ES	
memory		16 + EA	2	2-4	PUSH RETURN_CODE [SI]	

PUSHF	**PUSHF** (no operands) Push flags onto stack				Flags	O D I T S Z A P C
Operands		**Clocks**	**Transfers***	**Bytes**	**Coding Example**	
(no operands)		10	1	1	PUSHF	

RCL	**RCL** destination,count Rotate left through carry				Flags	O D I T S Z A P C X X
Operands		**Clocks**	**Transfers***	**Bytes**	**Coding Example**	
register, 1		2	—	2	RCL CX, 1	
register, CL		8 + 4/bit	—	2	RCL AL, CL	
memory, 1		15 + EA	2	2-4	RCL ALPHA, 1	
memory, CL		20 + EA + 4/bit	2	2-4	RCL [BP].PARM, CL	

RCR	**RCR** designation,count Rotate right through carry				Flags	O D I T S Z A P C X X
Operands		**Clocks**	**Transfers***	**Bytes**	**Coding Example**	
register, 1		2	—	2	RCR BX, 1	
register, CL		8 + 4/bit	—	2	RCR BL, CL	
memory, 1		15 + EA	2	2-4	RCR [BX].STATUS, 1	
memory, CL		20 + EA + 4/bit	2	2-4	RCR ARRAY [DI], CL	

REP	**REP** (no operands) Repeat string operation				Flags	O D I T S Z A P C
Operands		**Clocks**	**Transfers***	**Bytes**	**Coding Example**	
(no operands)		2	—	1	REP MOVS DEST, SRCE	

REPE/REPZ	**REPE/REPZ** (no operands) Repeat string operation while equal/while zero				Flags	O D I T S Z A P C
Operands		**Clocks**	**Transfers***	**Bytes**	**Coding Example**	
(no operands)		2	—	1	REPE CMPS DATA, KEY	

* For the 8086, add four clocks for each 16-bit word transfer with an odd address. For the 8088, add four clocks for each 16-bit word transfer. Mnemonics © Intel, 1978.

REPNE/REPNZ	**REPNE/REPNZ** (no operands) Repeat string operation while not equal/not zero			Flags	O D I T S Z A P C
Operands	Clocks	Transfers*	Bytes		Coding Example
(no operands)	2	—	1		REPNE SCAS INPUT LINE

RET	**RET** optional-pop-value Return from procedure			Flags	O D I T S Z A P C
Operands	Clocks	Transfers*	Bytes		Coding Example
(intra-segment. no pop)	8	1	1		RET
(intra-segment. pop)	12	1	3		RET 4
(inter-segment. no pop)	18	2	1		RET
(inter-segment. pop)	17	2	3		RET 2

ROL	**ROL** destination.count Rotate left			Flags	O D I T S Z A P C X X
Operands	Clocks	Transfers	Bytes		Coding Examples
register. 1	2	—	2		ROL BX, 1
register. CL	8 + 4/bit	—	2		ROL DI, CL
memory. 1	15 + EA	2	2-4		ROL FLAG BYTE [DI],1
memory. CL	20 + EA + 4/bit	2	2-4		ROL ALPHA , CL

ROR	**ROR** destination.count Rotate right			Flags	O D I T S Z A P C X X
Operand	Clocks	Transfers*	Bytes		Coding Example
register. 1	2	—	2		ROR AL, 1
register. CL	8 + 4/bit	—	2		ROR BX, CL
memory. 1	15 + EA	2	2-4		ROR PORT STATUS, 1
memory. CL	20 + EA + 4/bit	2	2-4		ROR CMD WORD, CL

SAHF	**SAHF** (no operands) Store AH into flags			Flags	O D I T S Z A P C R R R R R
Operands	Clocks	Transfers*	Bytes		Coding Example
(no operands)	4	—	1		SAHF

SAL/SHL	**SAL/SHL** destination,count Shift arithmetic left/Shift logical left			Flags	O D I T S Z A P C X X
Operands	Clocks	Transfers*	Bytes		Coding Examples
register,1	2	—	2		SAL AL,1
register, CL	8 + 4/bit	—	2		SHL DI, CL
memory,1	15 + EA	2	2-4		SHL [BX].OVERDRAW, 1
memory, CL	20 + EA + 4/bit	2	2-4		SAL STORE COUNT, CL

* For the 8086, add four clocks for each 16-bit word transfer with an odd address. For the 8088, add four clocks for each 16-bit word transfer. Mnemonics © Intel, 1978.

SAR	**SAR** destination,source Shift arithmetic right			Flags	O D I T S Z A P C X X X U X X
Operands	**Clocks**	**Transfers***	**Bytes**		**Coding Example**
register, 1	2	—	2		SAR DX, 1
register, CL	8 + 4/bit	—	2		SAR DI, CL
memory, 1	15 + EA	2	2-4		SAR N BLOCKS, 1
memory, CL	20 + EA + 4/bit	2	2-4		SAR N BLOCKS, CL

SBB	**SBB** destination,source Subtract with borrow			Flags	O D I T S Z A P C X X X X X X
Operands	**Clocks**	**Transfers***	**Bytes**		**Coding Example**
register, register	3	—	2		SBB BX, CX
register, memory	9 + EA	1	2-4		SBB DI, [BX].PAYMENT
memory, register	16 + EA	2	2-4		SBB BALANCE, AX
accumulator, immediate	4	—	2-3		SBB AX, 2
register, immediate	4	—	3-4		SBB CL, 1
memory, immediate	17 + EA	2	3-6		SBB COUNT [SI], 10

SCAS	**SCAS** dest-string Scan string			Flags	O D I T S Z A P C X X X X X X
Operands	**Clocks**	**Transfers***	**Bytes**		**Coding Example**
dest-string	15	1	1		SCAS INPUT LINE
(repeat) dest-string	9 + 15/rep	1/rep	1		REPNE SCAS BUFFER

SEGMENT†	**SEGMENT** override prefix Override to specified segment			Flags	O D I T S Z A P C
Operands	**Clocks**	**Transfers***	**Bytes**		**Coding Example**
(no operands)	2	—	1		MOV SS:PARAMETER, AX

SHR	**SHR** destination,count Shift logical right			Flags	O D I T S Z A P C X X
Operands	**Clocks**	**Transfers***	**Bytes**		**Coding Example**
register, 1	2	—	2		SHR SI, 1
register, CL	8 + 4/bit	—	2		SHR SI, CL
memory, 1	15 + EA	2	2-4		SHR ID BYTE [SI] [BX], 1
memory, CL	20 + EA + 4/bit	2	2-4		SHR INPUT WORD, CL

SINGLE STEP†	**SINGLE STEP** (Trap flag interrupt) Interrupt if TF = 1			Flags	O D I T S Z A P C 0 0
Operands	**Clocks**	**Transfers***	**Bytes**		**Coding Example**
(no operands)	50	5	N/A		N/A

---

* For the 8086, add four clocks for each 16-bit word transfer with an odd address. For the 8088, add four clocks for each 16-bit word transfer.

† ASM-86 incorporates the segment override prefix into the operand specification and not as a separate instruction. SEGMENT is included only for timing information.

† SINGLE STEP is not an instruction; it is included only for timing information.

Mnemonics © Intel, 1978.

STC	STC (no operands) Set carry flag			Flags	O D I T S Z A P C 1
Operands	Clocks	Transfers*	Bytes	Coding Example	
(no operands)	2	—	1	STC	

STD	STD (no operands) Set direction flag			Flags	O D I T S Z A P C 1
Operands	Clocks	Transfers*	Bytes	Coding Example	
(no operands)	2	—	1	STD	

STI	STI (no operands) Set interrupt enable flag			Flags	O D I T S Z A P C 1
Operands	Clocks	Transfers*	Bytes	Coding Example	
(no operands)	2	—	1	STI	

STOS	STOS dest-string Store byte or word string			Flags	O D I T S Z A P C
Operands	Clocks	Transfers*	Bytes	Coding Example	
dest-string	11	1	1	STOS PRINT LINE	
(repeat) dest-string	9 + 10/rep	1/rep	1	REP STOS DISPLAY	

SUB	SUB destination,source Subtraction			Flags	O D I T S Z A P C X X X X X X
Operands	Clocks	Transfers*	Bytes	Coding Example	
register, register	3	—	2	SUB CX, BX	
register, memory	9 + EA	1	2-4	SUB DX, MATH__TOTAL [SI]	
memory, register	16 + EA	2	2-4	SUB [BP + 2], CL	
accumulator, immediate	4	—	2-3	SUB AL, 10	
register, immediate	4	—	3-4	SUB SI, 5280	
memory, immediate	17 + EA	2	3-6	SUB [BP].BALANCE, 1000	

TEST	TEST destination,source Test or non-destructive logical and			Flags	O D I T S Z A P C 0 X X U X 0
Operands	Clocks	Transfers*	Bytes	Coding Example	
register, register	3	—	2	TEST SI, DI	
register, memory	9 + EA	1	2-4	TEST SI, END__COUNT	
accumulator, immediate	4	—	2-3	TEST AL, 00100000B	
register, immediate	5	—	3-4	TEST BX, 0CC4H	
memory, immediate	11 + EA	—	3-6	TEST RETURN__ CODE, 01H	

* For the 8086, add four clocks for each 16-bit word transfer with an odd address. For the 8088, add four clocks for each 16-bit word transfer. Mnemonics © Intel, 1978.

WAIT	**WAIT** (no operands) Wait while TEST pin not asserted			Flags	O D I T S Z A P C
Operands	**Clocks**	**Transfers***	**Bytes**	**Coding Example**	
(no operands)	3 + 5n	—	1	WAIT	

XCHG	**XCHG** destination,source Exchange			Flags	O D I T S Z A P C
Operands	**Clocks**	**Transfers***	**Bytes**	**Coding Example**	
accumulator, reg16	3	—	1	XCHG AX, BX	
memory, register	17 + EA	2	2-4	XCHG SEMAPHORE, AX	
register, register	4	—	2	XCHG AL, BL	

XLAT	**XLAT** source-table Translate			Flags	O D I T S Z A P C
Operands	**Clocks**	**Transfers***	**Bytes**	**Coding Example**	
source-table	11	1	1	XLAT ASCII_TAB	

XOR	**XOR** destination,source Logical exclusive or			Flags	O D I T S Z A P C 0 X X U X 0
Operands	**Clocks**	**Transfers***	**Bytes**	**Coding Example**	
register, register	3	—	2	XOR CX, BX	
register, memory	9 + EA	1	2-4	XOR CL, MASK_BYTE	
memory, register	16 + EA	2	2-4	XOR ALPHA [SI], DX	
accumulator, immediate	4	—	2-3	XOR AL, 01000010B	
register, immediate	4	—	3-4	XOR SI, 00C2H	
memory, immediate	17 + EA	2	3-6	XOR RETURN_CODE, 0D2H	

---

* For the 8086, add four clocks for each 16-bit word transfer with an odd address. For the 8088, add four clocks for each 16-bit word transfer. Mnemonics © Intel, 1978.

D The Assembler Directives

Assembler directives are commands executed at assembly time, not run time. They do not generate CPU instructions; they create constants, set aside memory locations, and give the assembler information about your program. They can define portions of your program that will not be assembled, define macros, and display information on the screen during assembly. A brief summary of the directives follows.

Directive	Meaning
AND	Logical AND
ASSUME	Designates segment registers
BYTE	Defines byte data size
COMMENT	Block comment
.CREF	Symbol listing for cross reference
DB	Defines byte storage
DD	Defines double word of four bytes
DQ	Defines quadruple word of eight bytes
DT	Defines ten bytes
DW	Defines word storage
DWORD	Defines double-word (32-bit) data size
DUP	Replicates a string
ELSE	Alternate conditional block
END	End of source program
ENDIF	End of conditional block
ENDM	End of macro
ENDP	End of procedure
ENDS	End of segment or structure
EQ	Logical equals
EQU	Assigns (equates) a constant
EVEN	Sets even address
EXITM	Exits macro
EXTRN	Defines external references
FAR	Designates label outside segment
GE	Logical greater-than or equal
GROUP	Associates segments with group name
GT	Logical greater-than
HIGH	High half of word
IF	Conditional block

Directive	Meaning
IF1	Conditional first pass
IF2	Conditional second pass
IFB	Conditional parameter missing
IFDEF	Conditional if defined
IFDIF	Conditional if two parameters different
IFE	Conditional if zero
IFIDN	Conditional if two parameters are the same
IFNB	Conditional if parameter not missing
INCLUDE	Inserts source code from another file
IRP	Indefinite-repeat macro
IRPC	Indefinite-repeat character macro
LABEL	Creates symbol
LE	Logical less-than or equal
LENGTH	Determines length of symbol
LOCAL	Defines local symbol in macro
LOW	Low half of word
LT	Logical less-than
.LALL	Lists macro statements
.LFCOND	Lists conditional block
.LIST	Lists program
MACRO	Defines macro
NAME	Defines program name
MASK	Bit mask for record field
MOD	Use modulus
NAME	Defines module name
NE	Logical not-equal
NEAR	Designates label within segment
NOT	Logical complement
OFFSET	Offset in segment
OR	Logical OR
ORG	Sets instruction pointer
%OUT	Displays string on video screen
PAGE	Starts new page and sets size
PROC	Starts procedure

Directive	Meaning
PTR	Used with BYTE, WORD, DWORD, NEAR, and FAR to specify size of label or variable
PUBLIC	Makes global symbol
.RADIX	Sets radix
RECORD	Defines record type
REPT	Repeats macro
.SALL	Disables macro listing
SEG	Segment value associated with symbol
SEGMENT	Defines segment
SHL	Logical shift left
SHORT	Forward short jump
SHR	Logical shift right
SIZE	Determines size of label
.SFCOND	False conditionals not listed
STRUC	Defines structure
SUBTTL	Defines subtitle
.TCOND	Default listing of conditional blocks
TITLE	Defines program title
XOR	Logical exclusive-OR
.XALL	Lists macros that create code or data
.XCREF	Turns off cross-reference listing
.XLIST	Turns off program listing
WIDTH	Determines width of record field
WORD	Defines word-size data
=	Assigns value to symbol
$	Current offset

E The BIOS Interrupts

The BIOS interrupt vectors are four-byte addresses that refer to routines located in the ROM BIOS. They are accessed with the instruction

    INT X

where X is the vector number.

Vector	Address	Function
5	14	Print screen
8	20	Timer
9	24	Keyboard scan code
10	40	Video screen
11	44	Equipment list
12	48	Memory size
13	4C	Disk service
14	50	Serial transfer
15	54	Cassette tape and TopView
16	58	Keyboard character
17	5C	Printer
18	60	ROM BASIC
19	64	Bootstrap loader
1A	68	Time of day
1B	6C	Keyboard break
1C	70	Timer

F The DOS Interrupts

The DOS interrupt vectors are four-byte addresses that refer to routines located in DOS. They are accessed with the instruction

INT X

where X is the vector number.

Vector	Address	Function
20	80	Terminate COM program
21	84	General DOS functions
22	88	Program terminate code
23	8C	Keyboard-break code
24	90	Error code
25	94	Absolute disk read
26	98	Absolute disk write
27	9C	Terminate, stay resident

The DOS
G Interrupt 21
Hex Functions

The Interrupt 21 hex functions perform common input and output services. They are accessed by placing the function number in the AH register and executing INT 21 hex.

AH	Function
0	Terminate
1	Keyboard input
2	Display character
3	Serial-port input
4	Serial-port output
5	Printer output
6	Direct keyboard input, direct display
7	Direct keyboard input without display
8	Keyboard input, no tabs, no display
9	Display string
A	Read keyboard buffer
B	Input status of keyboard
25	Change interrupt vector
30	Get DOS version number
31	Terminate, stay resident
35	Get interrupt vector
3C	Create file
3D	Open file
3E	Close file
3F	Read file or device
40	Write file or device
41	Delete file
43	Get or set file attributes
4A	Change allocated memory
4B	Load and execute program
4C	Terminate program
4D	Determine error code
56	Rename file

H The Keyboard
Scan Codes

The keys on the IBM PC keyboard are assigned numbers, called scan codes, ranging from 1 to 83. The IBM PC AT uses a different set of codes, ranging from 1 to 108. The numbers begin with the number and letter group, continue with the function keys, and finish with the cursor group. When a key is pressed, the keyboard processor transmits the corresponding scan code to the computer in the system unit. When a key is released, the scan code plus 80 hex is sent.

Hexadecimal	Decimal	PC Key	PC-AT Key
1	1	Esc	Tilde
2–B	2–11	1–9, 0	1–9, 0
C	12	Minus, underline	Minus, underline
D	13	Equal, plus	Equal, plus
E	14	Backspace	Backslash, vertical bar
F	15	Tab	Backspace
10	16	Q	Tab
11	17	W	Q
12	18	E	W
13	19	R	E
14	20	T	R
15	21	Y	T
16	22	U	Y
17	23	I	U
18	24	O	I
19	25	P	O
1A	26	Left bracket	P
1B	27	Right bracket	Left bracket
1C	28	Enter	Right bracket
1D	29	Ctrl	
1E	30	A	Ctrl
1F	31	S	A
20	32	D	S
21	33	F	D
22	34	G	F
23	35	H	G
24	36	J	H
25	37	K	J

Hexadecimal	Decimal	PC Key	PC-AT Key
26	38	L	K
27	39	Semicolon, colon	L
28	40	Quote	Semicolon, colon
29	41	Tilde	Quote
2A	42	Left shift	
2B	43	Backslash, vertical bar	Enter
2C	44	Z	Left shift
2D	45	X	
2E	46	C	Z
2F	47	V	X
30	48	B	C
31	49	N	V
32	50	M	B
33	51	Comma	N
34	52	Period	M
35	53	Slash, question mark	Comma
36	54	Right shift	Period
37	55	Asterisk, PrtSc	Slash, question mark
38	56	Alt	
39	57	Space bar	Right shift
3A	58	Caps Lock	Alt
3B	59	F1	
3C	60	F2	
3D	61	F3	Space bar
3E	62	F4	
3F	63	F5	
40	64	F6	Caps Lock
41	65	F7	F2
42	66	F8	F4
42	67	F9	F6
44	68	F10	F8
45	69	Num Lock	F10
46	70	Scroll Lock, Break	F1
47	71	Home	F3
48	72	Up arrow	F5

Hexadecimal	Decimal	PC Key	PC-AT Key
49	73	PgUp	F7
4A	74	Minus (far left)	F9
4B	75	Left arrow	
4C	76	Keypad 5	
4D	77	Right arrow	
4F	79	End	
50	80	Down arrow	
51	81	PgDn	
52	82	Ins	
53	83	Del	
5A	90		Esc
5B	91		Home
5C	92		Left arrow
5D	93		End
5F	95		Num Lock
60	96		Up arrow
61	97		Keypad 5
62	98		Down arrow
63	99		Ins
64	100		Scroll Lock
65	101		PgUp
66	102		Right arrow
67	103		PgDn
68	104		Del
69	105		Sys
6A	106		Asterisk, PrtSc
6B	107		Minus
6C	108		Plus

INDEX

Selections from The SYBEX Library

Technical

Assembly Language

PROGRAMMING THE 6502
by Rodnay Zaks
386 pp., 160 illustr., Ref. 0-135
Assembly language programming for the 6502, from basic concepts to advanced data structures.

6502 APPLICATIONS
by Rodnay Zaks
278 pp., 200 illustr., Ref. 0-015
Real-life application techniques: the input/output book for the 6502.

ADVANCED 6502 PROGRAMMING
by Rodnay Zaks
292 pp., 140 illustr., Ref. 0-089
Third in the 6502 series. Teaches more advanced programming techniques, using games as a framework for learning.

PROGRAMMING THE Z80®
by Rodnay Zaks
624 pp., 200 illustr., Ref. 0-069
A complete course in programming the Z80 microprocessor and a thorough introduction to assembly language.

PROGRAMMING THE 6809
by Rodnay Zaks and William Labiak
362 pp., 150 illustr., Ref. 0-078
This book explains how to program the 6809 microprocessor in assembly language. No prior programming knowledge required.

PROGRAMMING THE Z8000®
by Richard Mateosian
298 pp., 124 illustr., Ref. 0-032
How to program the Z8000 16-bit microprocessor. Includes a description of the architecture and function of the Z8000 and its family of support chips.

PROGRAMMING THE 8086™/8088™
by James W. Coffron
300 pp., illustr., Ref. 0-120
This book explains how to program the 8086 and 8088 microprocessors in assembly language. No prior programming knowledge required.

PROGRAMMING THE 68000™
by Steve Williams
250 pp., illustr., Ref. 0-133
This book introduces you to microprocessor operation, writing application programs, and the basics of I/O programming. Especially helpful for owners of the Apple Macintosh or Lisa.

Hardware

MICROPROCESSOR INTERFACING TECHNIQUES
by Rodnay Zaks and Austin Lesea
456 pp., 400 illustr., Ref. 0-029
Complete hardware and software interfacing techniques, including D to A conversion, peripherals, bus standards and troubleshooting.

THE RS-232 SOLUTION
by Joe Campbell
194 pp., illustr., Ref. 0-140
Finally, a book that will show you how to

correctly interface your computer to any RS-232-C peripheral.

FROM CHIPS TO SYSTEMS: AN INTRODUCTION TO MICROPROCESSORS

by Rodnay Zaks

552 pp., 400 illustr., Ref. 0-063

A simple and comprehensive introduction to microprocessors from both a hardware and software standpoint: what they are, how they operate, how to assemble them into a complete system.

MASTERING SERIAL COMMUNICATIONS

by Joe Campbell

250 pp., illustr., Ref. 0-180

This sequel to *The RS-232 Solution* guides the reader to mastery of more complex interfacing techniques.

Operating Systems

SYSTEMS PROGRAMMING IN C

by David Smith

275 pp., illustr., Ref. 0-266

This intermediate text is written for the person who wants to get beyond the basics of C and capture its great efficiencies in space and time.

REAL WORLD UNIX™

by John D. Halamka

209 pp., Ref. 0-093

This book is written for the beginning and intermediate UNIX user in a practical, straightforward manner, with specific instructions given for many business applications.

INTRODUCTION TO THE UCSD p-SYSTEM™

by Charles W. Grant and Jon Butah

300 pp., 10 illustr., Ref. 0-061

A simple, clear introduction to the UCSD Pascal Operating System for beginners through experienced programmers.

IBM PC and Compatibles

THE ABC'S OF THE IBM® PC

by Joan Lasselle and Carol Ramsay

143 pp., illustr., Ref. 0-102

This book will take you through the first crucial steps in learning to use the IBM PC.

THE BEST OF IBM® PC SOFTWARE

by Stanley R. Trost

351 pp., Ref. 0-104

Separates the wheat from the chaff in the world of IBM PC software. Tells you what to expect from the best available IBM PC programs.

THE IBM® PC-DOS HANDBOOK

by Richard Allen King

296 pp., Ref. 0-103

Explains the PC disk operating system. Get the most out of your PC by adapting its capabilities to your specific needs.

BUSINESS GRAPHICS FOR THE IBM® PC

by Nelson Ford

259 pp., illustr., Ref. 0-124

Ready-to-run programs for creating line graphs, multiple bar graphs, pie charts, and more. An ideal way to use your PC's business capabilities!

YOUR FIRST IBM® PC PROGRAM

by Rodnay Zaks

182 pp., illustr., Ref. 0-171

This well-illustrated book makes programming easy for children and adults.

DATA FILE PROGRAMMING ON YOUR IBM® PC

by Alan Simpson

219 pp., illustr., Ref. 0-146

This book provides instructions and examples for managing data files in BASIC. Programming design and development are extensively discussed.

THE IBM® PC CONNECTION
by James W. Coffron
264 pp., illustr., Ref. 0-127
Teaches elementary interfacing and BASIC programming of the IBM PC for connection to external devices and household appliances.

BASIC EXERCISES FOR THE IBM® PERSONAL COMPUTER
by J.P. Lamoitier
252 pp., 90 illustr., Ref. 0-088
Teaches IBM BASIC through actual practice, using graduated exercises drawn from everyday applications.

USEFUL BASIC PROGRAMS FOR THE IBM® PC
by Stanley R. Trost
144 pp., illustr., Ref. 0-111
This collection of programs takes full advantage of the interactive capabilities of your IBM Personal Computer. Financial calculations, investment analysis, record keeping, and math practice—made easier on your IBM PC.

SELECTING THE RIGHT DATA BASE SOFTWARE FOR THE IBM® PC

SELECTING THE RIGHT WORD PROCESSING SOFTWARE FOR THE IBM® PC

SELECTING THE RIGHT SPREADSHEET SOFTWARE FOR THE IBM® PC
by Kathleen McHugh and Veronica Corchado
100 pp., illustr., Ref. 0-174, 0-177, 0-178
This series on selecting the right business software offers the busy professional concise, informative reviews of the best available software packages.

ESSENTIAL PC-DOS
by Myril and Susan Shaw
300 pp., illustr., Ref. 0-176
Whether you work with the IBM PC, XT, PC*jr*, or the portable PC, this book will be invaluable both for learning PC-DOS and for later reference.

THE MS™-DOS HANDBOOK
by Richard Allen King
320 pp., illustr., Ref. 0-185
The differences between the various versions and manufacturer's implementations of MS-DOS are covered in a clear, straightforward manner. Tables, maps, and numerous examples make this the most complete book on MS-DOS available.

Languages

BASIC

YOUR FIRST BASIC PROGRAM
by Rodnay Zaks
182 pp., illustr. in color, Ref. 0-092
A "how-to-program" book for the first time computer user, aged 8 to 88.

FIFTY BASIC EXERCISES
by J. P. Lamoitier
232 pp., 90 illustr., Ref. 0-056
Teaches BASIC through actual practice, using graduated exercises drawn from everyday applications. Programs written in Microsoft BASIC.

BASIC FOR BUSINESS
by Douglas Hergert
224 pp., 15 illustr., Ref. 0-080
A logically organized, no-nonsense introduction to BASIC programming for business applications. Includes many fully-explained accounting programs, and shows you how to write your own.

EXECUTIVE PLANNING WITH BASIC
by X. T. Bui
196 pp., 19 illustr., Ref. 0-083
An important collection of business management decision models in BASIC,

including inventory management (EOQ), critical path analysis and PERT, financial ratio analysis, portfolio management, and much more.

BASIC PROGRAMS FOR SCIENTISTS AND ENGINEERS

by Alan R. Miller

318 pp., 120 illustr., Ref. 0-073

This book from the "Programs for Scientists and Engineers" series provides a library of problem-solving programs while developing the reader's proficiency in BASIC.

Pascal

INTRODUCTION TO PASCAL (Including Turbo Pascal™)

by Rodnay Zaks

450 pp., illustr., Ref. 0-319-8

In Zaks' classic style that has already helped a quarter of a million people learn Pascal, and now in a version that features Turbo Pascal.

INTRODUCTION TO TURBO PASCAL

by Douglas Stivison

268 pp., illustr., Ref. 0-269-8

This bestseller enhances the unique aspects of Turbo Pascal by concentrating on the extended applications capabilities offered, while giving a full introductory tutorial.

INTRODUCTION TO PASCAL (Including UCSD Pascal™)

by Rodnay Zaks

420 pp., 130 illustr., Ref. 0-066

A step-by-step introduction for anyone who wants to learn the Pascal language. Describes UCSD and Standard Pascals. No technical background is assumed.

THE PASCAL HANDBOOK

by Jacques Tiberghien

486 pp., 270 illustr., Ref. 0-053

A dictionary of the Pascal language, defining every reserved word, operator, procedure, and function found in all major versions of Pascal.

APPLE® PASCAL GAMES

by Douglas Hergert and Joseph T. Kalash

372 pp., 40 illustr., Ref. 0-074

A collection of the most popular computer games in Pascal, challenging the reader not only to play but to investigate how games are implemented on the computer.

PASCAL PROGRAMS FOR SCIENTISTS AND ENGINEERS

by Alan R. Miller

374 pp., 120 illustr., Ref. 0-058

A comprehensive collection of frequently used algorithms for scientific and technical applications, programmed in Pascal. Includes programs for curve-fitting, integrals, statistical techniques, and more.

DOING BUSINESS WITH PASCAL

by Richard Hergert and Douglas Hergert

371 pp., illustr., Ref. 0-091

Practical tips for using Pascal programming in business. Covers design considerations, language extensions, and applications examples.

Other Languages

UNDERSTANDING C

by Bruce H. Hunter

320 pp., Ref 0-123

Explains how to program in powerful C language for a variety of applications. Some programming experience assumed.

FIFTY PASCAL PROGRAMS

by Bruce H. Hunter

338 pp., illustr., Ref. 0-110

More than just a collection of useful programs! Structured programming techniques are emphasized and concepts such as data type creation and array manipulation are clearly illustrated.

FORTRAN PROGRAMS FOR SCIENTISTS AND ENGINEERS
by Alan R. Miller
280 pp., 120 illustr., Ref. 0-082
This book from the "Programs for Scientists and Engineers" series provides a library of problem-solving programs while developing the reader's proficiency in FORTRAN.

A MICROPROGRAMMED APL IMPLEMENTATION
by Rodnay Zaks
350 pp., Ref. 0-005
An expert-level text presenting the complete conceptual analysis and design of an APL interpreter, and actual listing of the microcode.

Computer Specific

Apple II—Macintosh

THE PRO-DOS HANDBOOK
by Timothy Rice/Karen Rice
225 pp., illustr., Ref. 0-230
All Pro-DOS users, from beginning to advanced, will find this book packed with vital information. The book covers the basics, and then addresses itself to the Apple II user who needs to interface with Pro-DOS when programming in BASIC. Learn how Pro-DOS uses memory, and how it handles text files, binary files, graphics, and sound. Includes a chapter on machine language programming.

THE MACINTOSH™ TOOLBOX
by Huxham, Burnard, and Takatsuka
300 pp., illustr., Ref. 0-249
This tutorial on the advanced features of the Macintosh toolbox is an ideal companion to The Macintosh BASIC Handbook.

THE MACINTOSH™ BASIC HANDBOOK
by Thomas Blackadar/Jonathan Kamin
800 pp., illustr., Ref. 0-257
This desk-side reference book for the Macintosh programmer covers the BASIC statements and toolbox commands, organized like a dictionary.

PROGRAMMING THE MACINTOSH™ IN ASSEMBLY LANGUAGE
by Steve Williams
400 pp., illustr., Ref. 0-263
Information, examples, and guidelines for programming the 68000 microprocessor are given, including details of its entire instruction set.

BASIC EXERCISES FOR THE APPLE®
by J.P. Lamoitier
250 pp., 90 illustr., Ref. 0-084
Teaches Applesoft BASIC through actual practice, using graduated exercises drawn from everyday applications.

THE APPLE II® BASIC HANDBOOK
by Douglas Hergert
250 pp., illustr., Ref. 0-115
A complete listing with descriptions and instructive examples of each of the Apple II BASIC keywords and functions. A handy reference guide, organized like a dictionary.

APPLE II® BASIC PROGRAMS IN MINUTES
by Stanley R. Trost
150 pp., illustr., Ref. 0-121
A collection of ready-to-run programs for financial calculations, investment analysis, record keeping, and many more home and office applications. These programs can be entered on your Apple II plus or IIe in minutes!

SYBEX COMPUTER BOOKS

are different.

Here is why . . .

At SYBEX, each book is designed with you in mind. Every manuscript is carefully selected and supervised by our editors, who are themselves computer experts. We publish the best authors, whose technical expertise is matched by an ability to write clearly and to communicate effectively. Programs are thoroughly tested for accuracy by our technical staff. Our computerized production department goes to great lengths to make sure that each book is well-designed.

In the pursuit of timeliness, SYBEX has achieved many publishing firsts. SYBEX was among the first to integrate personal computers used by authors and staff into the publishing process. SYBEX was the first to publish books on the CP/M operating system, microprocessor interfacing techniques, word processing, and many more topics.

Expertise in computers and dedication to the highest quality product have made SYBEX a world leader in computer book publishing. Translated into fourteen languages, SYBEX books have helped millions of people around the world to get the most from their computers. We hope we have helped you, too.

For a complete catalog of our publications:

SYBEX, Inc. 2344 Sixth Street, Berkeley, California 94710
Tel: (415) 848-8233 Telex: 336311